2.50

BLOOMSBURY

ATLAS OF THE WORLD

Bloomsbury Books
London

Cartography designed and produced by Euromap Ltd, Pangbourne, Berkshire.

This edition published 1993 by Bloomsbury Books, an imprint of The Godfrey Cave Group, 42 Bloomsbury Street, London, WC1B 3QJ.

ISBN 1 85471 139 3

Printed and bound by New Interlitho, Milan, Italy.

CONTENTS

USING THE ATLAS

A world atlas is a systematic and easily accessible summary of human knowledge of our planet Earth.

The *Bloomsbury Atlas of the World* admirably fits this bill, providing a new, convenient reference work that places at our fingertips up-to-date facts and figures reflecting the fast-changing world we live in today. It does this in three complementary ways: illustrated geographical information; visually stimulating and colourful map graphics; and the latest world data and statistics.

GEOGRAPHICAL INFORMATION (pages X-XXIII)
This introductory section, by use of illustrated and informative text, concisely summarizes recent scientific discoveries and conclusions about our physical world: our place in the universe; our neighbours in space; the origin, structure and dynamics of our planet; its enveloping atmosphere; and its vast oceans of water, so crucial to life on Earth.

MAPS OF THE WORLD (pages 1-48)
This focal section in full colour brings alive the 3-D art of the cartographer, with a map coverage that extends to every part of the world. Each continent is treated systematically. Each double-spread or single-page map has been planned carefully to include an entire physical region or political unit. Generous overlaps allow for continuity between maps.

Maps consist of different kinds of symbols. The symbolic language of the map is explained below.

Area symbols in one colour indicate the shape and size of a country on a map of a continent, or a natural feature such as a sea. Coloured area symbols show the height of land above sea level.

Line symbols show features such as roads, railways, rivers, and boundaries.

Point symbols show features (e.g. mountain peaks, heights in metres) and towns.

International boundary: the international boundary tells you where one country meets another one. The boundary often follows the line of a physical feature, such as a river.

Capital city: a capital city is shown on the map by an underlining in red. This distinguishes it from other towns and cities on the map.

Map colour: colour is used on maps to show various things. Each country is given a different colour from its neighbour on political maps. In the regional maps colour is used to show the height of land above sea level.

Latitude and longitude: lines of latitude and longitude help to indicate how far north or south of the Equator or how far east or west of Greenwich, London, a place is located.

Cities: cities and towns that are not capitals are shown by an open black circle or square, corresponding to the population size group of each location.

Mountains: the high peaks in mountain ranges are shown by a small black triangle. The name of a mountain and its height in metres are beside the triangle.

Rivers: rivers are shown on the map by a fine blue line. The name of the river will be found printed along this line.

Grid: places on a map can be found easily by using the grid letters and numbers at the edges of the map. These are needed when using the Index.

Map Scales: it is impossible to show an area at its true size on a map. All maps in this atlas are therefore drawn at a reduced scale. To fit the area to be shown on one page, many different scales are used. The amount of information given and the area covered by each map are affected by the scale of the map. For example, at a large scale (1 : 2 600 000) the London Basin is shown. At a medium scale (1 : 8 000 000) southern England is covered. At a small scale (1 : 25 000 000) we are able to map the British Isles, and at a very small scale (1 : 25 500 000) the continent of Europe.

There are many different ways of expressing the scale of a map. The *scale bar* gives a graphic linear measure. The *representative fraction* gives the scale ratio (for example, 1 : 8 000 000). A *statement of scale* can also be given (e.g. 4 miles to 1 inch).

Abbreviations: sometimes there is not enough space on a map to name a feature in full. The following abbreviations are commonly used in this atlas:

Arch.	Archipelago
C.	Cape
Hd.	Head
I.	Island, Isle
Is.	Islands
L.	Lake, Loch
Mt.	Mont, Mount
Mts.	Mountains
Ra.	Range
Str.	Strait

Abbreviations used for country names are listed on the world map or on individual continent maps.

WORLD DATA (pages 49-117)

This concluding section has two parts. First is a gazetteer of over 2500 important places and features in the world, arranged alphabetically. Each entry gives location and vital statistics of size: area, length, height, population, etc. Every country has an expanded description, with facts on climate, economy, government, religion and currency.

At the end of this atlas is an Index to most of the place names to be found on the maps. These names are arranged in alphabetical order. Each entry starts with the name of the place, followed in italic script by the country in which it is located. Then, in a column alongside, is first the number of the most appropriate page on which the name appears, usually the largest scale map. Next comes the alphanumeric reference of the map grid on that page. For example, the index entry for Berlin reads:

Berlin *Germany* 28C2

THE PLANET EARTH

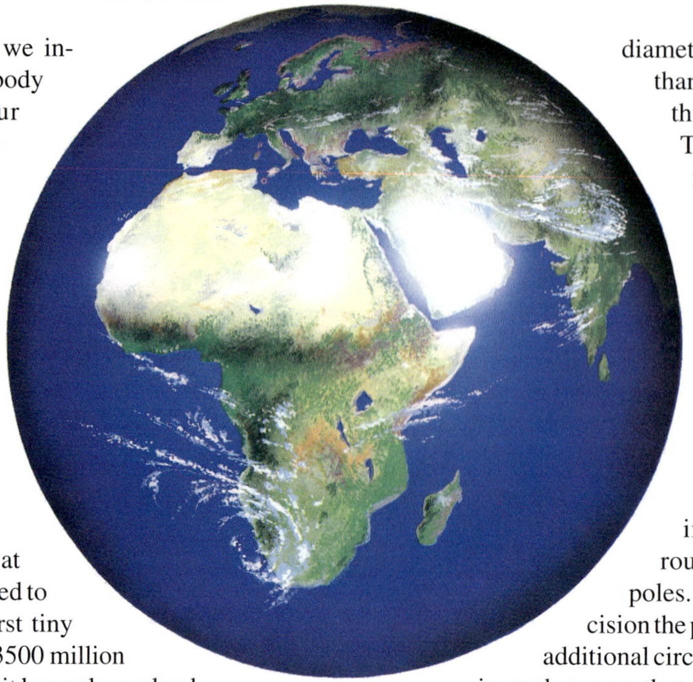

Earth is the planet which we inhabit, a nearly spherical body which every twenty-four hours rotates from west to east round an imaginary line called its axis. This axis has as its extremities, the north and south poles—and in the course of a year it completes a revolution round the sun.

The Earth is nearly 4600 million years old, and most probably took over 100 million years to form into a ball of rock, at which time the surface cooled to form the crust, with the first tiny signs of growth appearing 3500 million years ago. Life as we know it has only evolved over the last 40 to 50 million years.

Volcanic eruptions produced gases which formed the Earth's atmosphere—the layer of air surrounding the Earth containing mainly the gases oxygen, nitrogen, carbon dioxide and water vapour. The atmosphere is approximately 1000 km (620 miles) thick. This layer shields the earth from the harmful ultraviolet rays emanating from the sun and protects the Earth from extremes of temperature.

These eruptions also produced huge volumes of water vapour which condensed to fill the hollows in the Earth's crust to form the seas and oceans.

The Earth's surface layer of rock is known as the crust, around 65 km (40 miles) deep in areas of land mass, and 6 km (4 miles) deep under the oceans.

Beneath the crust is the mantle; a rock layer some 2900 km (1800 miles) thick.

The core of the Earth has two further layers; the outer core, and the inner core. The outer core is made up of molten iron, around 2000 km (1240 miles) deep. The inner core is of solid iron and nickel, a great ball at the centre of the Earth. To an observer, the visible part of the Earth appears as a circular and horizontal expanse. Accordingly, in remote antiquity, the Earth was regarded by man as a flat, circular body, floating on the waters. But gradually the spherical form of the Earth began to be suspected. The mere fact that the Earth could be circumnavigated did not prove it to be globular. Its surface, land and ocean, were explored and accurately mapped, and the relative distances and directions found to be consistent only with its possessing a spherical shape.

The Earth is not, however, an exact sphere, but is very slightly fattened at the poles, so as to have the form known as an oblate spheroid. In this way the polar diameter, or diameter from pole to pole, is shorter than the diameter at right angles to this—the equatorial diameter. The most accurate measurements make the polar diameter almost 42 km (27 miles) less than the equatorial, the equatorial diameter being 12,756 km (7926.7 miles), and the polar 12,714 km (7900 miles). The Earth is regarded as divided into two halves—the northern and the southern hemispheres—by the equator, an imaginary line going right round it midway between the poles. In order to indicate with precision the position of places on the Earth, additional circles are traced upon the surface in such a way that those of the one set all pass through both poles, while those of the other are drawn parallel to the equator. The former are called meridians, the latter parallels of latitude, and by reference to them we can state the latitude and longitude, and thus the exact position, of any place.

The surface of the Earth covers 511,000,000 sq km (196,900,000 sq miles) of which about 30% is dry land, the remaining 70% being water. The land is arranged into masses of irregular shape and size, the greatest connected mass being in the eastern hemisphere. The chief masses receive the name of continents, detached masses of smaller size being islands. The surface of the land is variously diversified, mountains, valleys, plains, plateaus and deserts. The water area of the Earth is divided into oceans, seas, bays, gulfs, etc, while rivers and lakes are regarded as features of the land surface. The great phenomena of the oceans are the currents and tides. The Earth's seas and oceans have an average depth of 3.5 km (2.2 miles).

The Earth, is one of nine planets which circle around the sun, completing its revolution in about 365 days and 6 hours. The orbit of the Earth is an ellipse.

Earth is the third planet from the sun and the only one which we know that supports life. Scientists and Astronomers estimate that there could be as many as 10,000 million galaxies which form the universe. The Sun is but one of around 100,000 million stars in our galaxy.

The Earth's daily motion about its own axis takes place in twenty-three hours, fifty-six minutes, and four seconds of mean time. This revolution brings about the alternation of day and night. As the axis on which the Earth rotates is inclined towards the plane of its path about the sun at an angle of 66.5°, and the angle between the plane of the ecliptic and the plane of the Earth's equator is therefore

23.5°, the sun ascends as seen from our northern latitudes, from 21st March to 21st June (the summer solstice), to about 23.5° above the celestial equator, and descends again towards the equator from 21st June to 23rd September. It then sinks till 22nd December (the winter solstice), when it is about 23.5° below the equator, and returns again to the equator by 21st March. This arrangement is the cause of the seasons, and the unequal measure of day and night during them.

For all places removed from the equator, day and night are equal only twice in the year (at the equinoxes). At the summer solstice in the northern hemisphere, the north pole of the Earth is turned towards the sun, and the south pole away from it, and for places within 23.5° of the North Pole there is a period of longer or shorter duration during which the sun is continually above the horizon throughout the twenty-four hours of each day. Round the South Pole there is an equal extent of surface within which the sun for similar periods is below the horizon. The reverse occurs at the winter solstice. The circles bounding these regions are called respectively the arctic and the antarctic circles, and the regions themselves the polar or frigid zones. Throughout a region extending to 23.5° on each side of the equator the sun is directly overhead at any place twice in the year. The circles which bound this region are called the tropics, that in the northern hemisphere being the tropic of Cancer, that in the southern the tropic of Capricorn, while the region between is the torrid zone. The regions between the tropics and the polar circles are the north and south temperate zones respectively.

The term "earth sciences" has entered our vocabulary, covering a synthesis of the traditional disciplines of geology, geophysics, geochemistry, oceanography and meteorology.

This new focus reflects worldwide concern that a greater understanding of the global elements of the structure of the Earth and its past will give the most valuable insight as to how the Earth's resources can be best sustained.

In comparison to the age of the Earth, man's relatively short existence has caused alarming levels of pollution, and the environment is under increasing stress.

Ozone forms a key layer in the upper atmosphere and there is concern over damage to it, caused by chlorofluorocarbons—chemicals, used by man which release chlorine into the upper atmosphere, destroying the ozone.

The World sustains more than 5,000 million people—a population which has doubled since the early 1950's, and it is believed by many experts that the population could double again within the next half-century. We must learn to sustain this growth, and face the growing ecological crisis.

EARTH FACTS AND FIGURES

Surface Area:	511,000,000 sq km (196,900,000 sq miles)
Land Area:	150,000,000 sq km (57,500,000 sq miles) 29.2% of The Surface of The Earth
Seas & Oceans Area:	361,000,000 sq km (139,400,000 sq miles) 70.8% of The Surface of The Earth
Mass:	6,000 Billion, billion tonnes
Diameter:	12756 km (7,926 miles) (At the Equator) 12714 km (7,900 miles) (At the Poles)
Circumference:	40,075 km (24,901 miles) (At the Equator)
Distance from the Sun:	149,500,000 km (93 million miles)
Rotation Period:	23 hours 56 mins 4.1 sec
Year:	365 days, 5 hours 48 mins 46 sec (complete orbit)
Age:	4,600 million years

THE SOLAR SYSTEM

The first astronomers, long ago, noticed five special "stars" that gradually moved through the constellations. The Greeks called them *planetoi*, the wanderers, from which came our word planet. Planets shine with a steady light, but real stars often twinkle. This is because a planet is, in fact, a disc of light, whereas a star is so distant that it is always just a point of light. The light from a point source shimmers as it passes through the Earth's atmosphere.

Planets are not like stars at all. The Sun is a typical star. It radiates heat and light of its own, but the planets shine only by the light they reflect from the Sun. Most stars are much larger than planets. The Sun is a thousand times more massive than the biggest planet, Jupiter. The twinkling stars are other suns, much farther away from Earth than any planet.

All the planets visible in the night sky are members of the Sun's family, or solar system. The five planets that can be seen without the aid of a telescope are Mercury, Venus, Mars, Jupiter and Saturn. Mercury is closest to the Sun. It is not easy to pick out because it is never far from the Sun in the sky. Venus is also closer to the Sun than is the Earth. This brilliant planet is seen at its best at dawn or dusk and so it is often called the morning star or evening star. Mars is the "Red Planet," so named because of its colour. Jupiter and Saturn, both of them giant planets, can often been seen shining with a steady yellow light.

After the invention of the telescope, astronomers found three, more distant planets. Uranus was discovered in 1781. Neptune in 1846 and Pluto in 1930. All nine planets travel in orbits around the Sun. They all journey in the same direction. The planets closest to the Sun take the least time in orbit. Mercury, nearest to the Sun, makes a circuit in only 88 days, Earth takes a year, and Jupiter almost 12 years.

Studying the motion of the planets, the German astronomer Johannes Kepler discovered in 1609 that the orbits of the planets are slightly stretched circles, called ellipses. An ellipse has two focal points. For each planetary orbit the Sun is at one of the focuses. This means that the distances of the planets from the Sun change slightly as they travel in their orbits.

Kepler found our how the planets move, but it was Isaac Newton, the seventeenth-century English mathematician, who realized that gravitational force holds the planets in their orbits. The Earth's gravity makes objects that are dropped fall to the ground. If the Sun's gravity did not constantly keep tugging at the planets, they would fly off into the depths of space.

The Sun's family has other members apart from planets. Swarming between Mars and Jupiter are thousands of asteroids or minor planets. Comets with their streaming tails approach the Sun from the farthest parts of the solar system. In addition, dust is scattered in the space between the planets, as well as stones called meteoroids. These space rocks burn up if they crash through the Earth's atmosphere, creating a meteor trail, or shooting star. Many of the planets have moons orbiting them, rather like miniature solar systems. Jupiter has at least sixteen moons, four of which can be seen in a small telescope. Gravitation holds the moons in their orbits around their planets, just as it keeps the whole of the Sun's family together.

The exploration of most of the planets in the solar system is a major scientific achievement of the twentieth century. Men in space have landed on the Moon, and brought back samples from its surface. The five planets that are visible to the naked eye — along with other moons from those of Mars to the satellites of Saturn—have been investigated and photographed by unmanned spacecraft.

THE PLANETS

Name	Distance from the Sun in millions of km (miles)	Distance from the Sun compared to Earth	Time to orbit the Sun in years	Mass compared to the Earth	Radius compared to the Earth
Mercury	58 (36)	0.39	0.24	0.06	0.38
Venus	108 (67)	0.72	0.62	0.82	0.95
Earth	149.5 (93)	1.00	1.00	1.00	1.00
Mars	228 (142)	1.52	1.88	0.11	0.53
Jupiter	778.5 (484)	5.20	11.86	318	11
Saturn	1427 (887)	9.54	29.46	95	9
Uranus	2870 (1783)	19.18	84	15	4
Neptune	4497 (2794)	30.06	165	17	4
Pluto	5900 (3706)	39.44	248	0.0024	0.28—0.34

This table lists the nine planets in the order of their distances from the Sun. Together with their moons, the asteroids and comets, these planets make up the solar system. The comparisons of the characteristics of the other planets to those of the Earth are given in decimal ratio, that is, Mars is 1.52 times farther from the Sun than is the Earth.

THE EARTH'S STRUCTURE

Man has been able to study the surface of his own planet for as long as the Earth has been inhabited. Yet it is strange to think that before orbiting spacecraft had actually returned colour photographs of Earth, nobody had predicted accurately what it would look like from space. Now the Earth can be seen and photographed as a beautiful blue and white planet. From beneath the spiraling patterns of brilliant white clouds the shapes of the continents come into view.

Many factors make the Earth unique in the solar system. It is the only planet with substantial amounts of liquid water. Oceans cover almost three-quarters of the surface. This vast quantity of water is a powerful force of erosion–the wearing away of the Earth's surface. Weather behaviour and long-term changes in climate gradually wear down the continental rocks. Mountains are eroded by glaciers, wind and rain. Mighty rivers etch channels through the rocks and lowland plains, carrying sediment away from one place and depositing it in another.

Erosion has given the Earth a quite different appearance from that of the other planets in the inner solar system. For example, there is little evidence now that Earth was once as pitted and meteorite craters as the Moon. But it is hard to imagine that Earth escaped this tremendous bombardment. Erosion by wind and water has helped heal such wounds.

Unlike the older rocky planets, the Earth has inner layers containing tremendous forces that are very active. Volcanoes and earthquakes, for example, permit Earth to let off pressure from friction and heat that build up inside as the great plates of rock comprising the Earth's surface slowly slide about. Earth-quakes, sudden, unpredictable and lethal though they may be, teach geologists about the inner structure of the Earth. Vibrations spreading out from an earthquake are measured and analyzed by scientific instruments all over the globe. These vibrations reveal that Earth is made of several layers. On top is a thin crust of rock that is

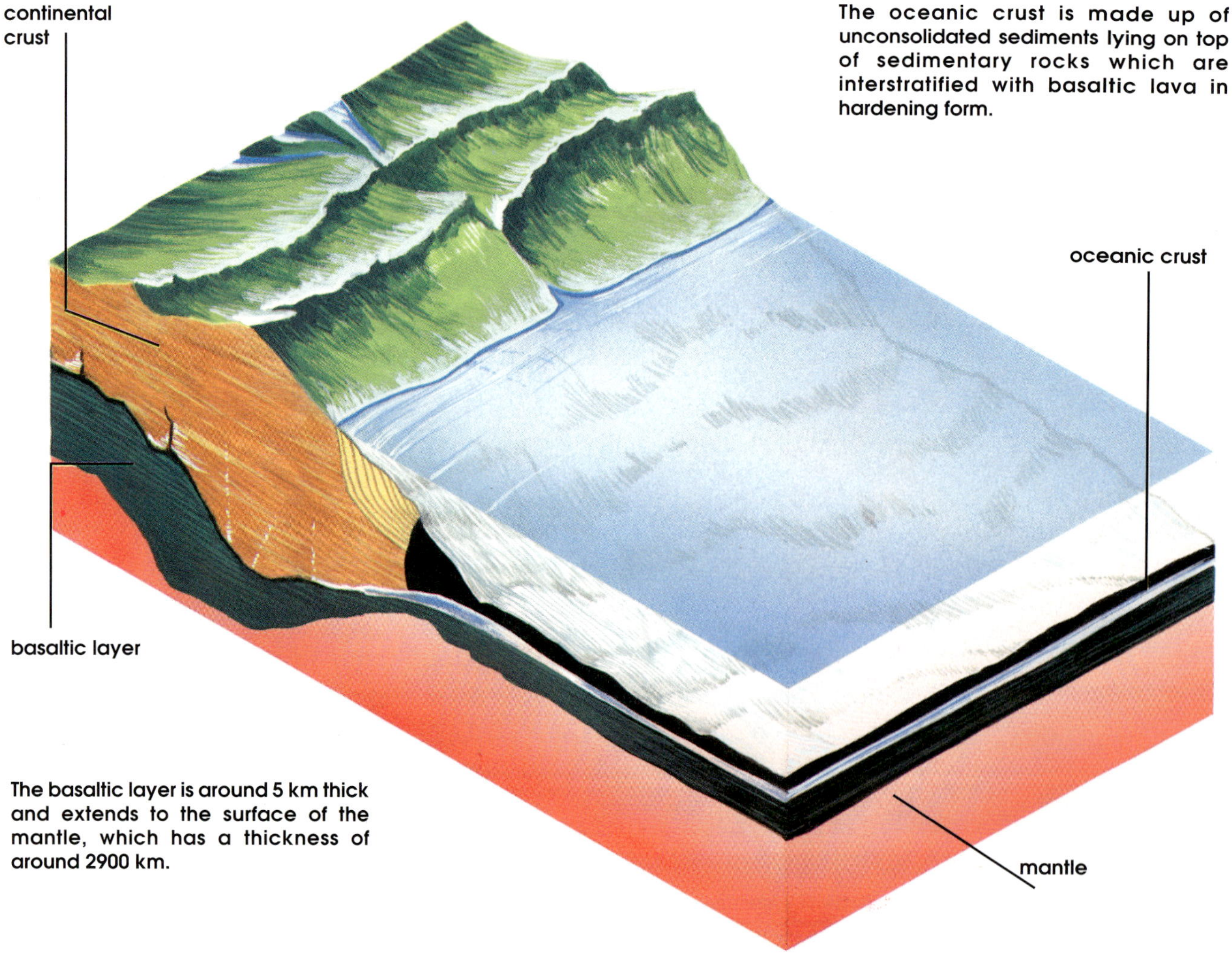

The oceanic crust is made up of unconsolidated sediments lying on top of sedimentary rocks which are interstratified with basaltic lava in hardening form.

The basaltic layer is around 5 km thick and extends to the surface of the mantle, which has a thickness of around 2900 km.

nowhere more than 65km (40 miles) thick. The crust lies atop a thick layer of rock 2900km (1800 miles) deep called the mantle. Inside that, there is a liquid core of hot iron 225 km (1400 miles) in diameter. Possibly the central part of this core is solid because of the immense pressure created by the weight of the overlying material.

Magnetism is generated by electric currents flowing through the liquid iron in the interior. On most planets a magnetic compass would be of no use for ending north. The compass works here because the Earth has its own magnetic field of influence. A compass needle lines up with the Earth's magnetism and points to the north.

Compared with most of the other rocky worlds in the solar system, Earth is a hive of geological activity. Mountains are constantly being thrust up, earthquakes make the globe tremble and volcanoes cough out liquid rock. Even the continents are slowly gliding about. Only Io, a moon of Jupiter, shows similar activity. Why does the Earth differ from Venus and Mars?

The answer is that the crust of the Earth consists of several large plates that will not keep still. Beneath the oceans and continents there is a rock layer that moves. According to theory, heat flowing from underneath the plates causes this motion, which is like that of a conveyor belt. The heat comes partly from the decay of radioactive rocks. In certain places the plates push into each other, and cause tremendous buckling. This crumpling of two continental plates has caused the information of the Alps and Himalayas. Along the west coast of North and South America the continental plates are being forced against the oceanic plates and this has formed a great range of coastal mountains from Alaska to southern Chile.

Another effect of these rock movements is to generate friction. This may melt the rock below the surface; molten material works its way upward through cracks and erupts as a volcano.

The motion of continental and oceanic plates is not noticeable in a human lifetime. But it is fast enough to change the face of the Earth. For example, all the present continents resulted when two enormous land masses shattered about 200 million years ago. South America and Africa are still moving about but a look at a map shows how they once fitted together.

This cutout diagram shows the inner structure of the Earth. The thickness of the Earth's crust may be likened proportionally to the skin of an apple. Beneath it lie the rocks of the mantle and the two- layered core, which is mostly liquid iron.

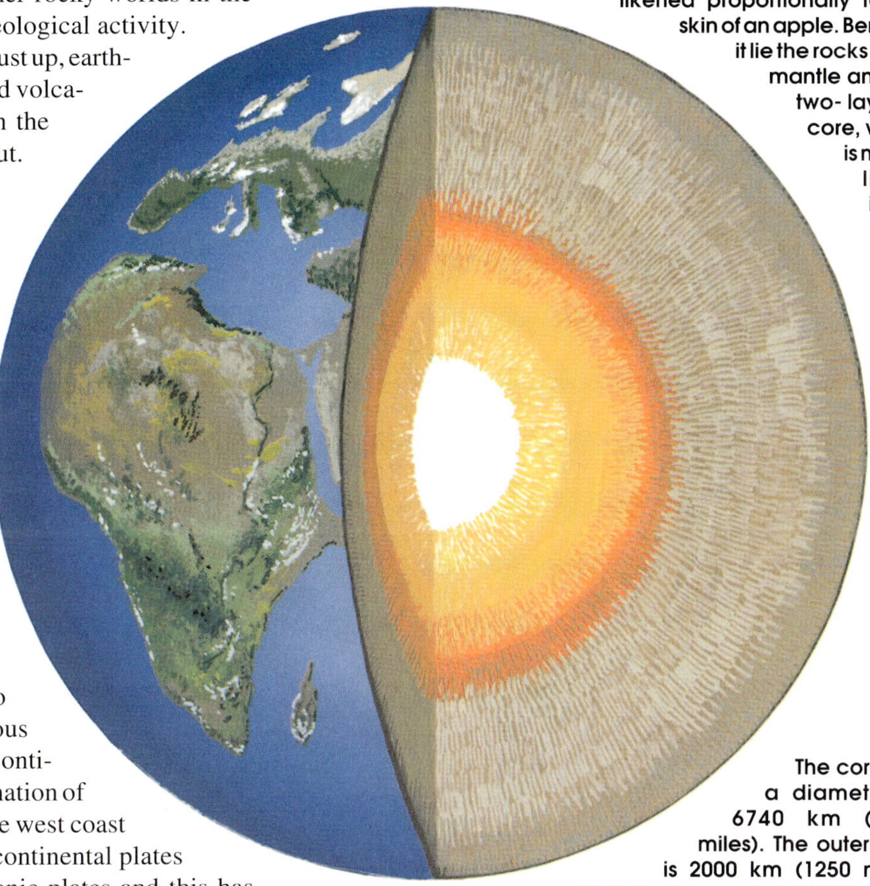

The core has a diameter of 6740 km (4200 miles). The outer core is 2000 km (1250 miles) thick, the inner core is 1370 km (850 miles) thick. The top 15 km (9.5 miles) of the crust is mostly made up of igneous rocks (those formed from molten magna) and metamorphic rocks (igneous or sedimentary rocks which have been changed by physical or chemical action). The dominant feature of landmass surface is sedimentary rock.

THE ATMOSPHERE

The atmosphere, which surrounds and sustains life, is the stage setting within which the drama of weather is played. Extending from the Earth's surface to perhaps 965 km (600 miles) or more into space, the atmosphere divides into several layers, each comprised of gases in varying quantities and densities. The predominant gases in the lowest layer, the troposphere, are oxygen, nitrogen, traces (about 0.03 per cent) of carbon dioxide and–most important for the weather–water vapour.

Virtually all of the weather as we know it–with constant changes from wet to dry, clear to cloudy, hot to cold, windy to still–and vice versa–takes place in the troposphere. This is mainly because all but the tiniest traces of water vapour –the stuff of which fog, clouds, rain and all other forms of precipitation is made–occur in the troposphere. Without this water vapour there would be no life.

The troposphere varies in thickness, from about eight kilometres over the Poles to about 16 km (10 miles) over the Equator. Above the troposphere there is very little water vapour. This is called the stratosphere, where supersonic aircraft fly with little danger of colliding with an ice crystal, which could do enormous damage. This atmospheric layer contains almost no clouds. Here too, oxygen and most of the other life-sustaining gases thin out.

As the altitude changes, so too does the temperature. This happens because the Earth and the water vapour in the troposphere act as radiators, absorbing and giving off the Sun's heat.

Beyond the troposphere, neither the Earth's heat nor water vapour is a factor in determining atmospheric temperature. In the stratosphere the temperature becomes warmer with increased altitude because of the dominance of solar radiation. Then in the next layer, the mesophere, the temperature turns cold again, in part because of the reaction of a gas called ozone that blocks out the Sun's ultraviolet rays. The temperature continues to drop until it reaches 85°C or more below zero. Then, at perhaps 80 km (50 miles) over the Earth, where the thermosphere begins, the gases–under the direct influence of the Sun–become so thinly concentrated that they all but disappear.

Although these upper layers contain no weather in the

This map shows the disaster that would be caused in Europe by a change in sea-level resulting from the melting of both polar ice-caps. Labels indicate the cities which would be submerged.

popular use of the term, they affect events in the troposphere by shielding the Earth from the searing rays of the Sun. In addition these upper layers together contribute about 25 per cent of the atmospheric weight that presses down upon the Earth's surface.

The troposphere contributes the other 75 per cent of the atmosphere's weight, through the presence of the relatively dense gases–including water vapour. Vapour enters the atmosphere by evaporation from oceans, seas, and lakes, and to a lesser extent from wet ground and vegetation. Heat is needed for evaporation to occur, and this heat is taken from the surrounding atmosphere and the surface of the Earth, which therefore becomes cooler.

This heat is not lost, but is stored in the vapour as hidden, or latent, heat. The vapour is carried by winds to higher levels of the atmosphere and to different parts of the world. As a result, water vapour may be found throughout the troposphere and over all regions, oceans and continents. Eventually, water vapour condenses into liquid water or solid ice and falls to the ground as precipitation–rain, snow or hail. In condensing, it releases its latent heat to the atmosphere. Thus if water evaporates into the air from a tropical ocean and winds then carry it to a temperate continent, where it condenses and falls as rain, this provides a very effective means of carrying not only water but also heat from places that have plenty to places that are short of both.

In the air around us, the temperature, pressure and moisture content are affected by the fourth critical ingredient that makes up our weather: the wind. As we know, wind is the name for a moving mass of air. Nearly everyone is familiar with winds that blow from north, south, east or west–that is across the Earth's surface, or horizontally. But winds also blow vertically–as bird-watchers know from seeing gulls or crows sail upwards on rising currents of warm air, or from watching a hawk sink down rapidly on a descending cold current.

Most vertical air currents are much gentler than horizontal winds. But they are vitally important, because they can generate many different types of weather. When air rises it expands, because the pressure on it becomes less. As it rises, the air cools. Because it cools, its moisture content increases. Eventually the rising air may reach a level at which it becomes saturated with moisture. If it rises still further, water vapour starts condensing to form clouds. nearly all clouds and rain originate in up-currents of air.

One reason why air starts to rise is because of temperature differences from place to place. Such differences are very marked on sunny days over land, when the air above some surfaces, such as asphalt or bare soil, becomes warmer than that over adjacent surfaces, such as trees or lakes. The warmer masses of air, which can be called bubbles, then start to rise. The air between the rising bubbles sinks to compensate. This type of air movement is called convection.

Once a bubble of air has started to rise, it will continue to do so as long as it remains warmer than its surroundings. As it rises, it cools, initially at a rate of 15°C per 90 metres. But it surroundings also cool with height. Eventually the bubble will reach its condensation level and clouds will start to form. The condensation in such clouds releases latent heat, making the rising air even warmer. This increases the difference in temperature between the rising air and the surrounding air. The atmosphere is then said to be unstable. As long as the atmosphere remains unstable, the bubble will grow bigger and rise further, producing a tall cloud. This cloud may become so saturated with moisture that rain or snow begins to fall from it.

On the other hand, if the rate of decrease of the temperature in the air surrounding the bubble is quite small, or if the temperature actually rises with height–as it sometimes does –then the rising air bubble will soon become colder than its surroundings. The bubble will then stop rising. In this situation the atmosphere is said to be stable. Bubbles may never reach their condensation level, in which case no clouds will form–or the bubble will produce only small, shallow clouds. When clouds do form, condensation may stop before the air becomes so saturated that precipitation begins. This is typically the case in stable air.

SEAS AND OCEANS

The water on the Earth's surface that now fills the oceans got there as part of a process that started with the origin of the Earth itself. This is the opinion of most Earth-scientists today. To understand that process, we need to know something about the origin of the solar system. The material from which the Earth and the other planets were later to be formed probably began as a cloud of gases spinning around the sun. These gases gradually condensed, making solid particles. Many of them collided, and built up larger and larger concentrations of matter.

The part that was eventually to become the Earth seems to have cooled and begun solidifying about 4.6 billion years ago, and as the spinning movement shaped matter into a ball, it contracted even further. Under these pressures, matter at the centre of the newly formed Earth began to heat up again and became molten. When this happened, water that had been contained inside the Earth was released to the surface as vapour and was added to the primitive atmosphere. When it cooled and condensed, it fell to the surface as rain and eventually formed the first oceans. We do not know how much of the water in the oceans came from this source. Estimates range from a third to almost all of it–there is no way we can determine the exact amount. Neither can we tell when this happened, but some indication comes from rocks. The oldest rock discovered so far on the Earth's surface is from Greenland and is 3.8 billion years old. It is a kind of rock formed from pebbles laid down under water and later compressed. This shows that water must already have condensed and fallen to Earth during the 800 million years that had passed since the Earth was formed.

The rest of the water in the oceans also came from the interior of the Earth, but was forced to the surface by volcanic eruptions and hot springs. There are many volcanoes and hot springs on land and even more in parts of the ocean, and they are still spewing out water. Only a small proportion of this water is new, or juvenile, water coming from deep inside the Earth for the first time. Most of it is

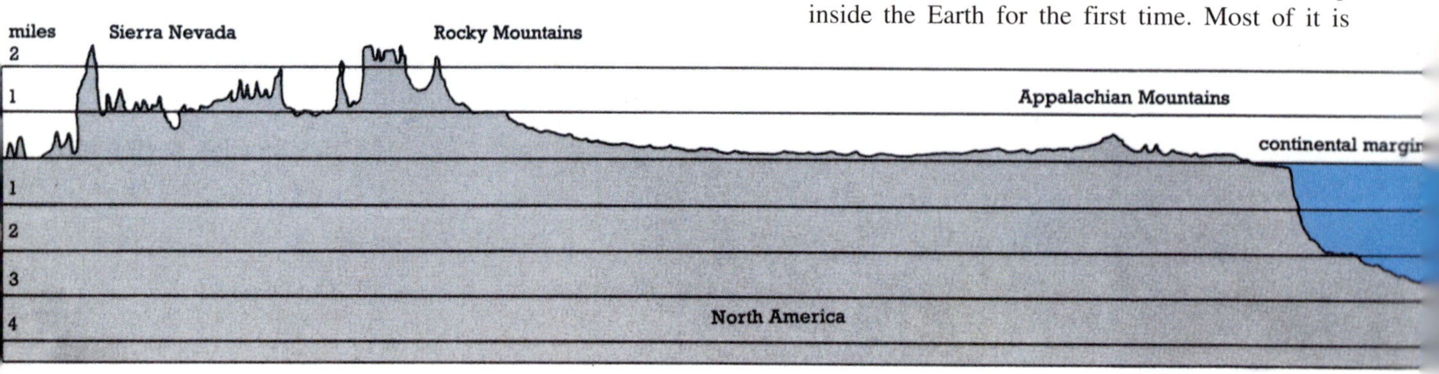

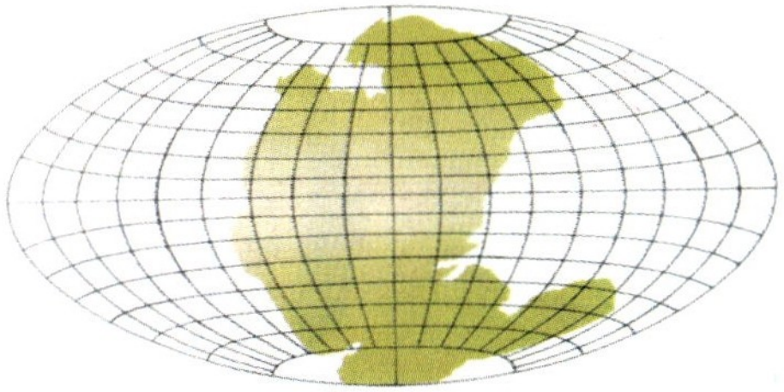

About 220 million years ago the present day continents formed a single supercontinent.

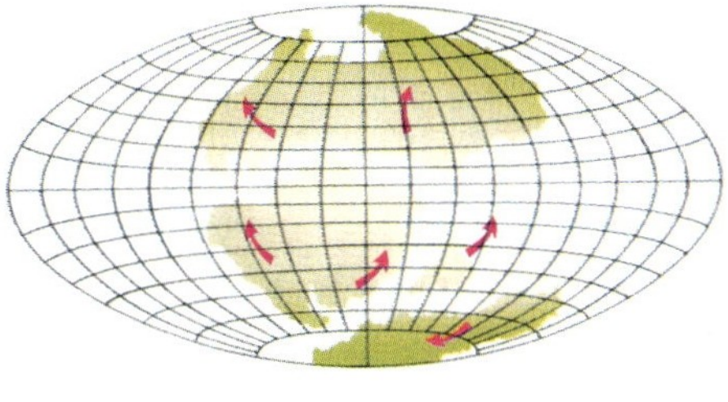

About 100 million years ago oceans began to appear in cracks as the supercontinent broke up and moved apart.

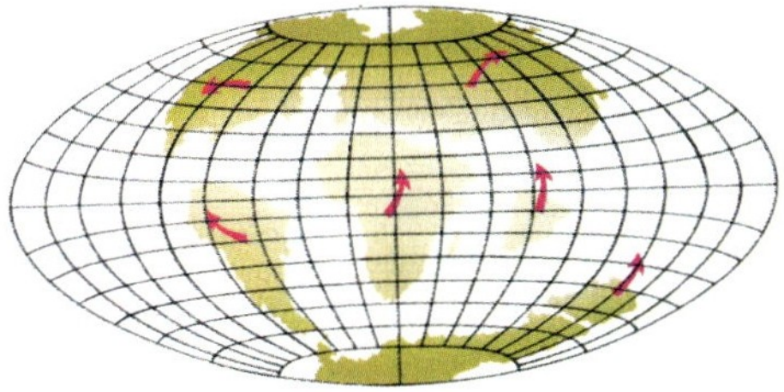

About 50 million years ago the Atlantic was growing in size, and India was migrating towards Asia.

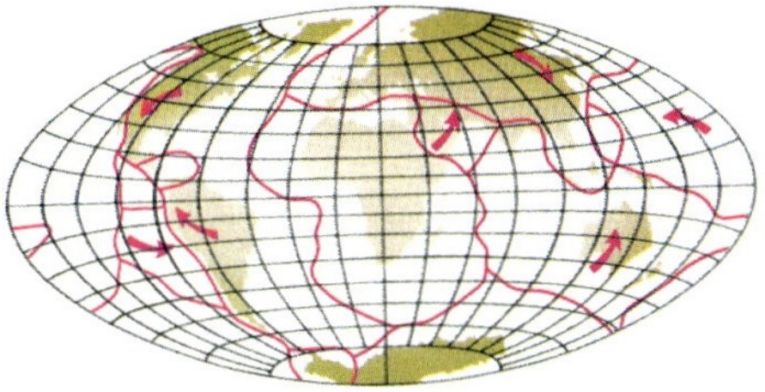

Today the margins of the plates are still active, some of them carrying the continents on their backs to new destinations.

groundwater or seawater that seeped down into the Earth, heated up through contact with hot rocks and then returned to the surface in a volcanic eruption or a hot spring. Although only a small proportion of this water is juvenile, the total amount of new water brought to the surface in the billions of years this process has been going on has been enough to help fill the oceans.

Was the water that came from the Earth's interior to fill the oceans the same salty seawater we know today? As far as we can tell, the oceans never had fresh water. Salt, or salinity, comes from gases and other substances dissolved in the water. When water first rose to the surface of the Earth as steam, it contained gases, some of which dissolved in the original oceans. Since then, volcanoes have supplied other gases along with water and added them to the oceans. Other substances in seawater reached and still reach the ocean by a different process. They come from rocks on land which slowly break down to produce tiny fragments that flow in rivers into the oceans.

Although the ocean, like the atmosphere, had very little oxygen up to about 1.9 billion years ago and had differing amounts of gases and metals in the past, the total amount of all dissolved substances in the ocean–and salinity–was probably similar to the present. And about 1 billion years ago the oceans reached a composition very similar to what it is today.

Just as substances are being added to seawater, so also are they being removed. If they were not, the concentration would go on building up. Water is still being added to the oceans by volcanoes, rain and rivers, and is being lost again by evaporation. The salinity of seawater remains at the same level because some of the solids sink to the bottom or are thrown into the air in sea spray. Salt particles attract water in the atmosphere and droplets grow on them, some of which are blown away over the land as rain. By these means, water and solids are recycled through the atmosphere, rivers, sediments, seawater, rock, and the Earth's interior to maintain the overall composition, of the oceans.

A comparison of the heights of land and ocean floor features on a line running across the USA and the North Atlantic to Africa. In this diagram the heights have been exaggerated in proportion to the width.

THE SUN

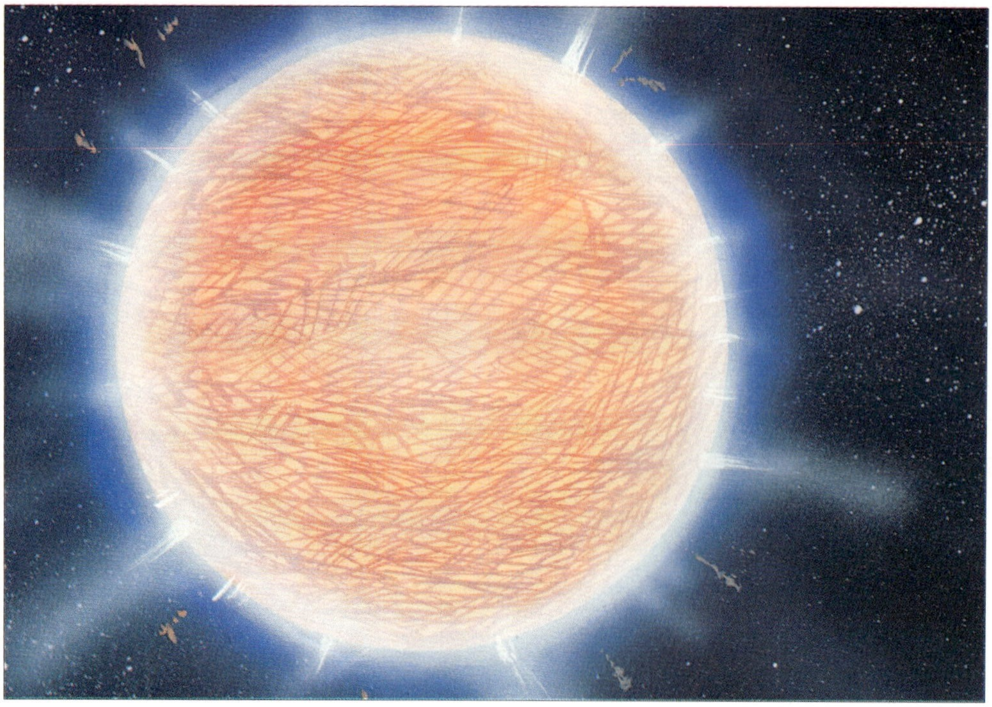

The gas inside the Sun is three-quarters hydrogen, the lightest gas. Deep inside the hot Sun, hydrogen atoms crowd together. In the jostling a group of them collides so violently with another group that they fuse together and make a completely different substance, helium. Each second, 650 million tons of hydrogen become helium. A small part of this mass of material is transformed in the process and reappears as pure energy, as Einstein has predicted would be the case. In one second, the Sun's mass falls by four million tons. In fifty million years the lost mass is equal to the mass of the Earth.

To the planets, animals and peoples of the Earth, the Sun is a unique and vital star. Every living thing on the Earth owes its existence to the fact that the Sun is nearby and keeps shining, and has done so for about five billion years. The energy from the burning of coal, oil and natural gas was once sun-energy. These fuels are the remains of plants and animals that grew in the warmth of sun-energy millions of years ago. The nearest star, apart from the Sun, is 300,000 times farther away, and the weak star energy we receive from it cannot possibly replace sun energy.

The Sun is far larger than the Earth and also a great deal more massive. One hundred and nine Earth-planets placed side by side would stretch from one side of the Sun to the other. Its volume is 1.3 million times greater than the Earth and the mass 330,000 times as much.

The distance from Earth to Sun is about 150 million km (93 million miles). Light and heat take eight minutes and twenty seconds to race across interplanetary space and reach the Earth from this distance. Although this seems a great separation, only a handful of stars exists within a million times this distance from the solar system.

The Sun's gravity pulls much harder than the Earth's gravity. A person who could venture to the surface of the Sun would weigh about one and a half tons. However, this is an impossible adventure since the Sun has no solid surface and the temperature there is about 10,000°F. This exceeds the melting temperature of every known substance. The temperature of the surface seems high, but inside the Sun it is much hotter. Its entire globe is a glowing mass of gas. At the centre the temperature is about 27 million degrees Fahrenheit.

Flashes of energy burst forth as the hydrogen turns to helium. The great density of matter traps the energy flashes inside the Sun. They wander through the interior for a million years or so before reaching the surface. The energy then streams off into space.

Along with the heat and light, the Sun emits radiation that can be harmful to living creatures. Ultraviolet rays and X-rays damage the cells in plants and animals. The Earth's blanket of atmosphere soaks up almost all of this radiation, although the small amount that reaches the ground on a fine day will make fair skin tan, or cause painful sunburn if exposure is too long. Astronauts journeying into space have to be protected from the Sun's harmful rays.

Sunspots look like holes in the fiery surface of the Sun. In fact they are areas that are about 3000°F cooler than the surrounding surface. This makes their temperature roughly 7000°F. Something that hot is actually extremely brilliant: sunspots only look dark because they are cooler and dimmer than the rest of the Sun. If a sunspot could be plucked from the Sun and examined separately it would seem a hundred times brighter than the full Moon. An average spot is 32,000 km (20,000 miles) across; most spots are more or less as big as the Earth, and huge spots span 145,000 km (90,000 miles.)

The chromosphere, the cool layer of atmosphere— above the yellow surface, can be seen readily only during total eclipses. The temperature in this thin layer is about 8000°F. Above the chromosphere is the intensely hot and invisible corona, where the temperature soars to an amazing two million degrees Fahrenheit. The gas in the corona is boiling away into space. This gas rush is called solar wind.

THE MOON

Moon soil is not all like Earth soil, it is made entirely from finely pulverized rock–the dust from meteoroid crashes. Moon soil has no water, decaying plant material or life. But it does contain something beautiful and unusual. Moon soil has many glass beads, emerald green and orange-red in colour, shaped like jewels and teardrops. These are made when a meteoroid impact sprays liquid rock in every direction. When the droplets of rock solidify, they turn glassy.

On the surface of the Moon a man weighs only one-sixth of his Earth weight. This is because the Moon's mass is a mere one-eightieth of the Earth's, so the gravitational pull is considerably smaller.

It was once feared that if a spacecraft landed on the Moon it would rapidly sink without trace into the deep dust layers. However, the lunar soil is well packed down to provide a reasonably firm surface. The main hazard of Moon travel is finding a smooth place to land. At close quarters the surface looks much like a bomb site, with small craters everywhere.

Moon rocks are distinctly different from Earth rocks. A geologist could easily tell them apart. The difference between them suggests that the Moon was once hotter than the Earth has ever been, and emphasizes the fact that the Moon has no air and no water. The oldest rocks found on the Moon are 4.6 billion years old. In comparison, the most aged rock yet discovered on Earth dates from only 3.8 billion years ago.

Astronauts left scientific apparatus on the Moon, including sensors that have detected numerous "moonquakes" as well as the impacts of meteoroids, some spacecraft and man-made debris slamming into the surface. Several small reflectors, like those on a car or bicycle, were placed on the Moon. Scientists can now measure the Moon's distance to within an inch or so by aiming a powerful laser beam at these reflectors and timing the beam's round trip from Earth to Moon and back again. This distance on the average is 385,000 km (240,000 miles.)

Geological maps of most of the surface are now available, a possibility undreamed of before about 1960. Samples mainly from the Apollo program, have been sent to laboratories throughout the world for very detailed examination. Nevertheless, this analysis of lunar material has shown that the surface has never supported life in the past. However, astronauts brought back to the Earth a piece of the Moon lander, *Surveyor 3*, which had landed on the Moon three years previously. Bacteria on this craft were still alive after several years of exposure to the harsh lunar environment. These bacteria did not flourish, but neither did they die. Thus there is a faint, extremely remote possibility that spacecraft are contaminating the Moon, planets and deep space with microscopic life from Earth even though the equipment is given a complete cleaning before its launch.

Two or three times a year, the full Moon moves into the Earth's shadow, and the Moon is eclipsed. During this so-called lunar eclipse, the shadowed part of the Moon looks dimly red because of Earth's atmosphere scatters reddish sunlight into the Earth's shadow. Eclipses do not take place every month because the Moon's orbit is tilted at an angle to the Earth's path around the Sun.

The Moon's gravitational pull has the important effect of creating ocean tides. The water surrounding the solid Earth is distorted into the shape of a squashed ball under the influence of the Moon's attraction. As the Earth spins on it axis, the bulges in the water seem to sweep around the Earth, causing two tides each day in most places. The Sun, too, influences the tides. When the Moon and the Sun are both pulling from the same direction, the highest tides are formed.

THE STARS

AUTUMN AND WINTER

A good starting point for recognizing stars in autumn is the constellation Cassiopeia. The five main stars of this group make the very obvious shape of the letter W, even though none of them reaches the first magnitude of brightness. This starry W is situated high in the sky during autumn evenings. Observers who are located at latitudes around 50° to 60° North see it right overhead.

Two stars in the W of Cassiopeia point to Cassiopeia's husband, Cepheus; and on the other side of the Cassiopeia is their daughter, Andromeda. The W is also a signpost to the large constellation of Pegasus, the winged horse. The principal stars in this constellation are part of a large square known as the Square of Pegasus. Looking for this square, bear in mind that it is large and that none of the stars is first magnitude.

Andromeda includes an object of unique interest. The great spiral galaxy M31 is just visible to the eye as a hazy patch of light. Two faint stars in the constellation of Andromeda lead to the galaxy M31, far beyond the edge of the Milky Way. Its light has taken two million years to reach the Earth. The M31 Galaxy is the most distant object visible to unaided human eyes. In a small telescope M31 is a soft glow of light.

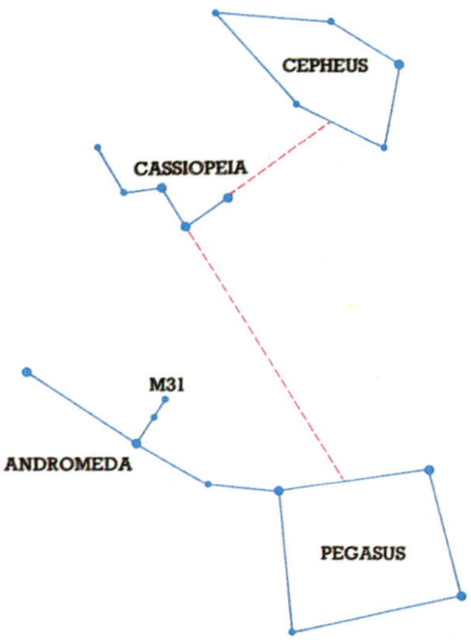

This typical star locator map shows how astronomers use the position of one constellation , and the stars within it, to locate other heavenly bodies. In the autumn sky of the northern hemisphere two arms of the W-shaped constellation Cassiopeia point to Cepheus (red line) and Pegasus. M31 can be found by following the map from Pegasus to Andromeda.

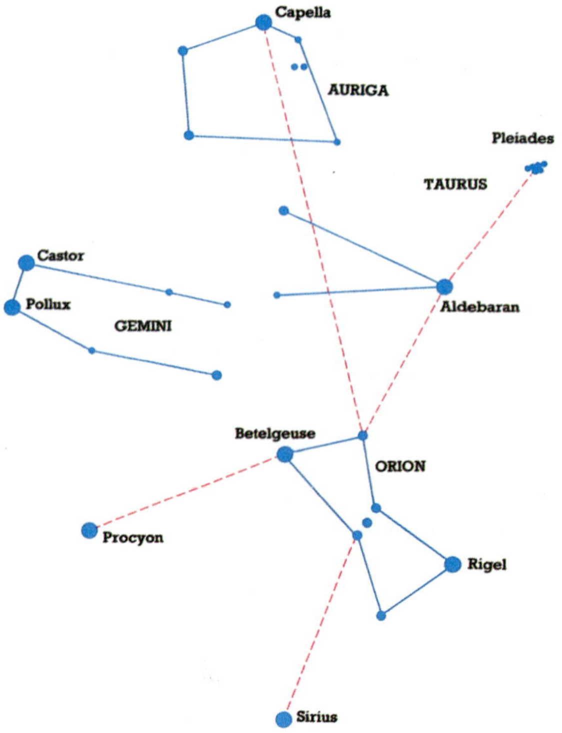

This locator map shows major stars and constellations that can readily be found after Orion has been identified in the winter sky. The dotted lines lead to Procyon and Sirius, to Capella in the constellation Auriga, and to the star Aldebaran and the Pleiades, a star cluster, in Taurus.

The bright constellations of winter, when the nights are long, are the best known, as well as being simple to learn.

One splendid view is that of the south on a January evening. Ahead is Orion, marching across the sky, with three stars forming a neat swordbelt for this mythical hunter. In Orion, seven stars of second magnitude and brighter make a memorable pattern. Betelgeuse, upper left, is distinctly red. It contrasts well with Rigel, lower right, which sparkles blue-white. Orion's belt points to twinkling Sirius, also called the Dog Star, the brightest star visible from northern latitudes. Procyon is a zero magnitude star, forming a triangle with Betelgeuse and Sirius. Near Orion's belt is a glowing cloud of gas, or nebula–a fine sight through binoculars.

Above Orion and Taurus, the Bull, and Gemini, the Twins. Aldebaran in Taurus is red, like Betelgeuse. Near the Bull's head lies the conspicuous cluster of stars called the Pleiades, or Seven Sisters. Six or seven stars can be seen by the unaided eye, but a small telescope or binoculars will bring dozens more into view. Higher still lies Auriga, the Charioteer, a constellation with the yellowish first magnitude star, Capella.

Leo Cancer Gemini Taurus Aries Pisces

SPRING AND SUMMER

In April the constellation Ursa Major reaches its highest point in the sky in the early evening. Observers between latitudes 50° and 60° North, in Canada or Alaska, for example, see it directly overhead. A section of Ursa Major, the Big Dipper, can be used to find three of the first magnitude stars in spring skies in the following manner.

Following the curve of the Big Dipper's tail leads to Arcturus, one of the brightest stars in the northern part of the sky. A reddish star, Arcturus belongs to the constellation of Boötes, the Herdsman. The eye, continuing to sweep in an arc from the Big Dipper through Arcturus, turns the observer's face to the south, and leads to Spica. This white star, the brightest in constellation Virgo, is first magnitude.

Yet another star of the first magnitude, Regulus, can also be seen by facing south. Regulus is the major star in the constellation of Leo, the Lion. It appears in the south in winter time and remains there through the spring. One way to find this star is to follow a line through the bowl of the Dipper, pointing away from the North Star. Regulus will be the brightest foot - just below the lion's head.

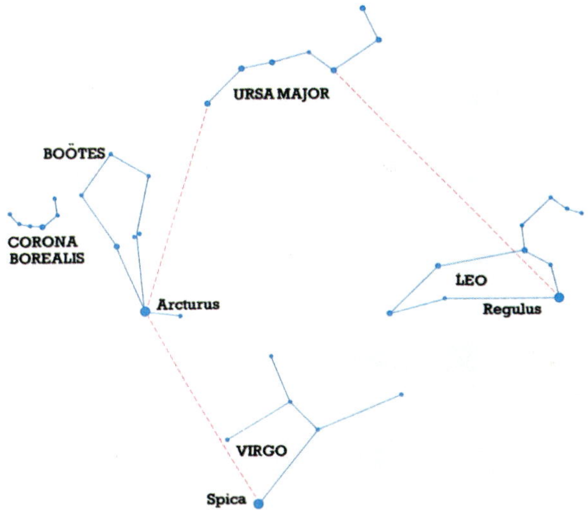

Stars in the Big Dipper (within Ursa Major or the Great Bear) can be used in the spring to find Regulus–the brightest star in the constellation of Leo–Arcturus, the brightest star in Boötes, and its neighbouring constellation of Corona Borealis, the Northern Crown. Arcturus, in turn, points to Spica, the brightest star in the constellation of Virgo.

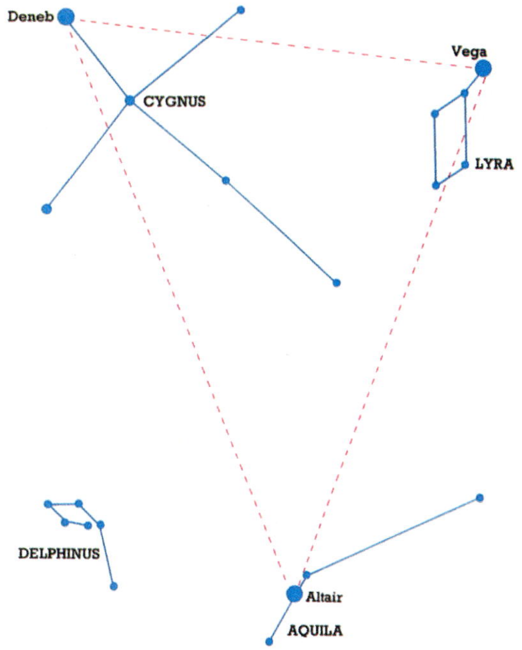

The locator map right traces a triangle of very bright stars that are visible in the northern hemisphere in summer: Deneb, in the constellation of Cygnus; Vega, in Lyra; and Altair, in Aquila. Stars in the small constellation of Dephinus are not nearly as bright as those of the triangle, but the compact constellation is easy to find near Altair.

In the skies on summer evenings three stars of first magnitude or brighter stand out: Deneb in Cygnus, Vega in Lyra, and Altair in Aquila. For an observer facing south, these map the Summer Triangle.

Deneb is the brightest star in the constellation of Cygnus, the Swan. This group of stars is sometimes called the Northern Cross. It lies right within the Milky Way. Binoculars or a small telescope can be swept slowly around this part of the sky. Rich star fields, many of the them thousands of light years away, will come into view. They make up the soft glow of light from the Milky Way. Close to Cygnus there are dark patches where dust clouds in deep space cut out the faint background of light from distant stars.

Vega is a member of the small constellation of Lyra, the Lyre, and Altair belongs to Aquila, the Eagle. The other stars in these two constellations are much fainter than Vega and Altair. The attractive grouping of stars making up Delphinus, the Dolphin, lies close to Aquila.

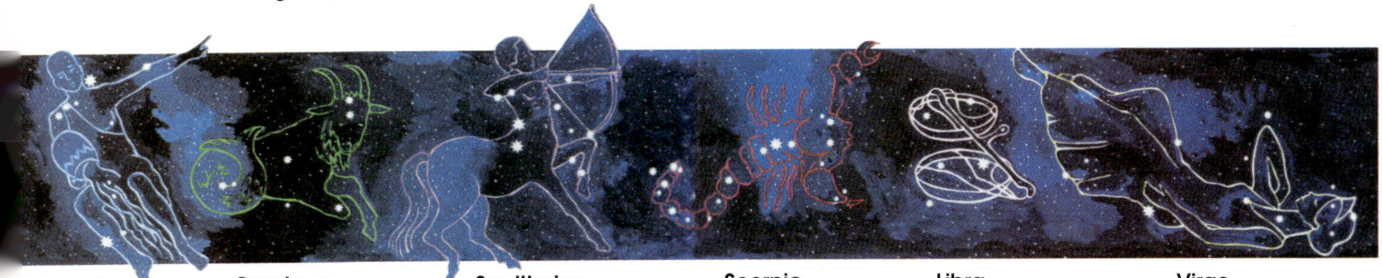

Aquarius Capricorn Sagittarius Scorpio Libra Virgo

NORTH & CENTRAL AMERICA

SOUTH AMERICA

EUROPE

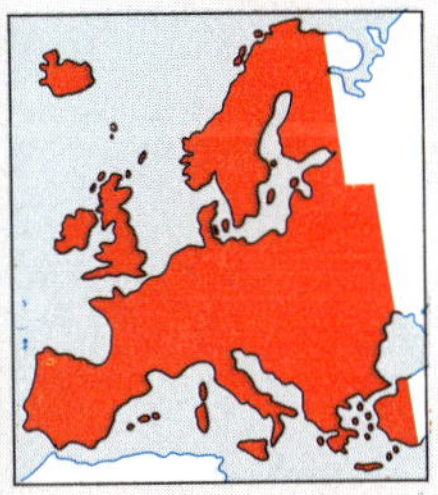

ASIA

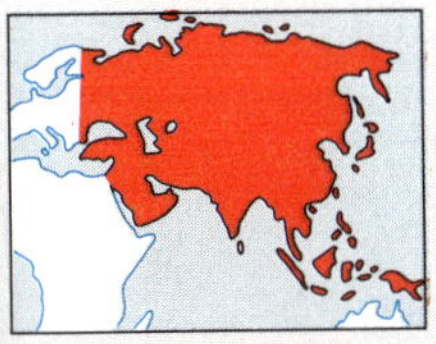

AFRICA

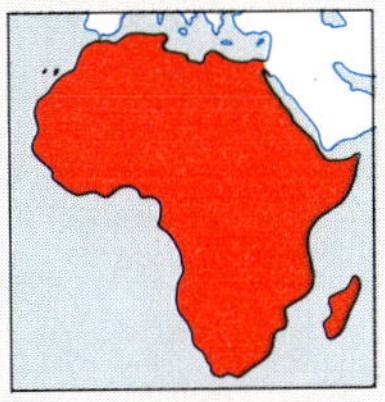

AUSTRALASIA & OCEANIA

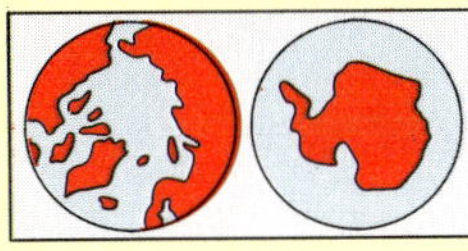

Roads – *at scales larger than 1:3 million*

Motorway/Highway
Other Main Road

– at scales smaller than 1:3 million

Principal Road: Motorway/Highway
Other Main Road
Main Railway

Towns & Cities

Population > 5,000,000
1-5,000,000
500,000-1,000,000
< 500,000

Paris National Capital
Airport
International Boundary
International Boundary – not defined or in dispute
Internal Boundary
River
Canal
Marsh or Swamp

Relief

▲ 1510 Peak (in metres)

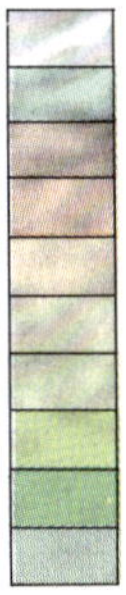

5000 metres (16405 feet)
4000 (13124)
3000 (9843)
2000 (6562)
1000 (3281)
500 (1641)
200 (656)
100 (328)
0
Land below sea level

Note – The 0-100 contour layer appears only at scales larger than 1:3 million

CONTENTS AND LEGEND

Cartography, designed and produced by Euromap Ltd, Pangbourne, England.

West from Greenwich
East from
ARCTIC
Bering Strait
Arctic Circle
Alaska (U.S.A.)
Gulf of Alaska
CANADA
Hudson Bay
Baffin Bay
GREENLAND (Denmark)
Godthåb
GREENLAND SEA
Svalbard (Nor.)
Reykjavik
ICELAND
Newfoundland
Ottawa
UNITED STATES OF AMERICA
Washington
Azores (Port.)
Bermuda (U.K.)
Tropic of Cancer
GULF OF MEXICO
MEXICO
México
Nassau
THE BAHAMAS
La Habana
CUBA
ATLANTIC
OCEAN
MICRONESIA
BELAU
STATES OF
FEDERATED
JAMAICA
Kingston
HAITI
DOM. REP.
Santo Domingo
Puerto Rico (U.S.A.)
Belmopan
BELIZE
GUATEMALA
Guatemala
HONDURAS
Tegucigalpa
EL SALVADOR
NICARAGUA
Managua
CARIBBEAN SEA
ANTIGUA
DOMINICA
ST. LUCIA
GRENADA
BARBADOS
TRINIDAD & TABAGO
COSTA RICA
San José
Panamá
PANAMA
Caracas
VENEZUELA
Georgetown
GUYANA
Paramaribo
SUR.
Cayenne
GUIANA (FRENCH)
COLOMBIA
Bogotá
PACIFIC
OCEAN
Equator
Islas Galápagos (Ecuador)
Quito
ECUADOR
PERU
Lima
BRAZIL
Brasília
BOLIVIA
Sucre
PARAGUAY
Asunción
Tropic of Capricorn
CHILE
ARGENTINA
Santiago
Buenos Aires
URUGUAY
Montevideo
Falkland Is. (U.K.) (Is Malvinas)
South Georgia (U.K.)
Tristan da Cunha (U.K.)
St. Helena (U.K.)
Ascension I. (U.K.)
Antarctic Circle
Madeira (Port.)
Islas Canarias (Sp)
CAPE VERDE
NORWAY
Oslo
SWEDEN
Stockholm
FINLAND
Helsinki
Tallinn
EST.
Riga
LAT.
LITH.
Vilnius
Moskva
DENMARK
København
UNITED KINGDOM
IRELAND
Dublin
London
NETH.
BEL.
LUX.
Bruxelles
Paris
FRANCE
Berlin
GERMANY
POLAND
Warszawa
BELARUS
Minsk
Praha
CZECH
Wien
AUS.
SLOV.
Budapest
HUNG.
SWZ.
SLO.
CRO.
BOS. HERZ.
YUGO.
Beograd
ROMANIA
București
UKRAINE
Kiyev
Kishinev
MOL.
BUL.
Sofiya
MAC.
ALB.
ITALY
Roma
PORTUGAL
Lisboa
Madrid
SPAIN
MEDITERRANEAN SEA
BLACK SEA
GREECE
Athínai
Ankara
TURKEY
CYPRUS
LEB.
Dimashq
ISRAEL
SYRIA
JORD.
Rabat
MOROCCO
Alger
Tunis
TUNISIA
Tarābulus (Tripoli)
ALGERIA
LIBYA
EGYPT
El Qâhira
Laâyoune
WESTERN SAHARA
MAURITANIA
Nouakchott
MALI
NIGER
CHAD
SUDAN
El Khartum
ERITREA
Asmera
Dakar
SENEGAL
GAMBIA
GUINEA BISSAU
Bamako
Niamey
BURKINA FASO
Ndjamena
GUINEA
Conakry
Freetown
SIERRA LEONE
Monrovia
LIBERIA
CÔTE D'IVOIRE
GHANA
TOGO
BENIN
Accra
NIGERIA
Abuja
CAMEROON
Yaoundé
CENTRAL AFRICAN REPUBLIC
Bangui
Malabo
E.G.
SÃO TOME AND PRINCIPE
GABON
CONGO
Brazzaville
Kinshasa
CABINDA (Angola)
ZAÏRE
RWANDA
BURUNDI
UGANDA
Kampala
KENYA
Nairobi
ETHI
Adis Abeba
TANZANIA
Dodoma
Luanda
ANGOLA
ZAMBIA
Lusaka
MALAWI
Lilongwe
Harare
ZIMBABWE
MOZAMBIQUE
NAMIBIA
Windhoek
Walvisbaai (S.A.)
BOTSWANA
Gaborone
Pretoria
Maputo
SWAZILAND
SOUTH AFRICA
LESOTHO
ALB - Albania
ARM - Armenia
AUS - Austria
AZER - Azerbaijan
BANG - Bangladesh
BEL - Belgium
BOS, HERZ. - Bosnia Herzegovina
BUL - Bulgaria
CAMB - Cambodia
CRO - Croatia
CZECH - Czech Republic
DOM. REP. - Dominican Republic
E.G. - Equatorial Guinea
EST - Estonia
GEOR - Georgia
HUNG - Hungary
JORD - Jordan
LAT - Latvia
LEB - Lebanon
LITH - Lithuania
LUX - Luxembourg
MAC - Former Yug. Rep. of Macedonia
MOL - Moldova
NETH - Netherlands
SLO - Slovenia
SLOV - Slovakia
SUR - Suriname
SWZ - Switzerland
U.A.E. - United Arab Emirates
YUGO - Yugoslavia

OCEAN
RUSSIAN FEDERATION
KAZAKHSTAN
Ulaanbaatar
MONGOLIA
Alma-Ata
UZBEKISTAN
Bishkek
KYRGYZSTAN
Tbilisi
Baku
AZER.
TURKMENISTAN
Tashkent
Ashkhabad
TAJIKISTAN
Dushanbe
Tehrān
IRAN
Kābul
AFGHANISTAN
Islamabad
PAKISTAN
Baghdād
KUWAIT
BAHRAIN
QATAR
Riyād
U.A.E.
Masqat
ARABIA
OMAN
REPUBLIC OF YEMEN
San'a
DJIBOUTI
SOMALIA
Muqdisho
CHINA
Beijing
Pyongyang
N. KOREA
Sõul
S. KOREA
SEA OF JAPAN
JAPAN
Tōkyō
NEPAL
Kathmandu
Thimphu
BHUTAN
New Delhi
INDIA
Dhākā
BANG.
MYANMAR (BURMA)
Rangoon
Hanoi
LAOS
Vientiane
THAILAND
Bangkok
VIETNAM
CAMB.
Phnom Penh
HONG KONG (U.K.)
T'ai-pei
TAIWAN
EAST CHINA SEA
SOUTH CHINA SEA
Manila
PHILIPPINES
ARABIAN SEA
BAY OF BENGAL
Colombo
SRI LANKA
MALDIVES
Kuala Lumpur
MALAYSIA
BRUNEI
SINGAPORE
INDONESIA
Jakarta
SEYCHELLES
INDIAN
OCEAN
COMOROS
Antananarivo
MADAGASCAR
MAURITIUS
Réunion
SEA OF OKHOTSK
BERING SEA
Bering Strait
Aleutian Is.
Alaska (U.S.A.)
Arctic Circle
CANADA
GULF OF ALASKA
PACIFIC
OCEAN
Tropic of Cancer
Hawaii (U.S.A.)
Northern Mariana Is. (U.S.A.)
TRUST TERRITORY OF THE PACIFIC OCEAN
FEDERATED STATES OF MICRONESIA
BELAU
NAURA
KIRIBATI
Equator
PAPUA NEW GUINEA
Port Moresby
SOLOMON ISLANDS
TUVALU
WESTERN SAMOA
CORAL SEA
VANUATU
FIJI
Nouvelle Calédonie (Fr.)
TONGA
Tropic of Capricorn
AUSTRALIA
Canberra
TASMAN SEA
Tasmania
Wellington
NEW ZEALAND
Is. Kerguelen (Fr.)
ANTARCTICA
Antarctic Circle
Greenwich
60°
80°
100°
120°
140°
160°
180°
40°
20°
0°

NORTH AMERICA Political

Scale 1: 41 600 000

0 500 1000 1500 km

0 250 500 750 1000 miles

CANADA

0 200 400 600 800km 0 200 400 600 miles

Scale 1: 30 000 000

UNITED STATES OF AMERICA & MEXICO

Scale 1: 20 000 000

0 200 400 600 km

0 200 400 600 miles

UNITED STATES OF AMERICA & MEXICO

U. S. A. EASTERN STATES

Scale 1: 8 600 000

0 100 200 300 km

0 100 200 miles

U. S. A. EASTERN STATES

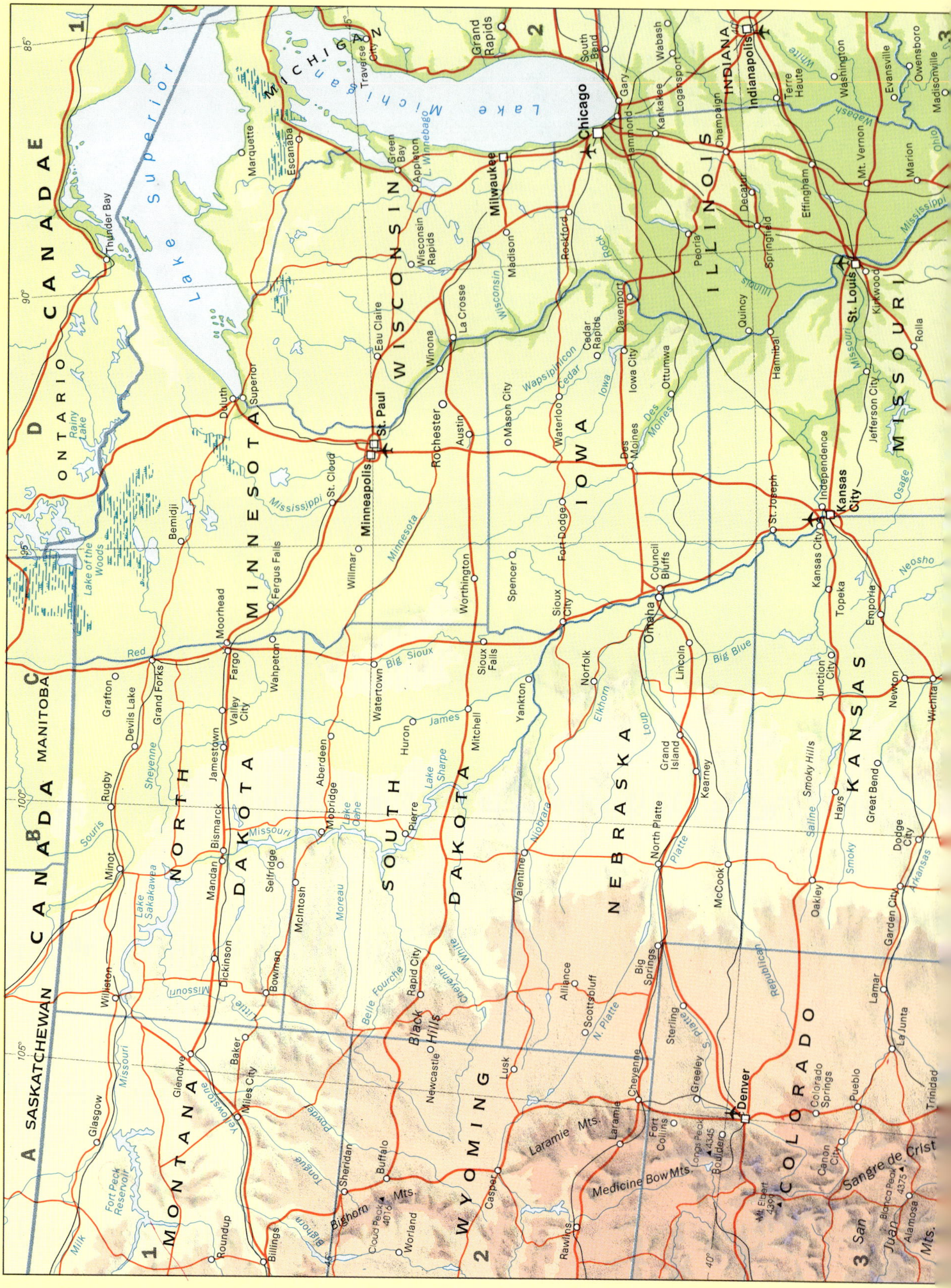

Scale 1: 8 600 000
0 100 200 300 km
0 100 200 miles

U. S. A. CENTRAL STATES

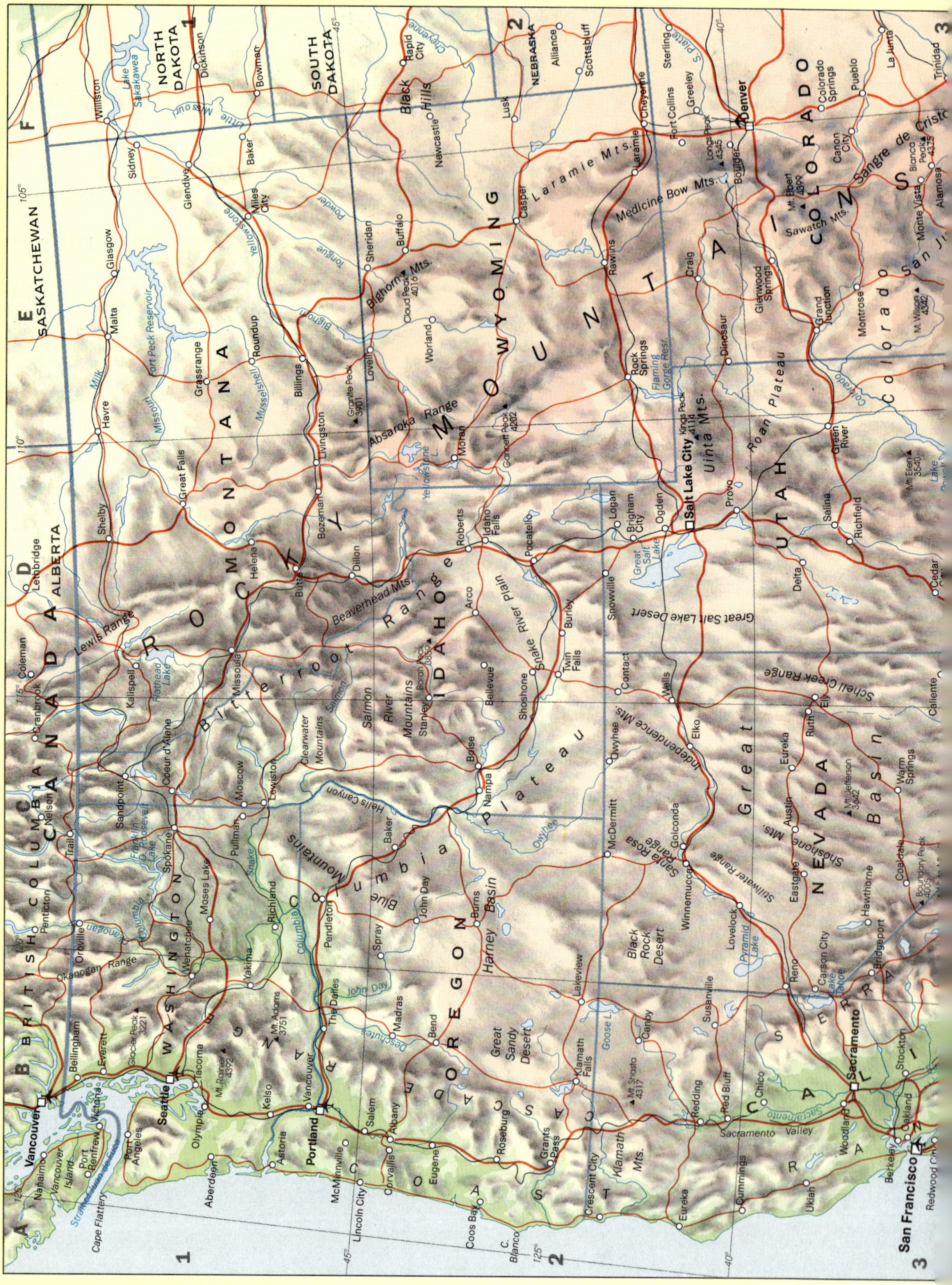

U. S. A. WESTERN STATES

Scale 1: 8 600 000

0 100 200 300km

0 100 200miles

U. S. A. WESTERN STATES

CENTRAL AMERICA & THE CARIBBEAN

Scale 1: 17 000 000
0 200 400 600km
0 200 400 miles

SOUTH AMERICA Political

Scale 1: 25 500 000

0 200 400 600 800 km

0 200 400 600 800 miles

SOUTH AMERICA

EUROPE Political

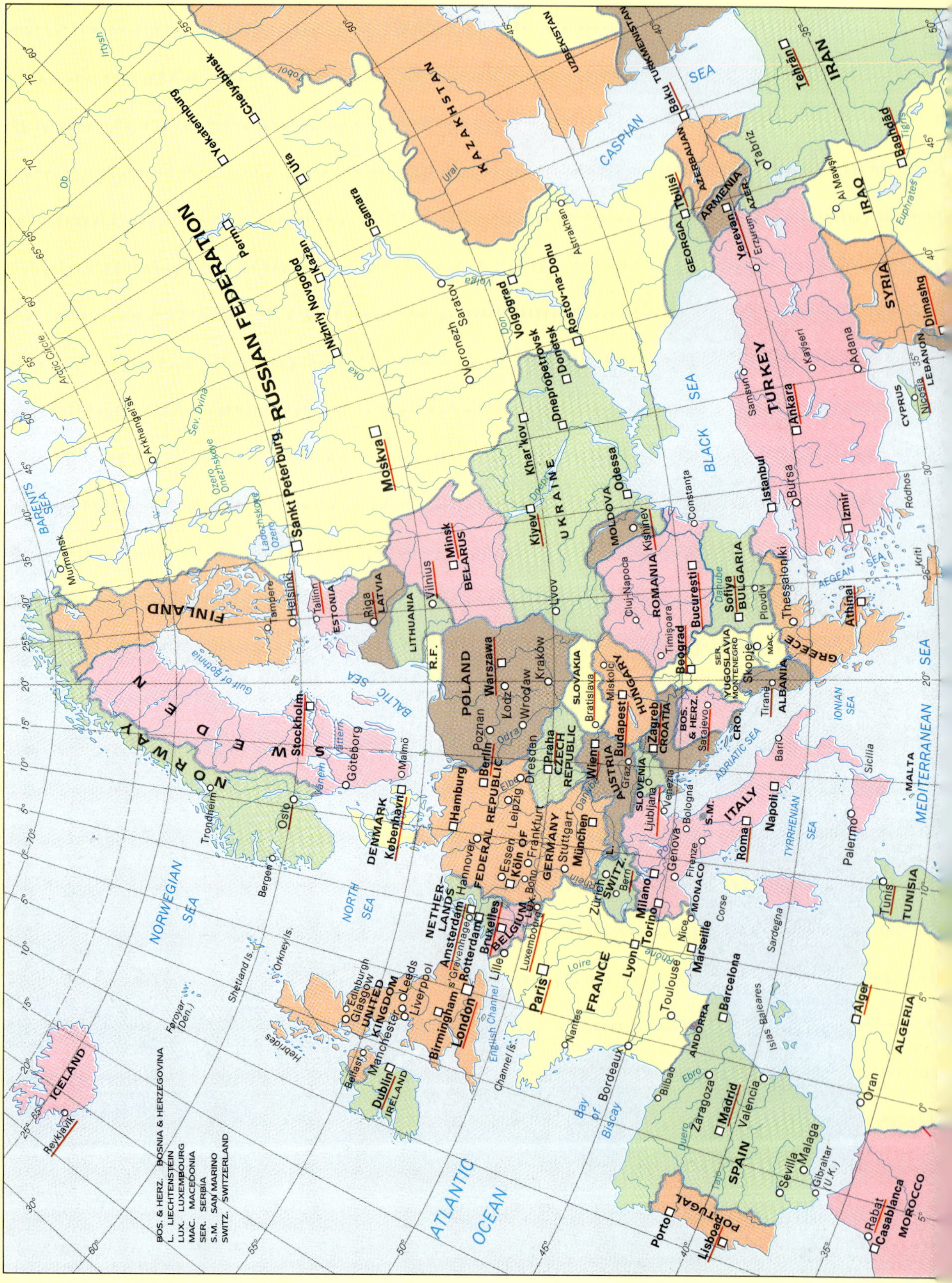

Scale 1: 25 500 000

0 200 400 600 800 km

0 200 400 600 miles

© Geddes & Grosset 0 100 200 300 km 0 100 200 miles **Scale 1: 8 000 000**

BRITISH ISLES

Scale 1: 2 600 000

0 200 400 600 800 km

0 200 400 600 800 miles

ENGLAND AND WALES

SCOTLAND

ATLANTIC OCEAN
NORTH SEA
ORKNEY
Orkney Islands
SHETLAND
Shetland Islands
HIGHLAND
GRAMPIAN
TAYSIDE
CENTRAL
FIFE
LOTHIAN
STRATHCLYDE
BORDERS
DUMFRIES AND GALLOWAY
NORTHUMBERLAND
CUMBRIA
DURHAM
TYNE AND WEAR
ENGLAND
SCOTLAND
WESTERN ISLES
LONDONDERRY
ANTRIM
TYRONE
NORTHERN IRELAND
Grampian Mountains
North West Highlands
Southern Uplands
Outer Hebrides
Inner Hebrides
North Minch
Little Minch
North Channel
Pentland Firth
Moray Firth
Firth of Forth
Firth of Tay
Firth of Clyde
Firth of Lorn
Solway Firth
Edinburgh
Glasgow
Aberdeen
Dundee
Inverness
Perth
Stirling
Kirkwall
Lerwick
Stornoway
Fort William
Oban
Carlisle
Belfast
Scale 1: 2 600 000

IRELAND

0 50 100 km
0 50 miles

Scale 1: 2 600 000

FRANCE
ENGLAND
BELGIUM
LUXEMBOURG
FEDERAL REPUBLIC OF GERMANY
SWITZERLAND
LIECHTENSTEIN
AUSTRIA
ITALY
MONACO
ANDORRA
SPAIN
English Channel
Bay of Biscay
Golfe de Gascogne
Golfe du Lion
MEDITERRANEAN SEA
LIGURIAN SEA
Channel Is. (U.K.)
Corse (Fr.)
NORMANDIE
BRETAGNE
MAINE
ANJOU
POITOU
PICARDIE
ARTOIS
CHAMPAGNE
LORRAINE
ALSACE
BOURGOGNE
FRANCHE-COMTÉ
NIVERNAIS
ORLÉANAIS
LIMOUSIN
AUVERGNE
Massif Central
GUYENNE
GASCOGNE
LANGUEDOC
DAUPHINÉ
SAVOIE
PROVENCE
PYRÉNÉES
ROUSSILLON
Paris
Lyon
Marseille
Bordeaux
Toulouse
Nantes
Lille
Strasbourg
Torino
Milano
Genève
Bruxelles
Luxembourg

SPAIN AND PORTUGAL

0 100 200 km 0 100 miles **Scale 1: 6 400 000**

Scale 1: 6 500 000

0 50 100 150 200 km   0 50 100 miles

Budapest
Debrecen
Karcag
Szolnok
Oradea
Székesfehérvár
Kecskemét
Kiskunfelegyháza
Salonta
Szekszárd
Pécs
Szeged
Makó
Arad
Subotica
VOJVODINA
Osijek
Timişoara
Novi Sad
Vršac
Bosanski Brod
Ruma
Beograd
(Belgrade)
Šabac
Tuzla
Loznica
BOSNIA
HERZEGOVINA
Zenica
Sarajevo
Konjic
Mostar
Kragujevac
Čačak
Svetozarevo
Paraćin
YUGOSLAVIA
Kruševac
SERBIA
Novi Pazar
Niš
Leskovac
Pirot
Kosovska-Mitrovica
Priština
Vranje
MONTENEGRO
Ivangrad
Peć
KOSOVO
Uroševac
Titograd
Kotor
Dubrovnik
Mljet
Shkodër
Kumanovo
Skopje
Titov Veles
MACEDONIA
Tiranë (Tirana)
Durrës
Ohrid
Bitola
Gevgelija
Berat
Korçe
Vlorë
Kastoria
Thessaloniki
Khalkidhiki
Katerini
Ólimbos
Lárisa
Vólos
Ioánnina
Kérkira
Kérkira (Corfu)
Igoumenitsa
GREECE
Árta
Lamía
Amfilokhía
Levkás
Mesolóngion
Kefallinía
Zákinthos
Pátrai
Kórinthos
Pelopónnisos
Pirgos
Tripolis
Argos
Kalámai
Pílos
Neápolis
Kíthira
Athínai
(Athens)
Piraiévs
Thívai
Khalkís
Évvoia
Skíros
Skópelos
Skíathos
Límnos
Áyios Evstrátios
Lésvos
Khíos
Sámos
Ikaría
Ándros
Tínos
Míkonos
Kéa
Síros
Kíthnos
Sérifos
Sífnos
Páros
Náxos
Mílos
Síkinos
Íos
Amorgós
Thíra
Anáfi
Astipálaia
Kálimnos
Léros
Kós
Tílos
Ródhos
Ródhos
(Rhodes)
Kárpathos
Kásos
Kríti
(Crete)
Khaniá
Iráklion
Timbákion
Akr. Sídheros
KIKLÁDHES
DHODHEKÁNISOS
AEGEAN SEA
Mirtoan Sea
Sea of Crete
IONIAN SEA
IÓNIOI NÍSOI
SEA
Strait of Otranto
Golfo di Taranto
C. Sta Maria di Leuca
Monopoli
Brindisi
Taranto
Gallipoli
Rizzuto
ALBANIA
Cluj-Napoca
Tîrgu Mureş
Turda
Sebeş
Sibiu
Deva
Caransebeş
Braşov
ROMANIA
Carpaţii Meridionali
Carpathian Mts.
Rîmnicu-Vîlcea
Piteşti
Cîmpina
Ploieşti
Drobeta-Turnu-Severin
Filiaşi
Craiova
Slatina
Caracal
Videle
Bucureşti
(Bucharest)
Giurgiu
Urziceni
Iaşi
Roman
Bacău
Bîrlad
Tecuci
Focşani
Galati
Brăila
Buzău
Hîrşova
Medgidia
Constanţa
Mangalia
Kishinev
MOLDOVA
Odessa
UKRAINE
Izmail
Vidin
Lom
Ruse
Razgrad
Ludogorie
Tolbukhin
Pleven
Byala
Šumen
Varna
Vratsa
Veliko Turnovo
Sofiya
(Sofia)
Stara Planina
Kazanlŭk
Sliven
Burgas
BULGARIA
Stara Zagora
Dimitrovgrad
Plovdiv
Michurin
Blagoevgrad
Kulata
Rodopi Planina
Edirne
Babaeski
Drama
Xánthi
Komotiní
Sérrai
Kaválla
Thásos
Alexandroúpolis
Samothráki
Gökçeada
Keşan
Çorlu
Istanbul
Üsküdar
Sea of Marmara
Marmara
Bandirma
Bursa
Gelibolu
Eceabat
Çanakkale
Balikesir
Edremit
Ayvalik
Akhisar
TURKEY
Manisa
İzmir
Selçuk
Denizli
Muğla
Bodrum
Marmaris
BLACK SEA
Dunav
Dunărea
Tisza
Mureş
Drina
Sava
Morava
Olt
Prut
Siret
Nestos
Strimon
Pinios
Thermaikos Kólpos
K. Strimonikos
K. Singitikos
K. Toronaíos
Messiniakós Kólpos
Lakonikós Kólpos
1836
1849
2245
2543
2169
2925
2252
2032
2522
2692
2702
2480
2503
2917
2033
1726
2456

Scale 1: 6 500 000

0 50 100 150 200km

0 50 100 miles

Gulf of Riga
Visby
Gotland
Ventspils
Riga
Jelgava
Dvina
LATVIA
Rezekne
Ostrov
Rzhev
Velikiye-Luki
RUSSIAN FEDERATION
Liepāja
Šiauliai
Panevežys
Daugavpils
Novopolotsk
Polotsk
Vitebsk
Smolensk
Klaipeda
Šilute
LITHUANIA
Ukmerge
Lepel'
Orsha
Kaunas
Vilnius
Borisov
Molodechno
Mogilev
Gulf of Danzig
Kaliningrad
Gusev
RUSSIAN FED.
Gdynia
Gdańsk
Elblag
Minsk
Lida
Augustow
Grodno
Neman
BELARUS
Bobruysk
Olsztyn
Grudziadz
Baranovichi
Dneprovskaya
Gomel
Soligorsk
Bydgoszcz
Toruń
Mława
Białystok
Rechitsa
POLAND
Włocławek
Mozyr
Warszawa
(Warsaw)
Siedlice
Bug
Brest
Kobrin
Pinsk
Pripyat
Nizmennost'
Chernigov
Konin
Kalisz
Łódź
Sarny
Nezhin
Radom
Lublin
Kovel'
Korosten
Kiyevskoye Vokhr
Kiyev
Kepno
Lutsk
Rovno
Kielce
Częstochowa
Zhitomir
Opole
Shepetovka
Bytom
Wisła
Belaya Tserkov
Gliwice
Sosnowiec
Berdichev
Rybnik
Katowice
Kraków
Rzeszów
Tarnów
Przemyśl
L'vov
UKRAINE
Khmel'nitskiy
Ternopol
Vinnitsa
Cherkassy
Smela
Ostrava
Beskidy Zachodnie
Podol'skaya Voz.
Pridneprovskaya Vozv.
Uman
Stryy
Žilina
2655
Ivano-Frankovsk
Kamenets Podolskiy
SLOVAKIA
Košice
Kolomyya
Uzhgorod
Chernovtsy
Nitra
Carpathian Mts
Prut
Bel'tsy
MOLDOVA
Dnestr
Miskolc
Nyíregyháza
Satu Mare
Suceava
Baia Mare
Iaşi
Kishinev
Győr
Debrecen
Budapest
Tisza
2102
Mureş
Roman
Odessa
Székesfehérvár
Szolnok
Karcag
Oradea
Balaton
Kecskemét
Cluj-Napoca
Bacău
HUNGARY
Salonta
1836
Tirgu Mureş
Kiskunfélegyháza
Turda
Birlad
1849
Szekszárd
Szeged
Makó
Tecuci
Pécs
Arad
Mureş
Sebeş
Focşani
Galati
Izmail
BLACK SEA
Sibiu
Braşov
Deva
Timişoara
ROMANIA
2245
2543
Carpatii Meridionali
Brăila
YUGOSLAVIA
Caransebeş
Osijek
Buzău
Novi Sad
Rîmnicu Vîlcea
Cîmpina
20°
25°
30°
45°
50°
55°
D
E
F
G
1
2
3

Scale 1: 9 600 000 0 100 200 300 kms 0 100 200 miles

ASIA Political

RUSSIAN FEDERATION, TRANSCAUCASIA AND CENTRAL ASIA

Scale 1: 27 000 000

0 200 400 600 800 1000 km

0 200 400 600 miles

OCEAN
LAPTEV SEA
EAST SIBERIAN SEA
CHUKCHI SEA
BERING SEA
SEA OF OKHOTSK
SEA OF JAPAN
YELLOW SEA
Bo Hai
O. Komsomolets
O. Oktyabr'skoy Revolyutsii
Severnaya Zemlya
O. Bol'shevik
Novosibirskiye Ostrova
O. Faddeyevskiy
O. Novaya Sibir
O. Kotel'nyy
O. Bol'shoy Lyakhovskiy
O. Vrangelya
Chukotskiy Poluostrov
Khrebet Chukotskiy
St. Lawrence (U.S.A.)
Arctic Circle
Gory Byrranga
Ozero Taymyr
Poluostrov Taymyr
Gory Putorana
Khrebet Orulgan
Khrebet Cherskogo
Verkhoyanskiy Khrebet
Khrebet Kolymskiy
Koryakskiy Khrebet
Kamchatka
Sredinnyy Khrebet
Klyuchevskaya Sopka 4750
Ust'Kamchatsk
Petropavlovsk Kamchatskiy
Ust'Nera
Magadan
Zaliv Sheikhova
Okhotsk
Khrebet Dzhugdzhur
Indigirka
Kolyma
Lena
Aldan
Tunguska
Angara
Yenisey
Shilka
Amur
Ussuri
Sredne Sibirskoye Ploskogorye
FEDERATION
Suntar
Yakutsk
Aldan
Stanovoy Khrebet
Skovorodino
Belogorsk
Blagoveshchensk
Birobidzhan
Khabarovsk
Komsomol'sk na-Amure
Sovetskaya Gavan
Aleksandrovsk-Sakhalinskiy
Sakhalin
Yuzhno-Sakhalinsk
Kuril'skiye Ostrova (Kuril Is.)
Sikhote-Alin'
Xiao Hinggan Ling
Da Hinggan Ling
Yeniseysk
Bratsk
Krasnoyarsk
Ozero Baykal
Tulun
Cheremkhovo
Irkutsk
Angarsk
Ulan Ude
Yablonovyy Khrebet
Chita
Borzya
Manzhouli
Abakan
Zapadnyy Sayan
Vostochnyy Sayan
Kyzyl
Hövsgöl Nuur
Uvs Nuur
Ulaanbaatar (Ulan Bator)
Choybalsan
Hovd
Tsetserleg
MONGOLIA
Altay
Saynshand
GOBI
Hohhot
Baotou
Beijing
Tianjin
Shijiazhuang
Taiyuan
Jinan
Huang
Qingdao
CHINA
Yumen
Lop Nur
Qiqihar
Harbin
Oz. Khanka
Ussuriysk
Vladivostok
Nakhodka
Jilin
Changchun
Fushun
Shenyang
Anshan
Jinzhou
Lüda
Ch'ŏngjin
Hamhŭng
NORTH KOREA
Wŏnsan
P'yŏngyang
Sŏul (Seoul)
SOUTH KOREA
Taejŏn
Taegu
Kwangju
Pusan
Mokp'o
JAPAN
Wakkanai
Hokkaidō
Sapporo
Hakodate
Aomori
Sendai
Niigata
Honshū
Tōkyō
Yokohama
Kyōto
Nagoya
Kōbe
Ōsaka
Shikoku
Kita-Kyūshū
Fukuoka
Kyūshū
Kagoshima
1 2 3 4 5 6 7
L M N O P Q R S T U
C H I M N O P
100° 110° 120° 130° 140° 150° 160° 170° 80° 70° 60° 50° 40° 30° 180°

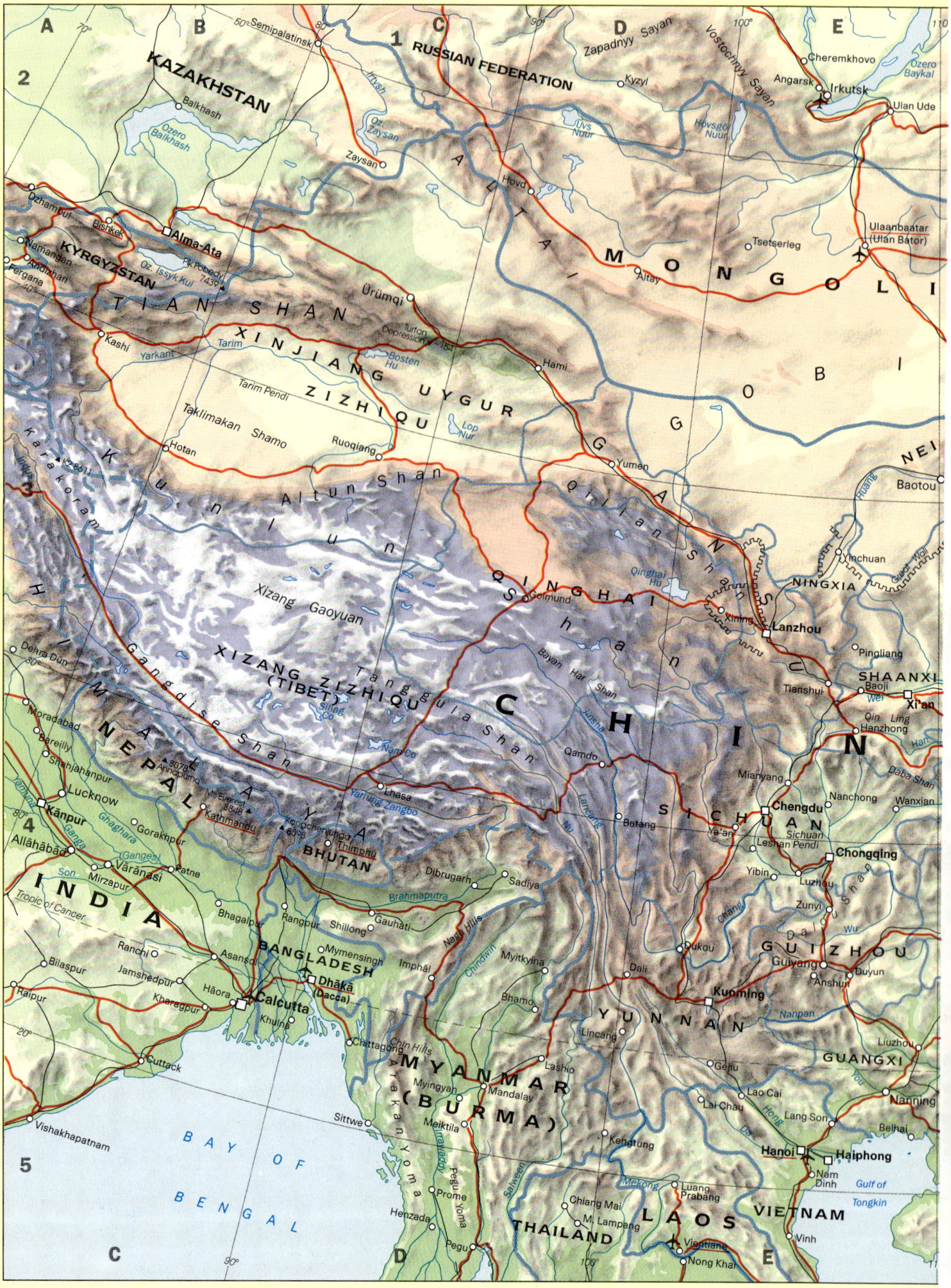

Scale 1: 19 500 000

0 200 400 600 800 km

0 100 200 300 400 500 miles

RUSSIAN FEDERATION
HEILONGJIANG
JILIN
LIAONING
MONGOL ZIZHIQU (INNER MONGOLIA)
HEBEI
SHANXI
SHANDONG
HENAN
JIANGSU
ANHUI
HUBEI
ZHEJIANG
HUNAN
JIANGXI
FUJIAN
GUANGDONG
NORTH KOREA
SOUTH KOREA
JAPAN
TAIWAN
SEA OF JAPAN
YELLOW SEA
EAST CHINA SEA
SOUTH CHINA SEA
PACIFIC OCEAN
Bo Hai
Yablonovyy Khrebet
Da Hinggan Ling
Xiao Hinggan Ling
Sikhote-Alin
Nansei-shotō (Ryūkyū Is.)
Honshū
Hokkaidō
Shikoku
Kyūshū
Sakhalin
Kuril Islands
La Pérouse Strait
Korea Strait
Taiwan Strait
Luzon Strait
Amur
Shilka
Ergun
Nen
Songhua
Ussuri
Khanka
Huang
Chang
Hui
Dongting Hu
Poyang Hu
Xi
Skovorodino
Chita
Borzya
Manzhouli
Hailar
Choybalsan
Saynshand
Erenhot
Belogorsk
Blagoveshchensk
Komsomol'sk na-Amure
Aleksandrovsk-Sakhalinskiy
Sovetskaya Gavan
Birobidzhan
Khabarovsk
Yuzhno-Sakhalinsk
Iturup
Kunashir
Wakkanai
Asahikawa
Sapporo
Otaru
Kushiro
Hakodate
Hegang
Jiamusi
Shuangyashan
Qiqihar
Harbin
Mudanjiang
Ussuriysk
Nakhodka
Vladivostok
Baicheng
Changchun
Jilin
Siping
Liaoyuan
Tonghua
Ch'ŏngjin
Chifeng
Shenyang
Fushun
Fuxin
Benxi
Liaoyang
Anshan
Jinzhou
Yingkou
Dandong
Zhangjiakou
Hohhot
Datong
BEIJING
Beijing (Peking)
Qinhuangdao
Tangshan
Tianjin
Lüda
Hamhŭng
Wŏnsan
P'yŏngyang
Kaesŏng
Sŏul (Seoul)
Taejŏn
Taegu
Kwangju
Mokp'o
Pusan
Cheju do
Baoding
Cangzhou
Shijiazhuang
Taiyuan
Yangquan
Xingtai
Dezhou
Handan
Jinan
Zibo
Weifang
Yantai
Qingdao
Changzhi
Linfen
Anyang
Jining
Xinxiang
Zhengzhou
Kaifeng
Sanmenxia
Luoyang
Xuzhou
Lianyungang
Qingjiang
Xuchang
Nanyang
Luohe
Bengbu
Huainan
Yangzhou
Nantong
Nanjing
Zhenjiang
Wuxi
Shanghai
Suzhou
Hefei
Wuhu
Xiangfan
Xinyang
Lu'an
Wuhan
Huangshi
Tongling
Anqing
Hangzhou
Ningbo
Shaoxing
Jinhua
Yichang
Shashi
Jiujiang
Jingdezhen
Qu Xian
Changde
Yiyang
Nanchang
Shangrao
Wenzhou
Changsha
Xiangtan
Zhuzhou
Fuzhou
Ji'an
Nanping
Shaoyang
Hengyang
Chen Xian
Ganzhou
Quanzhou
Zhangzhou
Xiamen
Guilin
Shaoguan
Wuzhou
Shantou
Foshan
Guangzhou
Kowloon
HONG KONG (U.K.)
Macau (Macao) (Port.)
Maoming
Zhanjiang
Haikou
Hainan Dao
Chi-lung
T'ai-pei
Chang-hua
Tái-nan
Kao-hsiung
Batan Is.
Babuyan Is.
C. Engaño
Aparri
Laoag
PHILIPPINES
Luzon
Sakishima guntō
Okinawa
Amami Ō-shima
Ōsumi-shotō
Kagoshima
Miyazaki
Kumamoto
Nagasaki
Sasebo
Kita-Kyūshū
Fukuoka
Hiroshima
Tokushima
Matsuyama
Kōchi
Matsue
Tottori
Okayama
Kōbe
Ōsaka
Sakai
Wakayama
Kyōto
Nagoya
Shizuoka
Hamamatsu
Fukui
Gifu
Kanazawa
Nagano
Kawasaki
Tōkyō
Chiba
Yokohama
Utsunomiya
Nagaoka
Niigata
Yamagata
Sendai
Ishinomaki
Akita
Morioka
Aomori
Hachinohe
CENTRAL JAPAN
1 : 10 000 000
0 100 200 km
0 50 100 150 miles
Mizusawa
Miyako
Hanamaki
Kamaishi
Sakata
Tsuruoka
Furukawa
Sado shima
Sanjō
Fukushima
Aizu-Wakamatsu
Kōriyama
Iwaki
Hitachi
Mito
Tsuchiura
Ashikaga
Takasaki
Takada
Takaoka
Toyama
Komatsu
Noto-hantō
Matsumoto
Okaya
Kōfu
Fuji-san 3776
Shimizu
Numazu
Odawara
Yokosuka
Bōsō-hantō
Wakasa wan
Tsuruga
Maizuru
Tottori
Himeji
Ōgaki
Okazaki
Toyohashi
Yokkaichi
Matsusaka
Ise
Kii-sanchi
Kii-suidō
Shingū
Mikuni-sammyaku
Kiso-sammyaku

Scale 1: 21 000 000

0 200 400 600 800km

0 100 200 300 400 500 miles

EAST CHINA SEA
Ningbo
Shaoxing
Wenzhou
Okinawa
Nansei - shotō (Ryūkyū Is.)
T'ai-pei
Chi-lung
Sakishima guntō
Chang-hua
TAIWAN
T'ai-nan
Kao-hsiung
Batan Is.
Luzon Strait
Babuyan Is.
C. Engaño
Laoag
Aparri
San Fernando
Baguio
Dagupan
Luzon
Cabanatuan
Quezon City
Manila
Naga
PHILIPPINES
Batangas
Legazpi
Mindoro
Masbate
Samar
Panay
Iloilo
Cebu
Leyte
Bacolod
Negros
Bohol
Butuan
SULU SEA
Cagayan de Oro
Mindanao
Davao
Zamboanga
Moro Gulf
Cotabato
Basilan
Jolo
General Santos
Sulu Arch.
Tawitawi
Kep. Talaud
CELEBES SEA
Kep. Sangihe
Morotai
Manado
Halmahera
Gorontalo
MOLUCCA SEA
Teluk Tomini
Kep. Togian
Waigeo
Manokwari
Biak
Sorong
Yapen
Poso
Obi
Teluk Cenderawasih
Jayapura
Wewak
BISMARCK SEA
Misoōl
Sulawesi (Celebes)
Kep. Banggai
Kep. Sula
SERAM SEA
MALUKU (MOLUCCAS)
Fakfak
IRIAN JAYA
Peguhungan Maoke
Pk. Jaya 5029
Sepik
Seram
Buru
Ambon
Kendari
Central Range
PAPUA
Madang
Mt. Hagen
4508 Mt. Wilhelm
New Guinea
NEW GUINEA
Lae
New Britain
Muna
Butung
BANDA SEA
INDONESIA
Kep. Kai
Wokam
Kep. Aru
Wau
Owen Stanley Range
Salayar
Trangan
D'Entrecasteaux Is.
Yamdena
Kepulauan Tanimbar
P. Dolak
Fly
Islands
Flores
Alor
Wetar
Babar
Tg. Vals
Merauke
Daru
Port Moresby
Alotau
Ruteng
Ende
Dili
Kep. Leti
ARAFURA SEA
Torres Strait
C. York
SAWU SEA
Timor
Kupang
Roti
AUSTRALIA
CORAL SEA
PACIFIC OCEAN
Ogasawara - shotō (Jap.)
Kazan - rettō (Jap.)
Iwo Jima
Tropic of Cancer
Northern Mariana Is.
Guam (U.S.A.)
Yap
U.S. TRUST TERRITORY OF THE PACIFIC ISLANDS
BELAU
Caroline Islands
Equator
Admiralty Is.
Bismarck Archipelago
E F G H
1 2 3 4 5
130° 140° 150°
20° 10° 0° 10°

Scale 1: 21 000 000

0 200 400 600 800 km

0 100 200 300 400 500 miles

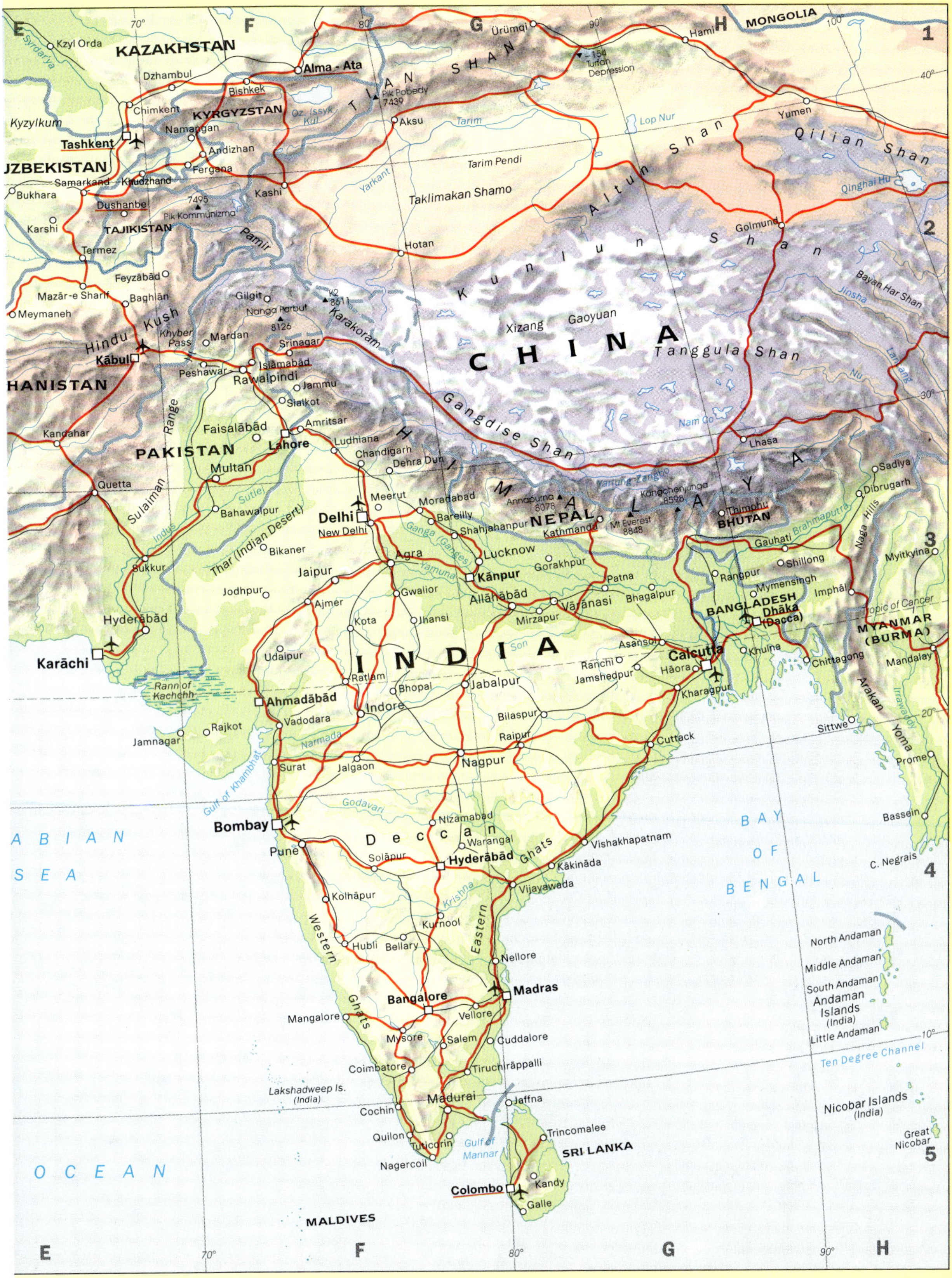

SOUTH ASIA AND THE MIDDLE EAST

Scale 1: 3 250 000

0 25 50 75 100 km

0 25 50 75 miles

0 400 800 1200 km 0 200 400 600 800 miles

Scale 1: 48 000 000

NORTHERN AFRICA

Scale 1: 23 500 000

0 200 400 600 800km

0 100 200 300 400 500miles

ITALY
Athinai
GREECE
Kriti
TURKEY
Izmir
Adana
Halab
Al Mawşil
Tehrān
CYPRUS
Nicosia
SYRIA
LEBANON
Beyrouth (Beirut)
Dimashq (Damascus)
IRAQ
Baghdād
IRAN
Eşfahān
Kūhhā-ye Zāgros
ISRAEL
Amman
Jerusalem
JORDAN
Al Başrah
Abādān
KUWAIT
An Nufūd
Al Baydā'O
Banghāzi
Gulf of Sirte
Tubruq
El Iskandarîya (Alexandria)
Port Said
Tanta
Suez Canal
El Gîza
Suez
El Qâhira (Cairo)
Sinai
Qattara Depression −133
El Faiyûm
G. Katherina 2637
Tabūk
El Minya
Asyût
Nile
BYA
Libyan Desert
EGYPT
Qena
Luxor
Aswân
Râs Banâs
Lake Nasser
SAUDI
ARABIA
Hijāz
Al Madīnah
Ar Riyāḑ (Riyadh)
Ad Dammām
BAHRAIN
QATAR
THE GULF
U.A.E.
Tropic of Cancer
Jiddah
Makkah
RED SEA
Wadi Halfa
Nubian Desert
besti
3415
Emi Koussi
Faya-Largeau
Port Sudan
Rub al Khālī
Atbara
Nile
Bodélé
Omdurman
Khartoum North
El Khartum (Khartoum)
Kassala
ERITREA
Mits'iwa
Asmera
Şan'ā
REPUBLIC OF YEMEN
Hadhramaut
Al Ḩudaydah
Al Mukallā
CHAD
Abéché
El Fasher
J. Marra 3071
SUDAN
El Obeid
Wad Medani
Gedaref
Dandkil −116
Ras Dashen 4620
Aseb
Ta'izz
Adan (Aden)
Gulf of Aden
Gonder
DJIBOUTI
Djibouti
Nyala
Bahr el Abiad (White Nile)
Bahr el Azraq
L. Tana
Desē
Berbera
Burco
Chari
Debre Mark'os
Ethiopian Highlands
Dire Dawa
Hārer
Hargeysa
Sarh
Bahr el Ghazal
Malakal
ETHIOPIA
Ādīs Ābeba (Addis Ababa)
Jima
Sudd
Wau
Jonglei Canal (under Construction)
CENTRAL AFRICAN REPUBLIC
Bambari
Bangassou
Bangui
Ubangi
Juba
L. Abaya
Shebele
SOMALIA
Uele
Aketi
Buta
Isiro
Mungbere
Arua
Gulu
Lake Turkana
Bumba
Impfondo
Zaire
Soroti
Albert
Mt. Elgon 4321
UGANDA
Ruwenzori Range
Kampala
Jinja
Kisangani
Kasese
KENYA
Eldoret
Kisumu
Mt. Kenya 5200
Juba
Muqdisho (Mogadishu)
Mbandaka
Entebbe
Nakuru
Equator
Kismaayo
L. Edward
Lake Victoria
Mbarara
Nairobi
Lualaba
Kigali
RWANDA
L. Mai-Ndombe
ZAÏRE
L. Kivu
L. Natron
Bukavu
Mwanza
Kilimanjaro 5895
INDIAN OCEAN
Bandundu
Kindu
BURUNDI
Bujumbura
L. Eyasi
Arusha
Moshi
Mombasa
Ilebo
Kigoma
Tabora
Masai Steppe
Tanga
Pemba
Kikwit
Kananga
Mbuji-Mayi
Kalémié
TANZANIA
Zanzibar
Lake Tanganyika
Dodoma
Dar es Salaam
Mwene Ditu
Kasai
L. Rukwa
20°
30°
40°
50°
10°
20°
30°
0°
F
G
H
J
1
2
3
4
5

SOUTHERN AFRICA

Scale 1: 23 500 000

0 200 400 600 800 km

0 100 200 300 400 500 miles

0 200 400 600 800 1000 km

0 200 400 600 miles

Scale 1: 29 000 000

AUSTRALASIA

Scale 1: 72 000 000

0 1000 2000 3000 km

0 1000 2000 3000 4000 5000 miles

CANADA
UNITED STATES OF AMERICA
MEXICO
GREENLAND (Den.)
ICELAND
Reykjavik
ALASKA (U.S.A.)
Anchorage
Gulf of Alaska
Kodiak I.
Edmonton
Calgary
Regina
Winnipeg
Vancouver
Seattle
Portland
Minneapolis
Chicago
Detroit
Toronto
Ottawa
Montréal
Boston
New York
Philadelphia
Baltimore
Washington
Pittsburgh
Cincinnati
St. Louis
Denver
San Francisco
Los Angeles
San Diego
Dallas
Atlanta
New Orleans
Houston
Miami
Hudson Bay
LABRADOR SEA
Newfoundland
ATLANTIC OCEAN
Bermuda (U.K.)
GULF OF MEXICO
Monterrey
Guadalajara
México
La Habana
CUBA
THE BAHAMAS
HAITI
DOMINICAN REPUBLIC
JAMAICA
BELIZE
GUATEMALA
Guatemala
HONDURAS
Tegucigalpa
San Salvador
EL SALVADOR
NICARAGUA
Managua
COSTA RICA
San José
PANAMA
Panamá
CARIBBEAN SEA
Caracas
VENEZUELA
Medellín
Bogotá
COLOMBIA
Quito
Guayaquil
ECUADOR
PERU
Lima
BRAZIL
BOLIVIA
La Paz
Sucre
PAR.
Asunción
CHILE
Santiago
ARGENTINA
Buenos Aires
URUGUAY
Montevideo
Patagonia
Tierra del Fuego
Falkland Is. (Islas Malvinas) (U.K.)
South Georgia (U.K.)
Honolulu
Hawaii
OCEAN
Palmyra (U.S.A.)
Kiritimati
Jarvis I. (U.S.A.)
French Polynesia
Îs. Marquises (Fr.)
Tahiti
Îs. Tuamotu (Fr.)
Pitcairn I. (U.K.)
Cook Is. (N.Z.)
I. de Pascua (Ch.)
Islas Galápagos (Ecuador)
Tropic of Cancer
Equator
Tropic of Capricorn

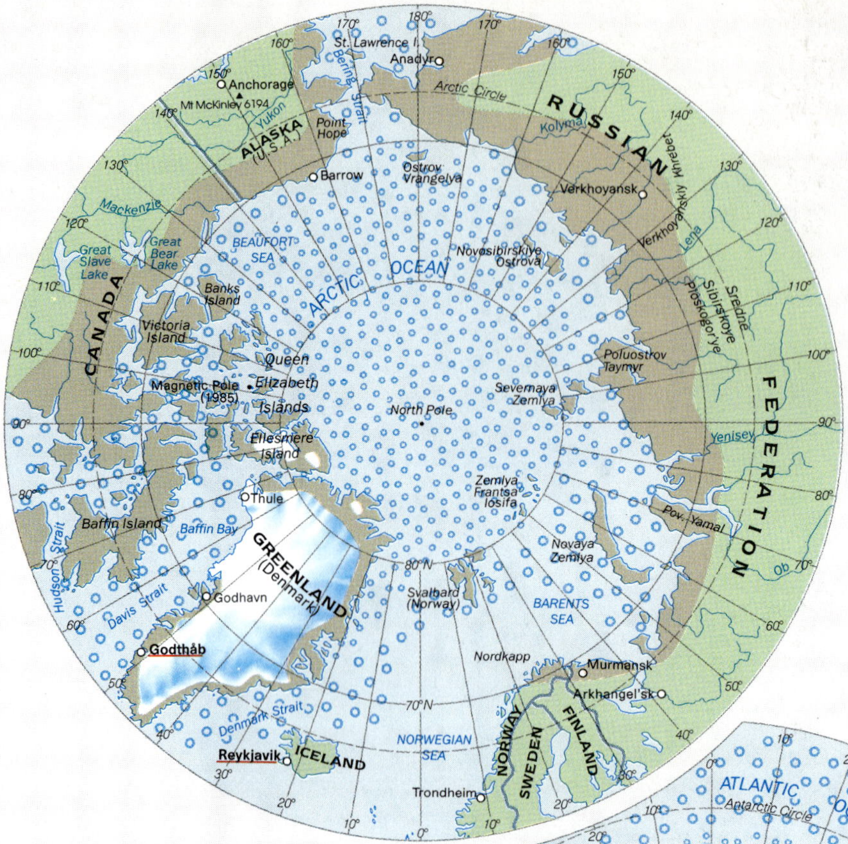

THE ARCTIC

Pack Ice
Drift Ice
Ice Cap
Permafrost

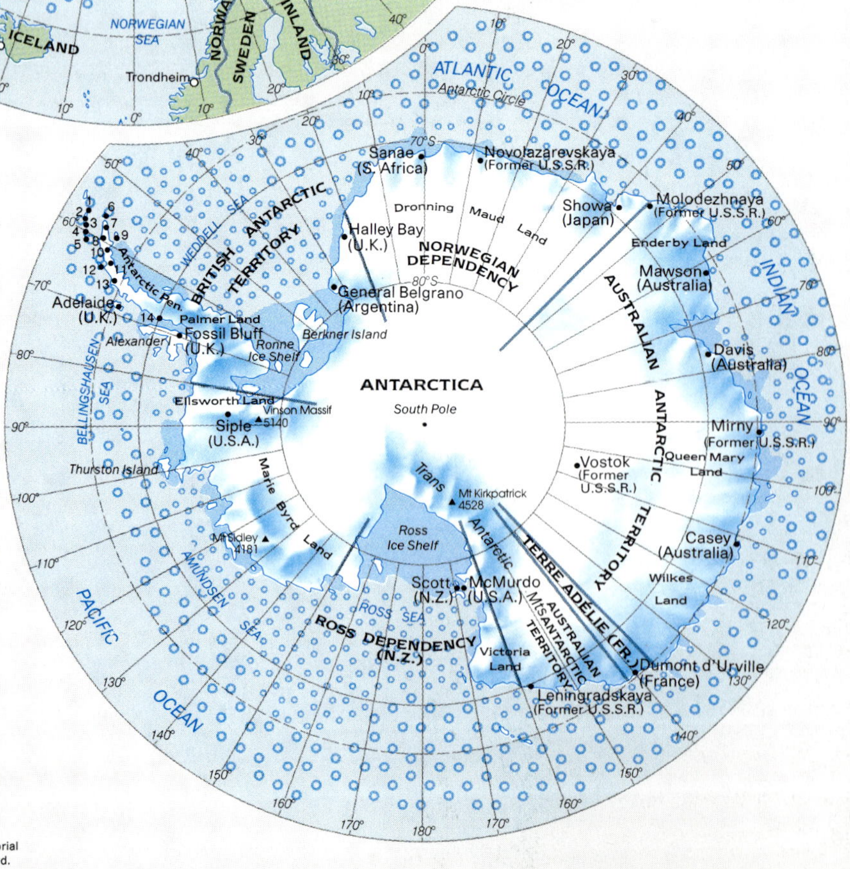

ANTARCTICA

Pack Ice
Drift Ice
Ice Cap
Ice Shelf

• Antarctic Research Stations

1 Arctowski (Poland)
2 Bellingshausen (Former U.S.S.R.)
3 Presidente Frei (Chile)
4 Artura Prat (Chile)
5 Deception (Argentina)
6 Petrel (Argentina)
7 Esperanza (Argentina)
8 General Bernado O'Higgins (Chile)
9 Vicecomodoro Marambio (Argentina)
10 Matienzo (Argentina)
11 Almirante Brown (Argentina)
12 Palmer (U.S.A.)
13 Faraday (U.K.)
14 San Martin (Argentina)

Note: Under the Antarctic Treaty of 1959 all territorial claims south of latitude 60°S have been suspended.

Scale 1: 60 000 000

0 400 800 1200 1600 km

0 200 400 600 800 1000 miles

GAZETTEER

Aachen (Aix-la-Chapelle) a historic university city and spa town in western Germany. (Pop. 250,000)
Aarhus *see* **Århus**.
Aba an industrial town in southern Nigeria. (Pop. 210,700)
Abadan a major oil-refining port on an island in the Shatt al Arab waterway, southern Iran. (Pop. 296,000)
Abeokuta an industrial town in western Nigeria. (Pop. 301,100)
Aberdeen a major North Sea oil city and fishing port in northeast Scotland, and the administrative centre of the Grampian region. (Pop. 214,000)
Aberdeenshire *see* **Grampian**.
Abidjan a major port and the chief city of Côte D'Ivoire. (Pop. 1,850,000)
Åbo *see* **Turku**.
Abruzzi a region of southern central Italy; its capital is Aquila. (Pop. 1,246,600)
Abu Dhabi the largest sheikhdom of the United Arab Emirates, of which the city of Abu Dhabi is the capital. (67,350 sq km/26,000 sq miles; pop. emirate 535,700/city 244,000)
Abuja the new capital of Nigeria, in the centre of the country, still under construction but inaugurated in 1992.
Acapulco a large port and beach resort on the Pacific coast of Mexico. (Pop. 800,000)
Accra the capital and main port of Ghana. (Pop. 1,045,400)
Aconcagua the highest mountain of the Andes, in Argentina. (6960 m/22,835 ft)
Adan *see* **Aden**.
Adana a city and province in southern Turkey. (Pop. city 776,000)
Ad Dawhah *see* **Doha**.
Addis Ababa (Adis Abeba) the capital of Ethiopia, in the centre of the country. (Pop. 1,500,000)
Adelaide the state capital of South Australia. (Pop. 969,000)
Aden (Adan) a major port in southern Yemen, formerly the capital of South Yemen. (Pop. 264,350)
Adirondack Mountains a mountain range in New York State, USA. The highest peak is Mount Marcy (1629 m/5344 ft).
Adis Abeba *see* **Addis Ababa**.
Adriatic Sea a branch of the Mediterranean Sea, between ITALY, SLOVENIA and CROATIA.
Aegean Sea a branch of the Mediterranean Sea between Greece and Turkey.
Afghanistan (*Area* 652,090 sq km (251,772 sq miles); *population* 15,810,000; *capital* Kabul; *other major cities* Herat, Kandahar, Mazar-i-Sharif; *form of government* People's Republic; *religions* Sunni Islam, Shia Islam; *currency* Afghani). A a landlocked country in southern Asia. The greater part of the country is mountainous with several peaks over 6000 m (19,686 ft) in the central region. The climate is generally arid with extremes of temperature. There is considerable snowfall in winter. The main economic activity is agriculture, and although predominantly pastoral, successful cultivation takes place in the fertile plains and valleys. Natural gas is produced in the north and over 90% of this is piped to the former USSR.
Africa the second largest continent in the world, with the Mediterranean Sea to the north, the Atlantic Ocean to the west and the Indian Ocean to the east. There are 52 nations within Africa, excluding Western Sahara. (30,300,000 sq km/ 11,700,000 sq miles; pop. 537,000,000)
Agadir a port and popular tourist resort in Morocco. (Pop. 111,000)
Agra a city in central India, and site of the Taj Mahal. (Pop. 747,000)
Ahmadabad (Ahmedabad) an industrial city in western India. (Pop. 2,548,000)
Ahvaz a port on the Karun River in southern Iran. (Pop. 471,000)
Aix-en-Provence a university city in southern France. (Pop. 129,000)
Ajman the smallest emirate of the United Arab Emirates. (65 sq km/25 sq miles; pop. emirate 42,000/ town 27,000)
Akron a city in northeast Ohio, USA. (Pop. city 226,900/metropolitan area 650,100)
Alabama a state in southern USA. The state capital is Montgomery. (133,667 sq km/51,606 sq miles; pop. 4,021,000)
Alaska the largest and most northerly state of the USA. The state capital is Juneau. (1,518,800 sq km/ 586,400 sq miles; pop. 521,000)
Albacete a town and province of southeastern Spain. (Pop. town 177,100)
Albania (*Area* 28,748 sq km (11,100 sq miles); *population* 3,200,000; *capital* Tirana (Tiranë); *other major cities* Durrës, Shkodër, Elbasan; *form of government* Socialist Republic; *religion* Constitutionally atheist but mainly Sunni Islam; *currency* Lek). A small mountainous country in the eastern Mediterranean. Its immediate neighbours are Greece and the former Yugoslavian republics of Serbia and Macedonia, and it is bounded to the west by the Adriatic Sea. The climate is typically Mediterranean, although winters are severe in highland areas. All land is state owned, with the main agricultural areas on the Adriatic coast and in the Korce Basin. Industry is also nationalized and output is small. The principal industries are agricultural product processing, textiles, oil products and cement.
Albany the capital city of New York State, USA. (Pop. 99,500)
Al Basrah *see* **Basra**.
Albert, Lake in the Great Rift Valley, is shared between Uganda and Zaïre. (Also known as Lake Mobuto Sese Seko.) (5180 sq km/ 2000 sq miles)
Alberta a province of western Canada; Edmonton is its capital. (661,190 sq km/ 255,285 sq miles; pop. 2,238,000)
Ålborg a city and port in northern Denmark. (Pop. 160,000)
Albuquerque a university city on the Rio Grande in New Mexico, USA. (Pop. 350,600)
Alcalá de Henares a town in central Spain, birthplace of Miguel de Cervantes (1547-1616), author of Don Quixote. (Pop. 142,900)
Alderney one of the CHANNEL ISLANDS.
Aleppo (Halab) an industrial city of ancient origins in Syria. (Pop. 905,944)
Alexandria the main port of Egypt, on the Nile delta. (Pop. 2,320,000)
Al Fujayrah the second smallest emirate in the United Arab Emirates. (117 sq km/45 sq miles; pop. emirate 38,000/town 760)
Al Furat *see* **Euphrates, River**.
Algarve the southern province of Portugal.
Algeria (*Area* 2,381,741 sq km (919,590 sq miles); *population* 25,360,000; *capital* Algiers (Alger); *other major cities* Oran, Constantine, Annaba; *form of government* Republic; *religion* Sunni Islam; *currency* Algerian dinar). A huge country in northern Africa, which fringes the Mediterranean Sea. Over four-fifths is covered by the Sahara Desert. Near the north coastal area the Atlas Mountains run east-west in parallel ranges. The climate in the coastal areas is warm and temperate with most of the rain falling in winter. Inland conditions become more arid, and temperatures range from 49°C during the day to 10°C at night. It is unproductive agriculturally, but possesses one of the largest reserves of natural gas and oil in the world.
Algiers (El Djazair, Alger) the capital of Algeria, on the Mediterranean coast. (Pop. 1,800,000)
Alicante a port and popular beach resort, and also the name of the surrounding province, on the Mediterranean coast of Spain. (Pop. town 251,400)
Alice Springs a desert settlement in the Northern Territory of Australia. (Pop. 18,400)
Aligarh a university town in central India. (Pop. 321,000)
Allahabad a holy city in India on the confluence of the rivers Ganges and Yamuna. (Pop. 650,000)
Alma-Ata (Almaty) a trading and industrial city and capital of KAZAKHSTAN. (Pop. 1,046,100)
Al Madinah *see* **Medina**.
Al Manamah the capital and main port of Bahrain. (Pop. 115,054)
Al Mawsil *see* **Mosul**.
Alps, The a mountain range in southern central Europe that spans the borders of Switzerland, France, Germany, Austria, Slovenia and Italy.
Alsace a region in the northeast of France.

Altai an area of high mountain ranges in central Asia on the borders of China and the Russian Federation at the western end of Mongolia.

Amalfi a small, picturesque town on a spectacular part of the west coast of Italy. (Pop. 6100)

Amarillo an industrial city in northwest Texas. (Pop. 162,900)

Amazon, River (Amazonas) the world's second longest river it rises in the Andes of Peru and flows east through Brazil to the Atlantic Ocean. (Length 6440 km/4000 miles)

Ambon (Amboina) an island and the capital of the so-called Spice Islands in the Maluku group in eastern central Indonesia. (813 sq km/314 sq miles; pop. 73,000)

America the continent lying between the Atlantic and Pacific Oceans, divided into three zones: North America (USA, Canada, Mexico and Greenland: 23,500,000 sq km/9,000,000 sq miles, pop. 354,000,000); Central America (between the southern Mexico border and the Panama-Colombia border with the Caribbean: 1,849,000 sq km/714,000 sq miles, pop. 63,000,000); and South America (south of the Panama-Colombia border: 17,600,000 sq km/6,800,000 sq miles, pop. 284,000,000).

American Samoa *see* **Samoa, American**.

Amiens an industrial city and capital of the Somme department of northern France. (Pop. 159,600)

Amindivi Islands *see* **Lakshadweep**.

Amman the capital of JORDAN, in the northeast of the country. (Pop. 1,232,600)

Amritsar an industrial city in northern India and home of the Golden Temple, the most sacred shrine of the Sikhs. (Pop. 595,000)

Amsterdam the capital and commercial centre of the Netherlands, a historic port set on the IJSSELMEER. (Pop. 712,300)

Amudar'ya, River a central Asian river forming much of the border between Tajikistan and Afghanistan before flowing through Uzbekistan into the Aral Sea. Its ancient name was Oxus. (Length 2620 km/1630 miles)

Amundsen Sea an arm of the South Pacific in Antarctica.

Amur, River (Heilong Jiang) a river which runs along the border between China and the Russian Federation, flowing east into the Pacific Ocean. (Length 4510 km/2800 miles)

Anatolia the historical name for the Asian part of Turkey.

Anchorage the largest city and port in Alaska, USA, on its southern coast. (Pop. 226,700)

Andalusia (Andalucía) a region of southwestern Spain, with a coast on the Mediterranean and Atlantic. (Pop. 6,441,800)

Andaman and Nicobar Islands two groups of islands in the Bay of Bengal, administered by India. (Pop. 188,700)

Andaman Sea a branch of the Bay of Bengal, lying between the Andaman Islands and Burma.

Andes a high mountain range that runs down the entire length of the western coast of South America. The highest peak is ACONCAGUA.

Andhra Pradesh a state in southeast India. The capital is Hyderabad. (275,088 sq km/106,184 sq miles; pop. 53,549,700)

Andorra (*Area* 453 sq km (175 sq miles); *population* 51,400; *capital* Andorra-la-Vella; *form of government* Co-principality; *religion* RC; *currency* Franc, Peseta). A tiny state, high in the eastern Pyrénées, between France and Spain. It consists of deep valleys and high mountain peaks which reach heights of 3000 m (9843 ft). Although only 20 km (12 miles) wide and 30 km (19 miles) long, the spectacular scenery and climate attract many tourists. Cold weather with heavy snowfalls in winter makes for ideal skiing. Tourism and the duty-free trade are now Andorra's chief sources of income.

Andorra-la-Vella the capital of ANDORRA. (Pop. 14,000)

Andros the largest of the islands of the Bahamas (4144 sq km/1600 sq miles; pop. 8900)

Angara, River a river in the Russian Federation flowing from Lake Baikal into the Yenisey River. (Length 1825 km/1135 miles)

Angel Falls a narrow band of water falling 979 m (3212 ft) from a high plateau in southeastern Venezuela to form the world's highest waterfall.

Anglesey an island off the northwestern tip of Wales. (715 sq km/276 sq miles; pop. 69,000)

Angola (*Area* 1,246,700 sq km (481,351 sq miles); *population* 10,020,000; *capital* Luanda; *other major cities* Huambo, Lobito, Benguela; *form of government* People's Republic; *religions* RC, Animism; *currency* Kwanza). Angola is situated on the Atlantic coast of west central Africa and lies about 10°S of the Equator. Its climate is tropical with temperatures constantly between 20°C and 25°C. The rainfall is heaviest in inland areas where there are vast equatorial forests. The country is also rich in minerals. Oil production is the most important aspect of the economy.

Anguilla an island in the Leeward Islands group of the Caribbean, now a self-governing British dependency. (91 sq km/35 sq miles; pop. 6500)

Angus *see* **Tayside**.

Anhui (Anhwei) a province of eastern China. Its capital is Hefei. (130,000 sq km/50,000 sq miles; pop. 48,030,000).

Anjou a former province of western France, in the valley of the River Loire.

Ankara the capital of Turkey, in the eastern central part of Asian Turkey. (Pop. 2,252,000).

Annaba (Bone) a historic town and seaport on the Mediterranean coast of Algeria. (Pop. 245,000)

Annapolis the capital of the state of Maryland, USA. (Pop. 31,900)

Annapurna a mountain of the Himalayas, in Nepal. (8172 m/26,810 ft)

Anshan a steel-manufacturing city in Liaoning province, northern China. (Pop. 1,250,000)

Antakya (Antioch) an ancient city in southern Turkey. (Pop. 109,200)

Antalya a port and resort on the Mediterranean coast of Turkey. (Pop. 258,100)

Antananarivo the capital of MADAGASCAR. (Pop. 663,000)

Antarctic Circle latitude 66° 32' south. At the southern winter solstice, the sun does not rise, nor does it set at the summer solstice, at this line, or in higher latitudes.

Antarctic Ocean (Southern Ocean) the waters that surround Antarctica made up of the southern waters of the Atlantic, Indian and Pacific Oceans.

Antarctica an ice-covered continent around the South Pole consisting of a plateau and mountain ranges reaching a height of 4500 m (15,000 ft). It is uninhabited apart from temporary staff at research stations. (14,000,000 sq km/5,100,000 sq miles)

Antigua and Barbuda (*Area* 440 sq km (170 sq miles); *population* 85,000; *capital* St. John's; *form of government* Constitutional Monarchy; *religion* Christianity (mainly Anglicanism); *currency* East Caribbean dollar). Located on the eastern side of the Leeward Islands, a tiny state comprising three islands—Antigua, Barbuda and the uninhabited Redonda. The climate is tropical although its average rainfall of 100 mm (4 inches) makes it drier than most of the other islands of the West Indies. On Antigua, many palm-fringed sandy beaches make it an ideal tourist destination. Barbuda is surrounded by coral reefs and is home to a wide range of wildlife.

Antioch *see* **Antakya**.

Antilles the major chain of islands in the Caribbean, divided into two groups: the Greater Antilles (which includes Cuba and Puerto Rico) to the west; and the Lesser Antilles (including e.g. Martinique and Barbados) to the east.

Antrim a county and town in Northern Ireland. (2831 sq km/1093 sq miles; pop. county 642,267/ town 22,242)

Antwerp (Antwerpen, Anvers) the capital of the province of Antwerp and the main port of Belgium. (Pop. 488,000)

Anvers *see* **Antwerp**.

Anyang an ancient city in HENAN province, China. (Pop. 500,000)

Aomori a port on HONSHU Island, Japan. (Pop. 294,000)

Apennines (Appennino) the mountain range which forms the "backbone" of Italy. The highest peak is Monte Corno (2912 m/9554 ft).

Apia the capital of WESTERN SAMOA. (Pop. 34,000)

Appalachian Mountains a chain of mountains which stretches 2570 km (1600 miles) down eastern North America from Canada to Alabama in the USA. The highest peak is Mount Mitchell (2037 m/6684 ft).

Appennino *see* **Apennines**.

Apulia *see* **Puglia**.

Aqaba the only port in Jordan, on the Gulf of Aqaba. (Pop. 35,000)

Aquitaine a region and former kingdom of southwestern France.

Arabian Gulf *see* **Gulf, The**.

Arabian Sea a branch of the Indian Ocean between India and Arabia.

Arafura Sea a stretch of the Pacific Ocean between New Guinea and Australia.

Aragon a region and former kingdom of northeast Spain.

Aral Sea a large, salty lake, to the east of the Caspian Sea, on the border between Uzbekistan and Kazakhstan. (64,750 sq km/25,000 sq miles)

Aran Islands (Oileáin Arann) three small islands, Inishmore, Inishmaan and Inisheer, off County Galway in the Republic of Ireland. (44 sq km/18 sq miles; Pop. 1380)

Ararat, Mount (Büjük Agri Dagi) the mountain peak in eastern Turkey where Noah's Ark is said to have come to rest. (5165 m/17,000 ft)

Arauca, River a major tributary of the Orinoco River which forms part of the border between Colombia and Venezuela. (Length 1000 km/620 miles)

Archangel (Arkhangel'sk) a port on the Dvina Delta on the White Sea in the Russian Federation. (Pop. 403,000)

Arctic the regions that lie to the north of the Arctic Circle.

Arctic Circle latitude 66° 32' north. The sun does not set above this line at the northern summer solstice, nor does it rise above this line at the winter solstice.

Arctic Ocean the ice-laden sea to the north of the Arctic Circle. (14,100,000 sq km/5,440,000 sq miles)

Ardabil a town in Iran, famous for its knotted carpets. (Pop. 222,000)

Ardennes a hilly and forested region straddling the borders of Belgium, Luxembourg and France.

Arequipa a city and department of Peru. (Pop. city 448,000)

Argentina (*Area* 2,766,889 sq km (1,068,296 sq miles); *population* 32,690,000; capital Buenos Aires; *other major cities* Cordoba, Rosaria, Mendoza, La Plata; *form of government* Federal Republic; *religion* RC; *currency* Austral). The world's eighth largest country, stretching from the Tropic of Capricorn to Cape Horn on the southern tip of the South American continent. To the west a massive mountain chain, the Andes, forms the border with Chile. The climate ranges from warm temperate over the Pampas in the central region, to a more arid climate in the north and west, while in the extreme south conditions although also dry are much cooler. A series of military regimes has resulted in an unstable economy.

Århus a port and the second largest city in Denmark. (Pop. 246,700)

Arizona a state in the southwest of the USA. The capital is Phoenix. (295,024 sq km/113,902 sq miles; pop. 3,137,000)

Arkansas a state in the south of the USA. The state capital is Little Rock. (137,539 sq km/53,104 sq miles; pop. 2,359,000)

Arkansas, River a tributary of the River Mississippi in the USA, flowing from the Rocky Mountains through the states of Kansas, Oklahoma and Arkansas. (Length 2335 km/1450 miles)

Arkhangel'sk *see* **Archangel.**

Armagh a county and city in Northern Ireland. (1254 sq km/484 sq miles; pop. county 118,820/city 12,700)

Armenia (1) the former independent kingdom that straddled the borders of modern Turkey, Iran, Georgia, and Azerbaijan.

Armenia (2) (*Area* 29,800 sq km (11,500 sq miles); *population* 3,267,000; *capital* Yerevan; *other major city* Kumayri (Leninkan); *form of government* Republic; *religion* Armenian Orthodox; *currency* Rouble). The smallest republic of the former USSR and part of the former kingdom of Armenia which was divided between Turkey, Iran and the former USSR. It declared independence from the USSR in 1991. It is a landlocked Transcaucasian republic, and its neighbours are Turkey, Iran, Georgia and Azerbaijan. It is very mountainous with many peaks over 3000 m (9900 ft). Agriculture is mixed in the lowland areas. Mining of copper, zinc and lead is important, and industrial development is increasing.

Arnhem a town in the Netherlands, scene of a battle in 1944 between British (and Polish) paratroops and the German army. (Pop. 128,600)

Arnhem Land an Aboriginal reserve in the Northern Territory of Australia.

Arno, River the main river of Tuscany in Italy, flowing westward through Florence to Pisa on the coast. (Length 245 km/152 miles)

Aruba a Caribbean island off the coast of Venezuela, formerly one of the Netherlands Antilles. The capital is Oranjestad. (193 sq km/75 sq miles; pop. 67,000; cur. Aruba guilder)

Arunachal Pradesh a union territory of northern India, bordering Tibet. The capital is Shillong. (Pop. 631,800)

Ascension Island a tiny volcanic island in the South Atlantic Ocean, forming part of the St Helena Dependencies. (Pop. 1625)

Ashkhabad the capital of Turkmenistan. (Pop. 347,000)

Asia the largest continent, bounded by the Arctic, Pacific and Indian Oceans, plus the Mediterranean and Red Seas (43,600,000 sq km/16,800,000 sq miles; pop. 3,075,000,000). East Asia is taken to mean those countries to the northeast of Bangladesh; South Asia refers to the countries on the Indian subcontinent; and Southeast Asia includes those countries to the southeast of China, including the islands to the west of New Guinea.

Asmara the main city of Eritrea in Ethiopia. (Pop. 430,000)

Assam a state in northeastern India. (99,680 sq km/38,476 sq miles; pop. 19,900,000)

Assisi a small town in Umbria, central Italy, and birthplace of St Francis (1182-1226). (Pop. 24,400)

Astrakhan a port near the Caspian Sea, situated on the delta of the River Volga. (Pop. 487,000)

Asturias a region of northern Spain. The capital is Oviedo. (Pop. 1,227,000)

Asunción the capital and the only major city of Paraguay. (Pop. 456,000)

Aswan a city in southern Egypt by the River Nile. The Aswan High Dam, completed 1971, is 13 km (8 miles) to the south. (Pop. 200,000)

Atacama Desert an extremely dry desert lying mainly in northern Chile.

Athabasca, River a river in Canada which flows north from the Rocky Mountains to Lake Athabasca. (Length 1231 km/765 miles)

Athens (Athinai) the historic capital, and the principal city, of Greece. (Pop. city 885,700/metropolitan area 3,027,300)

Atlanta the capital and largest city of Georgia, USA. (Pop. 426,100)

Atlantic Ocean the second largest ocean, lying between North and South America, Europe and Africa. (82,200,000 sq km/31,700,000 sq miles)

Atlas Mountains a series of mountain chains stretching across North Africa from Morocco to Tunisia.

Auckland the largest city and chief port of New Zealand, on North Island. (Pop. 769,600)

Augsburg a historic city in Bavaria, Germany. (Pop. 245,000)

Augusta (1) a city and river port on the Savannah River in Georgia, USA. (Pop. city 46,000/metropolitan area 368,300). (2) the state capital of Maine, USA. (Pop. 22,000)

Austin the capital city of Texas, USA. (Pop. city 397,000/metropolitan area 645,400)

Australasia a general term for Australia, New Zealand and neighbouring islands.

Australia (*Area* 7,686,848 sq km (2,967,892 sq miles); *population* 17,100,000; *capital* Canberra; *other major cities* Adelaide, Brisbane, Melbourne, Perth, Sydney; *form of government* Federal Parliamentary State; *religion* Christianity; *currency* Australian dollar). Australia, the world's smallest continental landmass, is a vast and sparsely populated island state in the southern hemisphere. The most mountainous region is the Great Dividing Range which runs down the entire east coast. Because of its great size, the climates range from tropical monsoon to cool temperate and there are also large areas of desert. Much of its wealth comes from agriculture, with huge sheep and cattle stations extending over large parts of the interior. Mineral extraction is also very important.

Australian Capital Territory the small region which surrounds Canberra, the capital of Australia. (2432 sq km/939 sq miles; pop. 240,000)

Austria (*Area* 83,853 sq km (32,376 sq miles); *population* 7,600,000; *capital* Vienna (Wien); *other major cities* Graz, Linz, Salzburg; *form of government* Federal Republic; *religion* RC; *currency* Schilling). A landlocked country in central Europe surrounded by seven nations. The wall of mountains across the centre of the country dominates the scenery. In the warm summers tourists come to walk in the forests and mountains and in the cold winters skiers come to the mountains which now boast over 50 ski resorts. Agriculture is based on small farms, many of which are run by single families. Dairy products, beef and lamb from the hill farms contribute to exports. More then 37% of Austria is covered in forest.

Auvergne a mountainous region of central France.

Avignon a historic city on the River Rhone in southern France, the seat of the Pope, 1309–77. (Pop. 177,500)

Avila a town and province in the mountainous central region of Spain, famous as the birthplace of St Teresa (1515-82). (Pop. Town 41,800)

Avon a county in the west of England; the county town is Bristol. (1338 sq km/517 sq miles; pop. 936,000)

Axios, River a river flowing through the Balkans to Greece and the Aegean Sea. (Length: 388km/ 241miles)

Ayers Rock a huge rock, sacred to the Aborigines, rising sharply out of the plains in the Northern Territory of Australia. (348 m/1142 ft)

Ayrshire *see* **Strathclyde**.

Ayutthaya a town with the extensive ruins of the city that was the capital of Thailand from 1350 to 1767. (Pop. 113,300)

Azarbaijan a region of northern Iran. Its population shares the same language as the people of neighbouring Azerbaijan. (Pop. 4,613,000)

Azerbaijan (*Area* 87,000 sq km (33,600 sq miles); *population* 6,506,000; *capital* Baku; *other major cities* Kirovabad, Sumgait; *form of government* Republic; *religions* Shia Islam, Russian Orthodox; *currency* Rouble). A republic of the former USSR, which declared itself independent in 1991. It is situated on the southwest coast of the Caspian Sea and shares borders with Iran, Armenia, Georgia and the Russian Federation. It is semi-arid, and 70% of the land is irrigated for the production of cotton, wheat, maize, potatoes, tobacco, tea and citrus fruits. It has rich mineral deposits, the most important being oil which is found in the Baku area.

Azores three groups of small islands in the North Atlantic Ocean, belonging to Portugal. The capital is Ponta Delgada. (2335 sq km/901 sq miles; pop. 336,100)

Baden-Baden a famous spa town in southwest Germany dating from Roman times. (Pop. 50,000)

Baden-Württemburg the southern state of Germany bordering France and Switzerland. (Pop. 9,241,000)

Baffin Bay a huge bay within the Arctic Circle between Baffin Island in Canada and Greenland.

Baffin Island a large, mainly ice-bound island in northeast Canada. (507,451 sq km/195,927 sq miles)

Baghdad the capital of IRAQ, in the centre of the country, on the River Tigris. (Pop. 3,300,000)

Bahamas (*Area* 13,878 sq km (5358 sq miles); *population* 256,000; *capital* Nassau; *other important city* Freeport; *form of government* Constitutional Monarchy; *religion* Christianity; *currency* Bahamian dollar). The Bahamas consist of an archipelago of 700 islands in the Atlantic Ocean off the southeast coast of Florida. The largest island is Andros, and the two most populated are Grand Bahama and New Providence where the capital, Nassau, lies. Winters are mild and summers warm. The islands have few natural resources. Tourism, which employs over two-thirds of the workforce, is the most important industry.

Bahrain (*Area* 678 sq km (262 sq miles); *population* 486,000; *capital* Manama; *form of government* Monarchy (Emirate); *religions* Shia Islam, Sunni Islam; *currency* Bahraini dollar). A GULF state comprising 33 low-lying islands situated between the Qatar peninsula and the mainland of Saudi Arabia. Bahrain Island is the largest, and a causeway links it to Saudi Arabia. The climate is pleasantly warm between December and March, but very hot from June to November. Most of Bahrain is sandy and fertile soil is imported from other islands. Oil was discovered in 1931, and revenues now account for about 75% of total revenue. Traditional industries include pearl fishing, boat building, weaving and pottery.

Baikal, Lake the world's deepest freshwater lake, and the largest by volume, situated in southeast Siberia in the Russian Federation. (31,500 sq km/12,150 sq miles)

Baile Atha Cliath *see* **Dublin.**

Baja California a huge 1300-km (800-mile) long peninsula belonging to Mexico which stretches south from California in the USA into the Pacific Ocean. (Pop. 1,400,000)

Bakhtaran formerly called Kermanshah, a large city in Iran on the old trading routes between Tehran and Baghdad. (Pop. 531,000)

Baku (Baky) a port on the Caspian Sea and the capital of the republic of Azerbaijan. (Pop. 1,661,000)

Balaklava *see* **Sevastopol.**

Balaton, Lake a lake in western Hungary. (601 sq km/232 sq miles)

Bâle *see* **Basle**.

Balearic Islands a group of islands in the western Mediterranean Sea belonging to Spain and famous as tourist resorts. The main islands are Majorca, Minorca, Ibiza, Formentera and Cabrera. (Pop. 685,000)

Bali a small island off the eastern tip of Java, the only island in INDONESIA to have preserved a predominantly Hindu culture intact. The main town and capital is Denpasar. (5591 sq km/2159 sq miles; pop. 2,470,000)

Balkans the southeastern corner of Europe, a broad, mountainous peninsula bordered by the Adriatic, Ionian, Aegean and Black Seas. Albania, Bulgaria, Greece, Romania, Slovenia, Croatia, Bosnia Herzegovina, the rest of the former Yugoslavia and European Turkey are in the Balkans.

Balkhash, Lake a massive lake in KAZAKHSTAN, near the border with China. (22,000 sq km/8500 sq miles)

Ballarat a historic gold-mining town in Victoria, Australia. (Pop. 62,600)

Baltic Sea a shallow sea in northern Europe, completely surrounded by land masses except for the narrow straits that connect it to the North Sea.

Baltimore the largest city in the state of Maryland, USA. (Pop. city 763,000/ metropolitan area 2,244,700)

Baluchistan a province of southwestern Pakistan, bordering Iran and Afghanistan. (Pop. 4,332,000)

Bamako the capital of MALI. (Pop. 405,000)

Bandar Abbas a port in southern Iran on the Strait of Hormuz, at the neck of The GULF. (Pop. 89,200)

Bandar Seri Begawan the capital of BRUNEI. (Pop. 50,000)

Banda Sea a part of the Pacific Ocean, in eastern Indonesia.

Bandung a large inland city in western Java, Indonesia. (Pop. 1,462,700)

Banffshire *see* **Grampian**.

Bangalore a large industrial city in central southern India. (Pop. 2,921,800)

Bangkok (Krung Thep) the capital of THAILAND, on the River Chao Phraya. (Pop. 5,900,000)

Bangladesh (*Area* 143,998 sq km (55,598 sq miles); *population* 113,340,000; *capital* Dacca (Dhaka); *other major cities* Chittagong, Khulna; *form of government* Republic; *religion* Sunni Islam; *currency* Taka). Bangladesh is bounded almost entirely by India and to the south by the Bay of Bengal. It is extremely flat and is virtually a huge delta formed by the Ganges, Brahmaputra and Meghna rivers. It is subject to devastating floods and cyclones. Most villages are built on mud platforms to keep them above water. The climate is tropical monsoon with heat, extreme humidity and heavy rainfall. The combination of rainfall, sun and silt from the rivers makes the land productive, and often three crops a year are grown.

Bangui the capital of the CENTRAL AFRICAN REPUBLIC. (Pop. 387,000)

Bangweulu, Lake a large lake in northern Zambia. (9800 sq km/3784 sq miles)

Banja Luka a city of ancient origins on the Vrbas River in northwest BOSNIA HERZEGOVINA. (Pop. 183,000)

Banjarmasin a port on the southern coast of Kalimantan, Indonesia. (Pop. 381,300)

Banjul the capital of the GAMBIA, formerly called Bathurst. (Pop. 42,000)

Barbados (*Area* 430 sq km (166 sq miles); *population* 260,000; *capital* Bridgetown; *form of government* Constitutional Monarchy; *religions* Anglicanism, Methodism; *currency* Barbados dollar). The most easterly island of the West Indies. Most of it is low-lying. The climate is tropical, but the cooling effect of the northeast trade winds prevents the temperatures rising above 30°C (86°F). Sugar is still the principal export, although tourism has now taken over as the main industry.

Barbuda *see* **Antigua and Barbuda**.

Barcelona the second largest city in Spain, and the name of the surrounding province. It is a major port on the Mediterranean Sea. (Pop. city 1,754,900)

Barents Sea a part of the Arctic Ocean to the north of Norway.

Bari a major port on the Adriatic coast of Italy. (Pop. 370,000)

Baroda *see* **Vadodara.**

Barossa Valley a wine-producing region in South Australia.

Barquisimeto an industrial city in western Venezuela. (Pop. 600,000)

Barranquilla the largest port on the Caribbean coast of Colombia. (Pop. 1,067,000)

Basel *see* **Basle**.

Bashkiria (Baskir Republic) a republic of the Russian Federation, in the southern Urals. The capital is Ufa. (143,500 sq km/55,400 sq miles; pop. 3,860,000)

Basle (Basel, Bâle) a city in northern Switzerland and the name of the surrounding canton. (Pop. city 200,000)

Basque Region an area straddling the border of Spain and France on the Atlantic coast.

Basra the second city of Iraq, and its main port. (Pop. 1,200,000)

Bassein a trading city on the delta of the Irrawaddy River in Burma. (Pop. 355,600)

Basseterre the capital of ST KITTS AND NEVIS. (Pop. 16,000)

Basse Terre the capital of the French island of GUADELOUPE, situated on the island called Basse Terre. (Pop. town 14,000/island 141,000)

Bass Strait the stretch of water spanning the 290 km (180 miles) which separate the mainland of Australia from Tasmania.

Bath a beautifully preserved spa town in the county of Avon, southwest England. (Pop.85,000)

Bathurst *see* **Banjul**.

Baton Rouge the state capital of Louisiana, USA, situated on the Mississippi River. (Pop. city 238,900/ metropolitan area 538,000)

Bavaria (Bayern) the largest state in Germany. (70,553 sq km/27,241 sq miles; pop. 10,958,000)

BAYEUX a market town in Normandy, France, and the home of the huge 11th-century tapestry depicting the Norman conquest of England. (Pop. 15,300)

Bayonne the capital of the French Basque region. (Pop. 129,730)

Beaufort Sea a part of the Arctic Ocean to the north of North America.

Beaujolais a famous wine-producing region of France situated on the River Saone between Lyons and Macon.

Bechuanaland the former name of BOTSWANA (until 1966).

Bedfordshire a county in central southern England; the county town is Bedford. (1235 sq km/477 sq miles; pop. 75,000)

Beijing (Peking) the capital of CHINA, in the northeast of the country. (Pop. 9,231,000)

Beirut (Beyrouth) the capital and main port of LEBANON. (Pop. 938,000)

Belarus (Belorussia, Byelorussia) (*Area* : 207,600 sq km (80,150 sq miles); *population* 9,878,000; *capital* Minsk; *other major cities* Gomel, Vitebsk, Mogilev; *form of government* Republic; *religions* Russian Orthodox, RC; *currency* Rouble). A republic of the former USSR, which declared itself independent in 1991. It borders Poland to the west, Ukraine to the south, Latvia and Lithuania to the north, and the Russian Federation to the east. It consists mainly of a low-lying plain, and forests cover approximately one third of it. The climate is continental with long severe winters and short warm summers. The main economic activity is agriculture. The production of peat is the main industry and is the main source of energy.

Belau a republic consisting of a group of islands in the western Pacific formerly known as Palau. It has an agreement of free association with the USA. Copper is the chief export and the main language is English. The capital is Koror. (494 sq km/191 sq miles; pop. 14,000; cur. US dollar)

Belém a major port of Brazil situated to the north of the mouth of the River Amazon. (Pop. 934,000)

Belfast the capital and largest city of Northern Ireland. (Pop. 360,000)

Belgium (*Area* 30,519 sq km (11,783 sq miles); *population* 9,930,000; *capital* Brussels; *other major cities* Antwerp, Ghent, Charleroi, Liege; *form of government* Constitutional Monarchy; *religion* RC; *currency* Belgian franc). A small country in northwest Europe with a short coastline on the North Sea. In the north, the land slopes until it reaches the flat and grassy coastlands. To the south of the Meuse river is the forested plateau area of the Ardennes. It is densely populated, industrial with few natural resources. Agriculture is based on livestock production but employs only 3% of the work force. Nearly all raw materials are now imported through the main port of Antwerp.

Belgrade (Beograd) the capital of SERBIA, on the confluence of the Rivers Danube and Sava. (Pop. 1,407,100)

Belize (*Area* 22,965 sq km (8867 sq miles); *population* 193,000; *capital* Belmopan; *other major city* Belize City; *form of government* Constitutional Monarchy; *religion* RC; *currency* Belize dollar). A small Central American country on the southeast of the Yucatan Peninsula. Its coastline on the Gulf of Honduras is approached through some 550 km (342 miles) of coral reefs and keys. The coastal area and north of the country are low-lying and swampy with dense forests inland. The subtropical climate is warm and humid and the trade winds bring cooling sea breezes. Rainfall is heavy, and hurricanes may occur in summer. The dense forests which cover most of the country provide valuable hardwoods such as mahogany. Most of the population make a living from forestry, fishing or agriculture.

Bellinghausen Sea a part of the Pacific Ocean off Antarctica, due south of South America.

Belmopan the capital of BELIZE. (Pop. 5000)

Belo Horizonte an industrial city, and the third largest city of Brazil, in the southeast of the country. (Pop. 1,777,000)

Belorussia *see* **Belarus**.

Belostock *see* **Bialystok**.

Benares *see* **Varanasi**.

Bengal a former Indian state which was divided in 1947 into two parts: West Bengal in India, and East Pakistan (now Bangladesh).

Bengal, Bay of the massive bay occupying the broad sweep of the Indian Ocean between India and Burma, to the south of Bangladesh.

Benghazi a major port on the Gulf of Sirte in Libya. (Pop. 485,000)

Benidorm a popular Mediterranean seaside resort of Spain. (Pop. 25,600)

Benin (*Area* 112,622 sq km (43,483 sq miles); *population* 4,760,000; *capital* Porto-Novo; *other major city* Contonou; *form of government* Republic; *religions* Animism, RC, Sunni Islam; *currency* Franc CFA). An ice cream cone-shaped country in West Africa with a very short coastline on the Bight of Benin. The coastal area has white sandy beaches backed by lagoons and low-lying fertile lands. In the northwest are grassy plateaux. The climate is tropical, and there are nine rainy months each year so crops rarely fail. Farming is predominantly subsistence, with yams, cassava, maize, rice, groundnuts and vegetables the main crops. The country is very poor, and lack of foreign investment prevents economic diversification.

Ben Nevis *see* **Grampian Mountains.**

Benue, River a river which flows through Cameroon and Nigeria to the Gulf of Guinea. (Length 1390 km/865 miles)

Benxi an industrial city in Liaoning, China. (Pop. 1,200,000)

Beograd *see* **Belgrade**.

Beqa'a a long, fertile valley running north to south in Lebanon, between the Lebanon and Anti-Lebanon Mountains.

Bergamo a historic and industrial city in northern Italy. (Pop. 121,000)

Bergen (1) an old port in southwest Norway, and now that country's second largest city. (Pop. 181,000). (2) *see* **Mons**.

Bering Sea a part of the Pacific Ocean between Alaska and eastern Russian Federation.

Bering Strait the stretch of sea, 88 km(55 miles) wide, that separates the Russian Federation from Alaska in the USA.

Berkshire a county of central southern England; the county town is Reading. (1256 sq km/485 sq miles; pop. 708,000)

Berlin the capital of GERMANY, in the north of the country on the River Spree. Until 1990 it was divided by the Berlin Wall. (Pop. 3,097,000)

Bermuda (*Area* 53 sq km (21 sq miles); *population* 59,066; *capital* Hamilton; *form of government* Colony under British administration; *religion* Protestantism; *currency* Bermuda dollar). A group of 150 small islands in the western Atlantic Ocean. The hilly limestone islands are the caps of ancient volcanoes rising from the sea bed. The climate is pleasantly warm and humid with rain spread evenly throughout the year. Many foreign banks and financial institutions operate from Bermuda to take advantage of the lenient tax laws. Its proximity to the USA and the pleasant climate have led to a flourishing tourist industry.

Berne (Bern) the historic capital of SWITZERLAND, and also the name of the surrounding canton. (Pop. city 150,000)

Berwickshire *see* **Borders**.

Besançon a town of ancient origins in the Jura region of eastern France. (Pop. 120,800)

Bethlehem a town in the West Bank area of Israel, celebrated by Christians as the birthplace of Jesus Christ. (Pop. 30,000)

Béthune an industrial town in northeastern France. (Pop. 259,700)

Beuten *see* **Bytom.**

Beyrouth *see* **Beirut**.

Bhopal an industrial city in central India. (Pop. 671,000)

Bhutan (*Area* 47,000 sq km (18,147 sq miles); *population* 1,400,000; *capital* Thimphu; *form of government* Constitutional Monarchy; *religion* Buddhism; *currency* Ngultrum). Bhutan is surrounded by India to the south and China to the north. It rises from foothills overlooking the Brahmaputra river to the southern slopes of the Himalayas, which rise to over 7500 m (24,608 ft) and make up most of the country. The climate is hot and wet on the plains but temperatures drop progressively with altitude, resulting in glaciers and permanent snow cover in the north. The valleys in the centre of the country are wide and fertile and about 95% of the workforce are farmers. The number of visitors is limited to 1500 each year.

Biafra *see* **Iboland**.

Bialystok (Belostock) a textile city in northeast Poland. (Pop. 240,000)

Bianco, Monte *see* **Blanc, Mont.**

Bielefeld an industrial city in western Germany. (Pop. 310,000)

Bielsko-Biala (Bielitz) an industrial city in southern Poland. (Pop. 172,000)

Bihar a state in northeast India. The capital is PATNA. (Pop. 69,914,700)

Bikini an atoll in the Marshall Islands, the site of US nuclear weapons tests between 1946 and 1962.

Bilbao a port and industrial city in the Basque region of northern Spain. (Pop. 433,000)

Bioko an island in the Gulf of Guinea (formerly Fernando Póo) now governed by EQUATORIAL GUINEA. (2017 sq km/780 sq miles; pop. 57,000)

Birmingham (1) the main city of the industrial West Midlands and the second largest city in the UK. (Pop. 976,000). (2) the largest city in the state of Alabama, USA. (Pop. city 279,800/metropolitan area 895,200)

Biscay, Bay of the broad bay, notorious for its rough weather, formed by the Atlantic Ocean between northern Spain and Brittany in northwest France.

Bishkek, formerly Frunze, the capital of KYRGYZSTAN. (Pop. 577,000)

Bismarck the state capital of North Dakota, USA. (Pop. city 47,600/metropolitan area 86,100)

Bismarck Sea a branch of the Pacific Ocean to the north of Papua New Guinea.

Bissau (Bissão) a port and the capital of GUINEA-BISSAU. (Pop. 109,000)

Black Country the industrial area of the British Midlands around Birmingham.

Black Forest (Schwarzwald) an extensive area of mountainous pine forests in southwest Germany.

Black Hills a range of hills rising to 2207 m(7242 ft) on the border between the states of South Dakota and Wyoming in the USA.

Blackpool the largest seaside holiday resort in the UK, in Lancashire. (Pop. 147,000)

Black Sea a sea lying between southeast Europe and western Asia; it is surrounded by land except for the Bosphorus channel, leading to the Mediterranean Sea.

Blanc, Mont (Monte Bianco) the highest mountain in Western Europe, on the border between France and Italy. (4808 m/15,770 ft)

Blantyre the largest city in Malawi. (Pop. 333,800)

Bloemfontein the judicial capital of South Africa, and the capital of the Orange Free State. (Pop. 256,000)

Blue Mountains (1) a range of mountains rising to 1100 m (3609 ft) in New South Wales in Australia, some 65 km (40 miles) from Sydney. (2) the mountains in eastern Jamaica rising to 2256 m (7402 ft) at Blue Mountain Peak. The region produces high quality coffee.

Bochum an industrial city in the Ruhr region of western Germany. (Pop. 410,000)

Bodensee *see* **Constance, Lake.**

Bodh Gaya a small town in eastern India which is the site of Buddhism's most revered shrine. (Pop. 15,700)

Bodrum a port on the southeastern coast of Turkey. (Pop. 13,090)

Bogotá the capital of COLOMBIA, set on a plateau of the eastern Andes in the centre of the country. (Pop. 5,789,000)

Bohemia formerly an independent kingdom (9th–13th centuries), now a western region of the CZECH REPUBLIC which includes the capital, Prague.

Bohol one of the Visayan Islands in the central area of the Philippines. (3862 sq km/1491 sq miles; pop. 759,370)

Boise the state capital of IDAHO, USA. (Pop. city 107,200/metropolitan area 189,300)

Bolivia (*Area* 1,098,581 sq km (424,162 sq miles); *population* 6,410,000; *capital* La Paz (administrative capital), Sucre (legal capital); *other major city* Cochabamba; *form of government* Republic; *religion* RC; *currency* Boliviano). A landlocked republic of central South America through which the great mountain range of the Andes runs. On the undulating Altiplano depression is the highest capital city in the world, La Paz. To the east and northeast of the mountains is a huge area of lowland containing tropical rainforests and wooded savanna. The northeast has a heavy rainfall while in the southwest it is negligible. Temperatures vary with altitude from extremely cold on the summits to cool on the Altiplano, where at least half the population lives. Although rich in natural resources, e.g. oil, tin, Bolivia is not a rich country because of lack of funds for their extraction.

Bologna the capital of Emilia Romagna, Italy. (Pop. 455,900)

Bolton a textile-manufacturing town in Lancashire, England. (Pop. 147,000)

Bombay a major port, the capital of Maharashtra state in central western India, and now India's most important industrial city. (Pop. 8,234,400)

Bonaire a Caribbean island off the coast of Venezuela and part of the NETHERLAND ANTILLES (288 sq km/111 sq miles; pop. 9700)

Bondi Beach a famous surfing beach in the suburbs of Sydney, Australia.

Bone *see* **Annaba.**

Bonin Islands a group of small volcanic islands in the Pacific Ocean belonging to Japan. (Pop. 2300)

Bonn the capital of former West Germany, it is the administrative centre of Germany until the government moves to Berlin. (Pop. 300,000)

Bophuthatswana one of the homelands declared by the government of South Africa to be an independent republic in 1977. It consists of seven separate territories. (44,109 sq km/17,030 sq miles; pop. 1,935,000)

Bordeaux a major port on the Gironde estuary in southwestern France. The region is famous for its wines. (Pop. 650,125)

Borders an administrative region of southern Scotland, created out of the old counties of Berwickshire, Peeblesshire, Roxburghshire, Selkirkshire and part of Midlothian. (4662 sq km/1800 sq miles; pop. 101,000)

Borkum *see* **Friesian Islands.**

Borneo one of the largest islands in the world, now divided between three countries. Most of the island is known as Kalimantan, a part of INDONESIA. The northern coast is divided into the two states of Sarawak and Sabah, which are part of MALAYSIA, and the small independent Sultanate of BRUNEI. (751,900 sq km/290,320 sq miles)

Bosnia Herzegovina (*Area* 51,129 sq km (19,736 sq miles); *population* 4,124,000; *capital* Sarajevo; *other major cities* Banja Luka, Tuzla; *form of government* Republic; *religions* Eastern Orthodox, Sunni Islam, RC; *currency* Dinar). A republic of former Yugoslavia, which was formally recognized as an independent state in 1992. It is very mountainous, and half the country is forested. One quarter of the land is cultivated, and corn, wheat and flax are the principal products of the north. In the south, tobacco, cotton, fruits and grapes are the main products. It has large deposits of lignite, iron ore and bauxite, but there is little industrialization.

Bosphorus the narrow strip of water, some 29 km (18 miles) long and no more than 4 km (2.5 miles) wide, which provides the navigable link between the Mediterranean and Black Seas by way of the Sea of Marmara. It separates the European part of Turkey from its Asian part.

Boston an Atlantic port and the state capital of Massachusetts, USA. (Pop. city 570,700/metropolitan area 2,820,700)

Botany Bay a bay now in the suburbs of Sydney, Australia, discovered by Captain James Cook in 1770.

Bothnia, Gulf of the most northerly arm of the Baltic Sea, bordered by Finland and Sweden.

Botswana (*Area* 581,730 sq km (224,606 sq miles); *population* 1,260,000; *capital* Gaborone; *other major cities* Mahalapye, Serowe, Francistown; *form of government* Republic; *religions Animism*, Anglicanism; *currency* Pula). A landlocked republic in southern Africa which straddles the Tropic of Capricorn.

Much of the west and southwest of the country forms part of the Kalahari Desert. In the north the land is marshy around the basin of the Okavango river. With the exception of the desert area, most of the country has a subtropical climate. The people are mainly farmers and cattle rearing is the main activity. Diamonds are an important revenue earner. About 17% of the land is set aside for wildlife preservation in national parks, game reserves, game sanctuaries and controlled hunting areas.

Bouaké the second largest city of the Côte d'Ivoire. (Pop. 640,000)

Bougainville the easternmost island belonging to PAPUA NEW GUINEA, and a part of, though politically separate from, the SOLOMON ISLANDS.

Bournemouth a coastal resort in DORSET, England. (Pop. 145,000)

Boyne, River a river flowing into the Irish Sea on the east coast of the Republic of Ireland. It was the site of a battle (1690) in which William of Orange defeated James II. (Length 115 km/70 miles)

Boyoma Falls a series of seven cataracts over 90 km (56 miles) where the Lualaba River beomes the Zaïre River. They were formerly called Stanley Falls after the British explorer Sir Henry Morton Stanley.

Brabant the central province of Belgium around the capital, Brussels. (3358 sq km/1297 sq miles; pop. 2,200,000)

Brac *see* **Dalmatia**.

Bradford a city in the county of West Yorkshire, England, which was the centre of the woollen industry in the 19th century. (Pop. 281,000)

Bragança a small inland medieval town in Portugal, and the original home of the family which ruled Portugal from 1640 to 1910. (Pop. 13,900)

Brahmaputra a major river of South Asia, flowing from the Himalayas in Tibet through Assam in northern India to join the River Ganges in Bangladesh. (Length 2900 km/1802 miles)

Braila a port in Romania on the River Danube, 140 km (87 miles) inland from the Black Sea. (Pop. 214,000)

Brasília the capital, since 1960, of BRAZIL. (Pop. 412,000)

Brazov an industrial city in central Romania. (Pop. 304,000)

Bratislava (Pressburg) the second largest city in the former Czechoslovakia, and the capital of the newly independent SLOVAKIA. (Pop. 402,000)

Braunschweig *see* **Brunswick**.

Brazil (*Area* 8,511,965 sq km (3,285,470 sq miles); *population* 115,600,000; *capital* Brasília; *other major cities* Belo Horizonte, Porto Alegre, Recife, Rio de Janeiro, Salvador, São Paulo; *form of government* Federal Republic; *religion* RC; *currency* Cruzeirois). The fifth largest country in the world, which covers nearly half of South America. The climate is mainly tropical, but droughts may occur in the northeast, where it is hot and arid. About 14% of the population is employed in agriculture, and the main products exported are coffee, soya beans and cocoa. It is rich in minerals and is the only source of high grade quartz crystal in commercial quantities.

Brazzaville the capital of the CONGO, on the River Zaïre. (Pop. 425,000)

Breconshire *see* **Powys.**

Breda a historic and manufacturing city in the Netherlands. (Pop. city 118,000/ Greater Breda 153,000)

Bremen a major port on the River Weser, near to the North Sea coast of Germany, and also the name of the surrounding state. (Pop. 550,000)

Bremerhaven a port on the North Sea coast of Germany. (Pop. 135,000)

Brescia a city in northern Italy. (Pop. 206,000)

Breslau *see* **Wroclaw**.

Brest (1) an important naval port situated on an inlet on the tip of Finistère in northwestern France. (Pop. 205,000). (2) **(Brzesc)** an inland port in BELARUS on the River Bug on the Polish border. (Pop. 214,000)

Brezhnev *see* **Naberezhnyye Chelny.**

Bridgeport a manufacturing city on the coast of the state of Connecticut, USA. (Pop. city 142,000/ metropolitan area 441,500)

Bridgetown the capital of BARBADOS. (Pop. 97,000)

Brighton a famous seaside resort on the south coast of England in the county of East Sussex. (Pop. 149,000)

Brindisi a port on the east coast of Italy at the southern end of the Adriatic Sea. (Pop. 92,000)

Brisbane a port on the east coast of Australia, and the state capital of Queensland. (Pop. 942,400)

Bristol a major city and port in southwest England, and the administrative centre of the county of Avon. (Pop. 399,000)

Britain *see* **Great Britain.**

British Columbia the western seaboard province of Canada. The capital is Victoria. (929,730 sq km/358,968 sq miles; pop. 2,744,000)

British Indian Ocean Territory the Chagos Archipelago, a group of five coral atolls in the middle of the Indian Ocean. (52 sq km/20 sq miles)

British Isles the name given to the group of islands in northwestern Europe formed by Great Britain and Ireland, and the surrounding islands.

British Virgin Islands *see* **Virgin Islands, British.**

Brittany (Bretagne) the region of France which occupies the extreme northwestern peninsula, pertruding into the Atlantic.

Brno (Brünn) an industrial city in the southeast of the Czech Republic. (Pop. 381,000)

Bromberg *see* **Bydgoszcz.**

Bruges (Brugge) a historic town and capital of the province of West Flanders, Belgium. (Pop. 120,000)

Brunei (*Area* 5,765 sq km (2,226 sq miles); *population* 267,000; *capital* Bandar Seri Begawan; *other major cities* Kuala Belait, Seria; *form of government* Monarchy (Sultanate); *religion* Sunni Islam; *currency* Brunei dollar). Brunei is a sultanate on the northwest coast of Borneo, bounded on all sides by the Sarawak territory of Malaysia, which splits the sultanate into two separate parts. Broad tidal swamplands cover the coastal plains and inland Brunei is hilly and covered with tropical forest. The climate is tropical with rainfall heaviest (5000 mm/197 inches) inland. The main crops grown are rice, vegetables and fruit, but economically the country depends on its oil industry, which accounts for almost all exports.

Brünn *see* **Brno**.

Brunswick (Braunschweig) a historic town in northern Germany, and the capital of the Dukes of Saxony. (Pop. 255,000)

Brussels (Brussel, Bruxelles) a historic city and the capital of BELGIUM. It plays a central role in Europe as the administrative headquarters for the European Community. (Pop. 1,000,000)

Bryansk an industrial city in the west of the Russian Federation. (Pop. 424,000)

Bucaramanga a city in the north of Colombia, close to the border with Venezuela. (Pop. 516,000)

Bucharest (Bucuresti) the capital of ROMANIA, in the southeast of the country. (Pop. 1,861,000)

Buckinghamshire a county in central southern England; the county town is Aylesbury. (1883 sq km/727 sq miles; pop. 609,000)

Budapest the capital of HUNGARY, comprising Buda and Pest, which lie on opposite sides of the River Danube. (Pop. 2,064,400)

Budweiss *see* **Ceské Budejovice**.

Buenos Aires the capital of ARGENTINA. (Pop. city 3,325,000/metropolitan area 9,948,000)

Buffalo a city and port in New York state situated at the eastern end of Lake Erie. (Pop. city 339,000/metropolitan area 1,205,000)

Bug, River a river which flows northwest from the Ukraine, forming the border with Poland before turning west into Poland and joining the Narew and Vistula rivers. (Length: 813 km/480 miles)

Büjük Agri Dagi *see* **Ararat, Mount**

Bujumbura the capital of BURUNDI, situated at the northern end of Lake Tanganyika. (Pop. 180,000)

Bukhara an old trading city in Uzbekistan. (Pop. 204,000)

Bulawayo the second city of Zimbabwe, in the southwest of the country. (Pop. 414,000)

Bulgaria (*Area* 110,912 sq km (42,823 sq miles); *population* 8,970,000; *capital* Sofia (Sofiya); *other major cities* Burgas, Plovdiv, Ruse, Varna; *form of government* Republic; *religion* Eastern Orthodox; *currency* Lev). Bulgaria is located on the east Balkan peninsula and has a coast on the Black Sea. It is bounded to the north by Romania, west by Serbia and Macedonia of the former Yugoslavia and south by Greece and Turkey. The centre of Bulgaria is crossed from west to east by the Balkan Mountains. The south has a Mediterranean climate with hot dry summers and mild winters. Further north the temperatures become more extreme, and rainfall is higher in summer. Bulgaria is an agricultural country, and a revolution in farming during the 1950s has led to great increases in output.

Burgas a major port on the Black Sea coast of Bulgaria. (Pop. 183,000)

Burgos an industrial town in northern Spain. (Pop. town 156,000)

Burgundy (Bourgogne) a region of central France, famous for its wine.

Burkina (Burkina Faso) (*Area* 274,200 sq km (105,869 sq miles); *population* 8,760,000; *capital* Ouagadougou; *form of government* Republic; *religions* Animist, Sunni Islam; *currency* Franc CFA). Burkina, a landlocked state in West Africa, on the southern fringe of the Sahara Desert, is made up of vast monotonous plains and low hills. Precipitation is generally low, the heaviest rain falling in the southwest, while the rest of the country is semi-desert. About 90% of the people live by farming, and food crops include sorghum, beans and maize. There is a great shortage of work, and many of the younger population go to Ghana and Côte d'Ivoire for employment.

Burma (Myanmar) (*Area* 676,578 sq km (261,227 sq miles); *population* 39,300,000; *capital* Yangon (formerly Rangoon); *other major cities* Mandalay, Moulmein, Pegu; *form of government* Republic; *religion* Buddhism; *currency* Kyat). The Union of Myanmar (formerly Burma) is the second largest country in Southeast Asia. Its heartland is the valley of the Irrawaddy. The north and west are mountainous and in the east the Shan Plateau runs along the border with Thailand. The climate is mainly tropical monsoon. Rice is the staple food and accounts for half the export earnings. Burma is rich in timber and minerals although not yet fully exploited.

Bursa a city in northwestern Turkey, and also the name of the surrounding province, of which it is the capital. (Pop. city 614,100)

Burundi (*Area* 27,834 sq km (10,747 sq miles); *population* 5,540,000; *capital* Bujumbura; *form of government* Republic; *religion* RC; *currency* Burundi franc). Burundi is a small densely populated country in central east Africa, bounded by Rwanda to the north, Tanzania to the east and south, and Zaïre to the west. It has a mountainous terrain, with much of the country above 1500 m (4921 ft). The climate is equatorial but modified by altitude. The soils are not rich but there is enough rain to grow the main food crops of bananas, sweet potatoes, peas, lentils and beans. The main cash crop is coffee, accounting for 90% of Burundi's export earnings.

Buryat Republic an autonomous republic of the Russian Federation, situated in the southeast, between Lake Baikal and Mongolia. (351,300 sq km/135,600 sq miles; pop. 985,000)

Bute *see* **Strathclyde.**

Bydgoszcz (Bromberg) a historic and industrial city in central Poland. (Pop. 357,700)

Byelorussia *see* **Belarus.**

Bytom (Beuthen) an industrial city in southwest Poland. (Pop. 238,100)

Byzantium *see* **Istanbul.**

Cadiz a port of Phoenician origins on the Atlantic coast of southern Spain; also the name of the surrounding province. (Pop. town 157,800)

Caen a city in the Normandy region of northern France. (Pop. 187,600)

Caerdydd *see* **Cardiff.**

Caernarfonshire *see* **Gwynedd.**

Cagliari the capital of the Italian island of Sardinia. (Pop. 232,800)

Cairngorms a range forming part of the Grampian Mountains in Scotland.

Cairns a port on the northeast coast of Queensland, Australia and a tourist resort catering for visitors to the Great Barrier Reef. (Pop. 48,000)

Cairo (El Qahira) the capital of Egypt, in the north of the country on the River Nile; it is the largest city in Africa. (Pop. 8,540,000)

Caithness *see* **Highland Region.**

Calabria the region which occupies the southern "toe" of Italy. The main town is Reggio Di Calabria. (Pop. 2,121,700)

Calais an old port in northern France situated on the narrowest part of the English Channel, opposite Dover in England. (Pop. 101,500)

Calcutta the largest city in India, a major port and industrial centre situated in the northeast of the country, on the Hugli River. (Pop. 9,194,000)

Calgary the second largest city of Alberta, Canada. (Pop. 593,000)

Cali an industrial city in southern Colombia. (Pop. 1,755,000)

Calicut (Kozhikode) a port on the west coast of southern India. (Pop. 546,100)

California the most populous state of the USA on the Pacific coast. The state capital is Sacramento, but Los Angeles is the biggest city. (411,015 sq km/ 158,693 sq km; pop. 26,365,000)

California, Gulf of (Sea of Cortes) the narrow inlet which separates the mainland part of Mexico from the peninsula of Baja California.

Callao the port serving Lima, the capital of Peru. (Pop. 440,500)

Calvados a department of northern France, a part of the region of Normandy. It is famous for its apple-based liqueur called Calvados. (Pop. 590,000)

Camargue the broad, flat area of sea marshes in the delta of the River Rhone in the centre of the Mediterranean coast of France.

Cambodia (*Area* 181,035 sq km (69,898 sq miles); *population* 8,300,000; *capital* : Phnom Penh; *other major cities* Kampong Cham, Battambang; *form of government* People's Republic; *religion* Buddhism; *currency* : Riel). Cambodia is a southeast Asian state on the Gulf of Thailand. The heart of the country is saucer-shaped, and gently rolling alluvial plains are drained by the Mekong river. The Dangrek Mountains form the frontier with Thailand in the northwest. It has a tropical monsoon climate, and about half of the land is tropical forest. Crop production depends entirely on the rainfall and floods, but production was badly disrupted during the civil war, and yields still remain low.

Cambrian Mountains a range which forms the "backbone" of Wales.

Cambridge (1) a famous university city in eastern England. (Pop. 95,300) (2) a city in Massachusetts, USA, home of Harvard University and the Massachusetts Institute of Technology. (Pop. 103,000)

Cambridgeshire a county in eastern England; the county town is Cambridge. (3409 sq km/1316 sq miles; pop. 578,700)

Cameron Highlands an upland area of Malaysia where tea and and vegetables are grown.

Cameroon (*Area* 475,442 sq km (183,568 sq miles); *population* 11,540,000; *capital* Yaoundé; *other major city* Douala; *form of government* Republic; *religions* Animism, RC, Sunni Islam; *currency* Franc CFA). Cameroon is a triangular-shaped country of diverse landscapes in west central Africa. It stretches from Lake Chad at its apex to the northern borders of Equatorial Guinea, Gabon and the Congo in the south. The climate is equatorial with high temperatures and plentiful rain. The majority of the population lives in the south where they grow maize and vegetables. In the drier north, where drought and hunger are well known, life is harder. Bananas, coffee and cocoa are the major exports.

Cameroon, Mount an active volcano in west Cameroon. (4095 m/13,435 ft)

Campania a region of central southern Italy, on the west coast around Naples. (Pop. 5,623,400)

Campinas a modern industrial town 75 km(47 miles) north of São Paulo in Brazil. (Pop. 665,000)

Canada (*Area* 9 ,976,139 sq km (3,851,787 sq miles); *population* 26,600,000; *capital* Ottawa; *other major cities* Toronto, Montréal, Vancouver, Québec; *form of government* Federal Parliamentary State; *religions* RC, United Church of Canada, Anglicanism; *currency* Canadian dollar). Canada, the second largest country in the world, is a land of great climatic and geographical extremes. It lies to the north of the United States and has both Pacific and Atlantic coasts. Climates range from polar conditions in the north, to cool temperate in the south with considerable differences from west to east. More than 80% of its farmland is in the prairies that stretch from Alberta to Manitoba. Forest reserves cover more than half the total land area. The most valuable mineral deposits (oil, gas, coal and iron ore) are found in Alberta. Most industry in Canada is associated with processing its natural resources.

Canary Islands a group of islands belonging to Spain, situated some 95 km (60 miles) off the coast of Western Sahara. The main islands are Gran Canaria, Tenerife, La Palma, Fuertaventura, Gomera, Lanzarote. (7273 sq km/2808 sq miles; pop. 1,444,600)

Canaveral, Cape a long spit of land on the east coast of the state of Florida, USA. It is the USA's main launch site for space missions and the home of the John F. Kennedy Space Center. For a time it was known as Cape Kennedy.

Canberra the capital of Australia, lying about halfway between Sydney and Melbourne in the southeast of the country. (Pop. 255,900)

Cancún a tiny island just off the Yucatan coast of Mexico, connected to the mainland by a causeway, and now a popular holiday resort. (Pop. 70,000)

Cannes a famous beach resort on the Côte d'Azur in southern France. (Pop.

72,800)

Cantabria a province on the Atlantic coast of northern Spain. (Pop. 510,800)

Canterbury a small cathedral city in Kent in southern England. (Pop. 36,000)

Canton *see* **Guangzhou.**

Cape Breton Island part of the province of Nova Scotia lying off the eastern coast of Canada. (10,349 sq km/3970 sq miles; pop. 170,000)

Cape Town a major port on the southwestern tip of South Africa, and the country's legislative capital. (Pop. 1,912,000)

Cape Verde (*Area* 4033 sq km (1575 sq miles); *population* 369,000; *capital* Praia; *form of government* Republic; *religion* RC; *currency* Cape Verde escudo). Cape Verde, one of the world's smallest nations, is situated in the Atlantic Ocean, about 640 km (400 miles) northwest of Senegal. It consists of 10 islands and five islets. Over 50% of the population live on São Tiago on which is Praia, the capital. Rainfall is sparse and the islands suffer from periods of severe drought. Agriculture is mostly confined to irrigated inland valleys. Fishing for tuna and lobsters is an important industry, but the economy is shaky, and Cape Verde relies heavily on foreign aid.

Capri a rocky island at the southern end of the Bay of Naples on the west coast of Italy, famous as a fashionable holiday retreat. (10.4 sq km/4 sq miles; pop. 16,500)

Caprivi Strip a narrow corridor of land, 450 km(280 miles) long, which belongs to Namibia and gives it access to the Zambezi River along the border between Botswana to the south and Angola and Zambia to the north.

Caracas the capital of VENEZUALA, in the northeast of the country. (Pop. 3,500,000)

Cardamom Mountains a range rising to 1813 m (5948 ft) which line the coast of Cambodia and separate the interior from the Gulf of Thailand.

Cardiff (Caerdydd) the capital of Wales, situated in the southeast of the principality, in South Glamorgan. (Pop. 281,000)

Cardiganshire *see* **Dyfed.**

Cardigan Bay the long, curving bay which, as part of the Irish Sea, forms much of the west coast of Wales.

Caribbean, The a term that refers to the islands lying within the compass of the Caribbean Sea.

Caribbean Sea a part of the western Atlantic Ocean, bounded by the east coast of Central America, the north coast of South America and the West Indies.

Carinthia (Kärnten) the southern state of Austria, which borders Italy and Slovenia. (9533 sq km/3681 sq miles; pop 536,730)

Carlow a landlocked county in the southeast of the Republic of Ireland. The county town is also called Carlow. (Pop. county 39,000)

Carlsbad *see* **Karlovy Vary**.

Carmarthenshire *see* **Dyfed**.

Carmel, Mount a ridge of land rising to 528 m(1746 ft) in northern Israel.

Caroline Islands a scattered group of islands in the western Pacific Ocean which now make up the Federated States of Micronesia and the separate state of Belau.

Carpathian Mountains a broad sweep of mountains stretching for nearly 1000 km (625 miles) down the border between Slovakia and Poland and into central Romania. They rise to 2663 m (8737 ft) at their highest point.

Carpentaria, Gulf of the broad gulf of shallow sea between the two hornlike peninsulas of northern Australia.

Carrara a town 50 km (31 miles) north of Pisa in Italy, famous for centuries for its marble quarries. (Pop. 68,500)

Carson City the state capital of Nevada, USA. (Pop. 35,900)

Cartagena (1) a major port on the Caribbean coast of Colombia. (Pop. 548,000). (2) a port of ancient origins on the Mediterranean coast of Spain. (Pop. 172,800)

Casablanca (Dar el Beida) the main port and largest city of Morocco. (Pop. 2,140,000)

Cascade Range a range of mountains stretching some 1125 km (700 miles) parallel to the coast of northern California in the USA and into southern Canada. The highest point is at Mount Rainier (4392 m/14,410 ft) in Washington State.

Caspian Sea the largest inland (salt) sea in the world, supplied mainly by the River Volga. It lies to the north of Iran, which shares its coasts with Azerbaijan, Georgia, Kazakhstan and Turkmenistan.

Cassai *see* **Kasai.**

Cassel *see* **Kassel.**

Castile (Castilla) a former kingdom of Spain, occupying most of the central area, now divided into two regions, Castilla-La Mancha and Castilla-León.

Castries the capital of St Lucia. (Pop. 45,000).

Catalonia (Cataluña) an autonomous region of Spain, in the northeast, centreing on Barcelona. (Pop. 5,958,000)

Catania a major port and the second largest city in Sicily. (Pop. 378,500)

Catskill Mountains a range of in New York State, USA, famed for their scenic beauty. The highest peak is Slide Mountain (1281 m/4204 ft).

Caucasus (Kavkaz) the mountainous region between the Black and Caspian Seas, bounded by the Russian Federation, Georgia, Armenia and Azerbaijan. It contains Europe's highest point, Mount Elbrus (5642m/18,510 ft).

Cauvery *see* **Kaveri.**

Cavan a county in the north of the Republic of Ireland, part of the ancient province of Ulster; Cavan is also the name of the county town. (1890 sq km/730 sq miles; pop. county 53,900)

Caveri *see* **Kaveri.**

Cawnpore *see* **Kanpur.**

Cayenne the capital of GUIANA (FRENCH). (Pop. 38,000)

Cayman Islands a group of three islands in the Caribbean Sea 240 km (150 miles) northwest of Jamaica which form a British Crown colony. The capital is Georgetown, on Grand Cayman. (260 sq km/100 sq miles; pop. 19,100)

Cebu one of islands in the central Philippines, forming part of the Visayan group; also the name of its capital city. (5088 sq km/1964 sq miles; pop. island 2,092,000/city 490,231)

Celebes *see* **Sulawesi.**

Celebes Sea a sea between the islands of eastern Indonesia and the Philippines.

Central African Republic (*Area* 622,984 sq km (240,534 sq miles); *population* 2,900,000; *capital* Bangui; *form of government* Republic; *religions* Animism, RC; *currency* Franc CFA). The Central African Republic is a landlocked country in central Africa. The terrain consists of an undulating plateau with dense tropical forest in the south and a semi-desert area in the east. The climate is tropical with little variation in temperature throughout the year. Most of the population live in the west and in the hot, humid south and southwest. Over 86% of the working population are subsistence farmers and the main crops grown are cassava, groundnuts, bananas, plantains, millet and maize. Gems and industrial diamonds are mined and vast deposits of uranium have been discovered.

Central Region a local government area of Scotland formed in 1975 out of the old counties of Clackmannanshire and parts of Perthshire and Stirlingshire. (2590 sq km/1000 sq miles; pop. 273,000)

Cephalonia *see* **Ionian Islands.**

Ceram *see* **Seram.**

Ceské Budejovice (Budweiss) a historic town in the south of Bohemia, Czech Republic, famous for its Budvar beer. (Pop. 92,800)

Ceuta a Spanish administered enclave in northern Morocco. (Pop. 80,000)

Cévennes the southern part of the Massif Central in France.

Ceylon *see* **Sri Lanka.**

Chad (*Area* 1,284,000 sq km (495,752 sq miles); *capital* N'Djamena; ; *other major cities* Sarh, Moundou; *form of government* Republic; *religions* Sunni Islam, Animism; *currency* Franc CFA). Chad, a landlocked country in the centre of northern Africa, extends from the edge of the equatorial forests in the south to the middle of the Sahara Desert in the north. It lies more than 1600 km (944 miles) from the nearest coast. In the far north of the country the Tibesti Mountains rise from the desert sand to heights of more than 3000 m (9843 ft). The southern part of Chad is the most densely populated and its relatively well-watered savanna has always been the country's most arable region. Recently, however, even here the rains have failed. Cotton ginning is the principal industry.

Chad, Lake a large lake in western Chad, on the border with Niger and Nigeria. (26,000 sq km/10,000 sq miles)

Chamonix a winter sports resort in France, just to the north of Mont Blanc. (Pop. 11,000)

Champagne a region of northeastern France famous for the sparking wine called champagne. It now forms part of the administrative region called Champagne-Ardennes.

Chandigarh a modern city in north India. (Pop. 422,800)

Changchun the capital of Jilin province, China. (Pop. 1,604,000)

Changhua a historic city in west Taiwan. (Pop. 1,206,400)

Chang Jiang (Yangtze) the world's third longest river. It rises in Tibet and flows across central China into the East China Sea. (Length 6380 km/3965 miles)

Changsha the capital of Hunan province, China. (Pop. 2,638,000)

Channel Islands a group of islands in the English Channel, close to the coast of France, which are British Crown dependencies. The main islands are Jersey and Guernsey, but the group also includes the smaller inhabited islands of Alderney, Sark and Herm. (Pop. 134,700)

Chao Phrya, River a river running from north to south down the west side of Thailand and through its capital, Bangkok. (Length 100 km/62 miles)

Chapala, Lake the largest lake in Mexico, near Guadalajara. (2460 sq km/950 sq miles)

Charleroi an industrial city in central Belgium. (Pop. 213,000)

Charleston (1) the state capital of West Virginia, USA (Pop. city 59,400/ metropolitan area 267,000). **(2)** An old port on the Atlantic coast of South Carolina, USA. (Pop. city 67,100/metropolitan area 472,500)

Charlotte Amalie the capital of the US Virgin Islands. (Pop. 11,800)

Charlottetown a port and the provincial capital of Prince Edward Island, Canada. (Pop. 45,000)

Chartres a market town, capital of the department of Eure-et-Loire, in northern France, 80 km (50 miles) west of Paris. It is famous for its early 13th-century cathedral, with original stained-glass windows. (Pop. 80,340)

Chattanooga an industrial city and railway town in Tennessee, USA. (Pop. city 164,400/metropolitan area 422,500)

Chechen-Ingush Republic one of the 16 autonomous republics of the Russian Federation. (19,300 sq km/7450 sq miles; pop. 1,204,000)

Cheju Do an island belonging to South Korea, lying some 90 km (56 miles) off its southern tip, and dominated by the sacred volcano, Mount Halla (1950 m/ 6398 ft). (1828 sq km/706 sq miles; pop. 463,000)

Chelyabinsk an industrial city in the Russian Federation. (Pop. 1,086,000)

Chemnitz an industrial city in southeast Germany, named Karl-Marx-Stadt in former Communist East Germany (until 1990). (Pop. 319,000)

Chengdu the capital of Sichuan province, China. (Pop. 2,470,000)

Chenstokhov *see* **Czestochowa.**

Chernobyl a city about 90 km (55 miles) north of Kiev, in the Ukraine. In April 1986 one of the reactors in its nuclear power station exploded, causing the world's worst nuclear accident.

Chesapeake Bay an inlet, 314 km (195 miles) long, on the east coast of the USA, shared by the states of Virginia and Maryland.

Cheshire a county in northwest England; the county town is Chester. (2322 sq km/897 sq miles; pop. 933,000)

Cheviot Hills a range of hills, 60 km (37 miles) long, which line the border between Scotland and the county of Northumberland in England.

Cheyenne the state capital of Wyoming, USA. (Pop. 50,900)

Chiang Mai *see* **Chiengmai.**

Chianti the winemaking region of central Tuscany, Italy.

Chiba a large industrial city on Honshu Island, Japan. (Pop. 788,900)

Chicago the largest city in the state of Illinois, and the third largest city in the USA (after New York and Los Angeles). (Pop. city 2,992,500/metropolitan area 8,035,000)

Chiengmai (Chiang Mai) the second largest city in Thailand, in the northwest of the country, famous for its temples and the crafts produced in the surrounding villages. (Pop. 200,700)

Chihuahua a city in northern central Mexico, and the name of the surrounding province, of which it is the capital. (Pop. city 410,000)

Chile (*Area* 756,945 sq km (292,256 sq miles); *population* 12,960,000; *capital* Santiago; *other major cities* Arica, Talcahuano, Viña del Mar; *form of government* Republic; *religion* RC; *currency* Chilean peso). Chile lies like a backbone of the South American continent. Its Pacific coastline is 4200 km (2610 miles) long. Because of its enormous range in latitude it has almost every kind of climate from desert conditions to icy wastes. Some 60% of the population live in the central valley where the climate is similar to southern California. The land here is fertile and the principal crops grown are wheat, sugar beet, maize and potatoes. Also in the central valley is one of the largest copper mines in the world, and accounts for Chile's most important source of foreign exchange.

Chiltern Hills a range to the northwest of London, England, rising to 260 m (850 ft).

China (*Area* 9,596,961 sq km (3,705,387 sq miles); *population* 1,114,000,000; *capital* Beijing (Peking); *other major cities* Chengdu, Guangzhou, Shanghai, Tianjin, Wuhan; *form of government* People's Republic; *religions* Buddhism, Confucianism, Taoism; *currency* Yuan). China, the third largest country in the world, covers a large area of east Asia. In western China most of the terrain is very inhospitable—in the northwest there are deserts which extend into Mongolia and the Russian Federation, and much of the southwest consists of the ice-capped peaks of Tibet. The southeast has a green and well-watered landscape comprising terraced hillsides and paddy fields. Most of China has a temperate climate, but in such a large country wide ranges of latitude and altitudes produce local variations. China is an agricultural country, and intensive cultivation and horticulture is necessary to feed its population of over one billion.

China Sea a part of the Pacific Ocean, off the east coast of China.

Chindwin, River a river in Burma, flowing parallel to the northwest border before joining the Irrawaddy River in the centre of the country. (Length 1130 km/700 miles)

Chios (Khios) a Greek island in the Aegean Sea, lying only 8 km (5 miles) from the coast of Turkey. (904 sq km/349 sq miles; pop. 49,900)

Chisinau *see* **Kishinev.**

Chittagong the main port of Bangladesh and its second largest city. (Pop. 1,392,000)

Chongqing (Chungking) an industrial city on the Chang Jiang river, China, and the largest city in Sichuan province. (Pop. 2,650,000)

Chonju a historic city in the southwest of South Korea. (Pop. 367,100)

Chonnam *see* **Kwangju.**

Christchurch the largest city on South Island, New Zealand. (Pop. 300,000)

Christmas Island (1) an island in the eastern Indian Ocean, 400 km (250 miles) to the south of Java, administered by Australia since 1958. (142 sq km/55 sq miles; pop. 3500). **(2)** (Kiritimati) is the Pacific Ocean's largest coral atoll, situated at the northeastern end of the Kiribati group. (432 sq km/167 sq miles; pop. 1300)

Chubu Sangaku a national park in central Honshu Island which contains two of the highest mountains in Japan, Mount Hotaka (3190 m/10,466 ft) and Mount Yari (3180 m/10,434 ft)

Chungking *see* **Chongqing.**

Churchill, River a river which flows into the Hudson Bay at the port of Churchill after a journey through Saskatchewan and Manitoba. (Length 1600 km/1000 miles)

Chuvash Republic one of the 16 autonomous republics of the Russian Federation. (18,300 sq km/7050 sq miles; pop. 1,314,000)

Cincinnati a city in the southwest of the state of Ohio, USA, on the Ohio River. (Pop. city 370,500/metropolitan area 1,673,500)

C.I.S. *see* **Commonwealth of Independent States.**

Ciskei a Bantu homeland for the Xhosa people declared independent by South Africa in 1981. (8300 sq km/3205 sq miles; pop. 728,400)

Citaltépetl a volcanic peak to the southeast of Mexico City, and at 5747 m (18,855 ft) the highest point in Mexico.

Clare a county on the west coast of Ireland; the county town is Ennis. (3188 sq km/1230 sq miles; pop. 87,500)

Clermont-Ferrand a city in Auvergne, central France. (Pop. 262,175)

Cleveland (1) a county of northeast England created in 1974 out of Durham and Yorkshire to administer the industrial region along the River Tees, known as Teeside (583 sq km/225 sq miles; pop. 565,000). **(2)** a port and industrial city on the southern side of Lake Erie, in Ohio, USA. (Pop. city 546,500/metropolitan area 1,867,000)

Cluj-Napoca a city of ancient origins in central Romania. (Pop. 260,000)

Clwyd a county in northeast Wales created in 1974 out of the county of Flintshire and parts of Merionethshire and Denbighshire. (2425 sq km/936 sq miles; pop. 395,000)

Clyde, River a river in Strathclyde region in southwest Scotland which flows northwest to form an estuary 100 km (60 miles) long, called the Firth of Clyde, with Glasgow at its head. (Length 170 km/105 miles)

Coast Ranges the mountains lining the western coast of the USA, stetching 1600 km(1000 miles) from the borders with Canada to Los Angeles. The highest point is in the San Jacinto Mountains (3301 m/10,831 ft)

Cobh a town and port in Cork Harbor on the south coast of Ireland, some 10 km (6 miles) from the city of Cork. (Pop. 6600)

Cochin a port on the southwestern tip of India. (Pop. 551,600)

Cochin China the name given to the region around the Mekong delta during the French occupation of Vietnam.

Cockburn Town the capital of Turks and Caicos. (Pop. 3200)

Cocos Islands (Keeling Islands) a cluster of 28 small coral islands in the eastern Indian Ocean, equidistant from Sumatra and Australia, and administered by Australia since 1955. (14 sq km/6 sq miles; pop. 700)

Cod, Cape a narrow, low-lying peninsula on the coast of Massachusetts, USA, where the Pilgrim Fathers landed in 1620.

Cologne (Köln) a city and industrial centre on the River Rhine, Germany. (Pop. 932,400)

Colombia (*Area* 1,138,914 sq km (439,735 sq miles); *population* 33,000,000; *capital* Bogotá; *other major cities* Barranquilla, Cali, Cartagena, Medellin; *form of government* Republic; *religion* RC; *currency* Peso). Colombia is situated in the northwest of South America. The Andes run north along its western, Pacific coast and gradually disappear toward the Caribbean Sea. Half of Colombia lies east of the Andes, and much of this region is covered in tropical grassland. Towards the Amazon Basin the vegetation changes to tropical forest. Very little of the country is under cultivation although much of the soil is fertile. The range of climates result in an extraordinary variety of crops of which coffee is the most important. Colombia is rich in minerals and produces about half of the world's emeralds.

Colombo a major port and the capital of Sri Lanka. (Pop. 600,000)

Colorado an inland state of central western USA; the state capital is Denver. (270,000 sq km/104,247 sq miles; pop. 3,231,000)

Colorado, River a river which rises in the Rocky Mountains in the state of Colorado, USA, and flows southwest to the Gulf of California, forming the Grand Canyon on its way. (Length 2330 km/1450 miles)

Colorado Springs a spa and resort city in the state of Colorado, USA. (Pop. city 247,700/metropolitan area 349,100)

Columbia the state capital of South Carolina. (Pop. city 98,600/metropolitan area 433,200)

Columbia, District of *see* **Washington D.C.**

Columbia, River flows northwards from its source in British Columbia, Canada, before turning south into Washington State, USA and entering the Pacific Ocean at Portland, Oregon. (Length 1950 km/1210 miles)

Columbus the state capital of Ohio, USA. (Pop. city 566,100/metropolitan area 1,279,000)

Commonwealth of Independent States (C.I.S.) an organization created in 1991 to represent the common interests of eleven independent states of the former USSR. The eleven member states are: Armenia, Azerbaijan, Belarus, Kazakhstan, Kyrgyzstan, Moldova, Russian Federation, Tajikistan, Turkmenistan, Ukraine and Uzbekistan. The former Soviet states of Estonia, Latvia, Lithuania and Georgia did not join the C.I.S. on gaining independence.

Comorin, Cape the southern tip of India.

Comoros (*Area* 2235 sq km (863 sq miles); *population* 503,000; *capital* Moroni; *form of government* Federal Islamic Republic; *religion* Sunni Islam; *currency* Comorian franc). The Comoros consist of three volcanic islands in the Indian Ocean situated between mainland Africa and Madagascar. The islands are mostly forested, and the tropical climate is affected by Indian monsoon winds from the north. Only small areas of the islands are cultivated, and most of this land belongs to foreign plantation owners. The chief product was formerly sugar cane, but now vanilla, copra, maize, cloves and essential oils are the most important products.

Conakry the capital of Guinea, a port partly located on the island of Tumbo. (Pop. 763,000)

Concord the state capital of New Hampshire, USA. (Pop. 30,900)

Congo (*Area* 342,000 sq km (132,046 sq miles); *population* 2,260,000; *capital* Brazzaville; *other major city* Pointe-Noire; *form of government* Republic; *religion* RC; *currency* Franc CFA). Congo is situated in west-central Africa, where it straddles the Equator. The Bateke Plateau has a long dry season but the Congo Basin is more humid and rainfall approaches 2500 mm (98 inches) each year. About 62% of the total land area is covered with equatorial forest from which valuable hardwoods such as mahogany are exported. Cash crops such as coffee and cocoa are mainly grown on large plantations. Oil offshore accounts for most of the Congo's revenues.

Congo, River *see* **Zaïre, River.**

Connaught (Connacht) one of the four old Irish provinces.

Connecticut a state on the northeastern seaboard of the USA, in New England; the capital is Hartford. (12,973 sq km/5009 sq miles; pop. 3,174,000)

Connemara a famously beautiful part of County Galway on the west coast of Ireland centreing upon the distinctive peaks of the Twelve Bens.

Constance, Lake (Bodensee) surrounded by Germany to the north, Switzerland to the south and Austria to the east. (536 sq km/207 sq miles)

Constanta a major port on the Black Sea coast of Romania. (Pop. 283,600)

Constantine (Qacentina) an ancient walled city in the northeastern corner of Algeria. (Pop. 430,500)

Constantinople *see* **Istanbul**.

Cook, Mount the highest mountain in New Zealand, on South Island. (3753 m/ 12,316 ft)

Cook Islands a group of 15 islands in the South Pacific, independent since 1965 but associated with New Zealand. The capital is Avarua. (240 sq km/93 sq miles; pop. 17,700; cur. Cook Islands dollar/ New Zealand dollar = 100cents)

Cook Strait the strait that separates North Island and South Island of New Zealand, 26 km (16 miles) across at its widest point.

Cooper Creek a river flowing into Lake Eyre in South Australia from its source in central Queensland. The upper stretch is known as the Barcoo River. (Length 1420 km/800 miles)

Copacabana a famous beachside suburb of Rio de Janeiro, Brazil.

Copenhagen (København) a port and the capital of Denmark, located on the islands of Zealand and Amager. (Pop. 641,900)

Coral Sea a part of the Pacific Ocean, off the northeast coast of Australia.

Córdoba (Cordova) (1) a city in southern Spain, famous for its cathedral which was built originally as a mosque; also the name of the surrounding province. (Pop. city 284,700) (2) the second city of Argentina, and the name of the surrounding province. (Pop. city 969,000)

Corfu (Kérkira) the most northerly of the Ionian Islands, in western Greece; the capital is also called Corfu. (592 sq km/229 sq miles; pop. 97,100)

Corinth (Korinthos) a town in the Peloponnese in western Greece, built near the Corinth Ship Canal. (Pop. 22,700)

Cork the second largest city in the Republic of Ireland, at the head of a large natural harbour which cuts into the southern coast. Also the name of the county of which it is the county town. (County 7459 sq km/2880 sq miles; pop. county 402,300; pop. city 136,300)

Cornwall the county occupying the southwestern tip of England; the county town is Truro. (3546 sq km/1369 sq miles; pop. 432,000)

Coromandel Coast the coast of southeastern India around Madras.

Coromandel Peninsula the central peninsula reaching northwards from North Island, New Zealand.

Corpus Christi a port in Texas on the Gulf of Mexico. (Pop. city 258,100/ metropolitan area 361,300)

Corsica (Corse) a large island in the Mediterranean Sea lying to the north of Sardinia, governed by France. (8680 sq km/3350 sq miles; pop. 240,000)

Corunna (La Coruña) a port and manufacturing town in northwest Spain, and also the name of the surrounding province. (Pop. town 232,400)

Costa Brava a strip of coastline to the northeast of Barcelona in Spain, famous for its beaches and its popular resorts.

Costa Rica (*Area* 51,100 sq km (19,730 sq miles); *population* 2,910,000; *capital* San José; *other major city* Límon; *form of government* Republic; *religion* RC; *currency* Costa Rican colon). With the Pacific Ocean to the south and west and the Caribbean Sea to the east, Costa Rica is sandwiched between the Central American countries of Nicaragua and Panama. Much of the country consists of volcanic mountain chains which run northwest to southeast. The climate is tropical with a small temperature range and abundant rain. The most populated area is the Valle Central, which was first settled by the Spanish in the 16th century. Coffee and bananas are grown commercially and are the major agricultural exports.

Costa Smeralda the "emerald coast" on the northeast side of the island of Sardinia, famed for its watersports and its upmarket resorts.

Côte d'Azur the coast of southeast France, famous for its beaches and resorts such as St Tropez, Cannes and Nice.

Côte d'Ivoire (*Area* 322,463 sq km (124,503 sq miles); *population* 12,100,000; *capital* Yamoussoukro; *other major cities* Abidjan, Bouaké, Daloa; *form of government* Republic; *religions* Animism, Sunni Islam, RC; *currency* Franc CFA). A former French colony in west Africa, Côte d'Ivoire is located on the Gulf of Guinea with Ghana to the east and Liberia to the west. In the east there are coastal plains which are the country's most prosperous region. The climate is tropical and affected by distance from the sea. Côte d'Ivoire is basically an agricultural country. It is the world's largest producer of cocoa and the fourth largest producer of coffee. These two crops bring in half the country's export revenue.

Cotonou a port and the main business centre of Benin. (Pop. 488,000)

Cotswold Hills a range in west central England, lying east of the Severn.

Coventry an industrial city in the West Midlands of England. (Pop. 315,900)

Cracow (Krakow) the third largest city in Poland, and the capital during medieval times. (Pop. 520,700)

Craiova an industrial city in southwest Romania. (Pop. 228,000)

Cremona a town on the River Po in central northern Italy, famous for its violins, especially those of Antonio Stradivari (?1644-1737). (Pop. 80,800)

Crete (Krití) the largest and most southerly of the islands of Greece, with important ruins of the Minoan civilization at Knossos. The capital is Heraklion. (8366 sq km/3229 sq miles; pop. 502,100)

Crimea (Krym) a diamond-shaped peninsula jutting out into the northern part of the Black Sea and part of the Ukraine. (25,900 sq km/10,000 sq miles; pop. 2,309,000)

Croatia (Hrvatska) (*Area* 56,538 sq km (21,824 sq miles); *population* 4,601,500; *capital* Zagreb; *other major cities* Rijeka, Split; *form of government* Republic; *religions* RC, Eastern Orthodox; *currency* Dinar). Croatia, a republic of former Yugoslavia, declared itself independent in 1991 and was formally recognized in 1992. Western Croatia lies in the Dinaric Alps. The eastern region is low-lying and agricultural. Over one third of the country is forested and timber is a major export. Deposits of coal, bauxite, copper, oil and iron ore are substantial, and most of the republic's industry is based on the processing of these. In Istria in the northwest and on the Dalmatian coast tourism is a major industry.

Crozet Islands a group in the Southern Ocean, forming part of the French Southern and Antarctic Territories. (300 sq km/116 sq miles)

Cuango, River *see* **Kwango, River.**

Cuba (*Area* 110,861 sq km (42,803 sq miles); *population* 10,580,000; *capital* Havana (La Habana); *other major cities* Camaguey, Holguin, Santiago de Cuba; *form of government* Socialist Republic; *religion* RC; *currency* Cuban peso). Cuba is the most westerly of the Greater Antilles and lies about 140 km (87 miles) south of the tip of Florida. Cuba is as big as all other Caribbean islands put together and is home to a third of the whole West Indian population. The climate is warm and generally rainy, and hurricanes are liable to occur between June and November. The island consists mainly of extensive plains and the soil is fertile. The most important product grown and processed is sugar.

Cubango, River *see* **Kavango, River.**

Cúcuta a city in northern Colombia on the border with Vene-zuela. (Pop. 516,000)

Cuenca a city in southern Ecuador, founded by the Spanish in 1557, but also the site of a number of important Inca ruins. (Pop. 272,500)

Cuernavaca an old resort town in the mountains 80km (50miles) to the south of Mexico City. (Pop. 557,000)

Cumberland *see* **Cumbria.**

Cumbria a county in northwest England, created in 1974 from the old counties of Cumberland, Westmorland and a part of Lancashire. (6809 sq km/2629 sq miles; pop. 483,000)

Curaçao an island in the Caribbean lying just off the coast of Venezuela but a part of the Netherlands Antilles. (444 sq km/171 sq miles; pop. 170,000)

Curitaba an industrial city in southern Brazil. (Pop. 1,442,000)

Cuzco a city set in the Andes mountains in Peru, and the name of the surrounding province. It was a centre of the Inca empire, and there are numerous Inca remains in the region, including Machu Picchu. (Pop. city 184,600)

Cyclades (Kikládhes) a group of some 220 islands in the middle of the Aegean Sea belonging to Greece. The best known are Tínos, Andros, Mílos, Míkonos, Delos, Náxos, Paros, Ios and Síros. (Pop. 88,400)

Cyprus (*Area* 9251 sq km (3572 sq miles); *population* 698,800; *capital* Nicosia; *other major cities* Limassol, Larnaca; *form of government* Republic; *religions* Greek Orthodox, Sunni Islam; *currency* Cyprus pound). Cyprus is an island which lies in the eastern Mediterranean. It has a long thin panhandle and is divided from west to east by two parallel ranges of mountains, which are separated by a wide central plain open to the sea at either end. It has very hot dry summers and warm damp winters. This contributes towards the great variety of crops grown on the island. Fishing is a significant industry, but above all the island depends on visitors, and it is tourism which has led to a recovery in the economy since 1974.

Czechoslovakia *see* **Czech Republic; Slovakia.**

Czech Republic (*Area* 78,864 sq km (30,449 sq miles); *population* 10,291,900; *capital* Prague (Praha); *other major cities* Brno, Ostrava, Plzen; *form of government* Republic; *religions* RC, Protestantism; *currency* Koruna). The Czech Republic was newly constituted on January 1,1993, with the dissolution of the 74-year-old federal republic of Czechoslovakia that it had previously formed with Slovakia. It is a landlocked country at the heart of central Europe. Natural boundaries are formed by the Sudeten Mountains in the north, the Ore Mountains to the northwest, and the Bohemian Forest in the southwest. The climate is humid continental with warm summers and cold winters. Agriculture is highly developed and efficient. Major crops are sugar beet, wheat and potatoes. Over a third of the labour force is employed in industry, the most important being iron and steel, coal, machinery, cement and paper.

Czestochowa (Chenstokhov) an industrial city in southern Poland. (Pop. 244,100)

Dacca *see* **Dhaka.**

Dagestan an autonomous republic of the Russian Federation lying to the west of the Caspian Sea. The capital is Makhachkala. (50,300 sq km/19,400 sq miles; pop. 709,000)

Dakar the main port and capital of Senegal. (Pop. 1,000,000).

Dalian *see* **Lüda.**

Dakota *see* **North Dakota; South Dakota.**

Dal, Lake the most famous of the lakes of Kashmir, India, by Srinagar.

Dallas a city in northeast Texas, USA. (Pop. city 974,200/metropolitan area 2,203,700)

Dalmatia (Dalmacija) the coast of Croatia, on the Adriatic Sea. The main islands of the coast are Krk, Rab, Losinj, Brac, Hvar, Korcula and Mljet. The principal tourist centre is Dubrovnik.

Damascus (Dimashq) the capital of Syria, an oasis town. (Pop. 1,042,000)

Damavand, Mount an extinct volcano, and the highest peak in the Elburz Mountains, Iran. (5670 m/18,600 ft)

Danube, River (Donau) the longest river in Western Europe, rising in the Black Forest in Germany, and passing through Austria, Slovakia, Hungary and Serbia of former Yugoslavia, forming much of the border between Bulgaria and Romania before turning north and forming a delta on the Black Sea. (Length 2850 km/1770 miles)

Danzig *see* **Gdansk.**

Dardanelles the narrow ribbon of water, some 80 km(50 miles) long, in Turkey which connects the Aegean Sea to the Sea of Marmara (and from thence the Black Sea). Gallipoli is on the peninsula to the north. The Dardanelles were known as the Hellespont to the ancient Greeks.

Dar el Beida *see* **Casablanca.**

Dar es Salaam the largest town and main port of Tanzania. It was the national capital until 1974. (Pop. 757,346)

Darién the eastern province of Panama, a narrow neck of land on the border with Colombia, and the only gap in the Pan-American Highway, which otherwise runs from Alaska to Chile.

Darjiling (Darjeeling) a town in West Bengal, India near the border with Nepal, famous for its tea. (Pop. 282,200)

Darling, River a river flowing from southern Queensland through New South Wales in Australia before converging with the Murray River. (Length 3057 km/1900 miles)

Dartmoor an area of moorland in Devon, England. (945 sq km/365 sq miles)

Darwin the capital of the Northern Territory, Australia. (Pop. 50,000)

Datong (Tatung) an industrial city in Shanxi province, China. (Pop. 800,000)

Davao a city in the southern part of the island of Mindanao, Philippines, and now that country's second largest city. (Pop. city 540,000)

Davis Strait the broad strait, some 290 km (180 miles) across at its narrowest, separating Baffin Island in Canada and Greenland.

Dayr az Zawr the largest town in eastern Syria, on the River Euphrates. (Pop. 332,000)

Dead Sea a small sea on the border between Israel and Jordan into which the River Jordan flows and does not exit. It is one of the lowest places on Earth (396 m/1299 ft below normal sea level) and the body of water with the world's highest salt content. (1049 sq km/395 sq miles)

Death Valley a low-lying desert area in eastern California, USA.

Debrecen an agricultural and industrial centre in eastern Hungary, which has grown up around the original medieval town. (Pop. 207,000)

Deccan the broad, triangular plateau which forms much of the southern part of India.

Dehra Dun a town in northern India, in the foothills of the Himalayas. It is famous as the supposed home of the Hindu god Shiva, and also for the military academy established by the British in the 1930s. (Pop. 293,000)

Delaware a state on the east coast of the USA, and the second smallest in the USA after Rhode Island. The capital is Dover. (5328 sq km/2057 sq miles; pop. 622,000)

Delft a small city in central western Netherlands, famous since the 16th century for its distinctive blue and white pottery. (Pop. 86,300)

Delhi, including New Delhi, the capital of India, in the north of the country, on the Yamuna River. (Pop. 5,729,300)

Delphi the ruins of the Temple of Apollo on Mount Parnassos, 166 km (102 miles) northwest of Athens, Greece. It was the seat of the most important oracle of ancient Greece

Demerara, River a river in central Guyana which flows through the capital, Georgetown. It has given its name to the type of brown sugar which is grown in the region. (Length 320 km/200 miles)

Denbighshire *see* **Clwyd; Gwynedd.**

Den Haag *see* **Hague, The.**

Denmark (*Area* 43,077 sq km (16,632 sq miles); *population* 5,140,000; *capital* Copenhagen (København); *other major cities* Ålborg, Århus, Odense; *form of government* Constitutional Monarchy; *religion* Lutheranism; *currency* Danish krone). Denmark is a small European state lying between the North Sea and the entrance to the Baltic. It consists of a western peninsula and an eastern archipelago of 406 islands, only 89 of which are populated. It has warm sunny summers and cold cloudy winters. The scenery is very flat, low-lying and monotonous, but the soils are good and a wide variety of crops can be grown. Animal husbandry is, however, the most important activity, its produce including the famous Danish bacon and butter. It produces a wide range of manufactured goods and is famous for its imaginative design of furniture, silverware and porcelain.

Denmark Strait the arm of the North Atlantic Ocean which separates Iceland from Greenland, some 290 km (180 miles) apart.

Denpasar the capital of the island of Bali, Indonesia. (Pop. 82,140)

Denver the state capital of Colorado, USA. (Pop. city 504,600/metropolitan area 1,582,500)

Derby a city of Saxon and Danish origins in the county of Derbyshire, England. (Pop. 215,000)

Derbyshire a county in north central England; the county town is Matlock. (2631 sq km/1016 sq miles; pop. 911,000)

Derry *see* **Londonderry.**

Des Moines the state capital of Iowa, USA. (Pop. city 190,800/metropolitan area 377,100)

Detroit a major industrial city and Great Lakes port in the state of Michigan, USA. (Pop. city 1,089,000/metropolitan area 4,315,800)

Devon a county in southwest England; the county town is Exeter. (6715 sq km/2593 sq miles; pop. 980,000)

Dhahran a commercial centre for petroleum extraction business with an important international airport in eastern Saudi Arabia. (Pop. 25,000)

Dhaka (Dacca) the capital of Bangladesh, on the delta of the Rivers Ganges and Brahmaputra. (Pop. 3,458,600)

Dhanbad a city in northeast India and a centre for the coal mining industry of the Damodar Valley. (Pop. 433,100)

Dhaulagiri, Mount a peak of the Himalayas in Nepal. (8172 m/26,810 ft)

Dhodhekanisos *see* **Dodecanese.**

Dijon the historic capital of the Bourgogne region (Burgundy) in western central France, famous in particular for its mustard. (Pop. 221,900)

Dimashq *see* **Damascus.**

Diyarbakir a city on the River Tigris in southeastern Turkey, and the name of the province of which it is the capital. (Pop. city 305,300)

Djerba *see* **Jerba.**

Djibouti (*Area* 23,200 sq km (8958 sq miles); *population* 484,000; *capital* Djibouti; *form of government* Republic; *religion* Sunni Islam; *currency* Djibouti franc). Djibouti is situated in northeast Africa and is bounded almost entirely by Ethiopia, except in the southeast where it shares a border with Somalia. Its coastline is on the Gulf of Aden. The climate is hot, among the world's hottest, and extremely dry. Only a tenth of the land can be farmed even for grazing so it has great difficulty supporting its modest, mostly nomadic population.

Dnepr, River *see* **Dnieper, River.**

Dnepropetrovsk an industrial and agricultural city on the River Dnieper in the Ukraine. It was formerly (1787-96 and 1802-1920) known as Ekaterinoslav. (Pop. 1,140,000)

Dnestr, River *see* **Dniester, River**.

Dnieper (Dnepr), River the third longest river in Europe after the Volga and the Danube, flowing south through the Russian Federation and the Ukraine to the Black Sea via Kiev. (Length 2285 km/1420 miles)

Dniester (Dnestr), River a river flowing through the Ukraine and Moldova to the Black Sea. (Length 1411 km/877 miles)

Dodecanese (Dhodhekanisos) a group of twelve islands belonging to Greece in the eastern Aegean Sea near the coast of Turkey. They include Samos, Patmos, Kalimnos, Karpathos, Kos and Rhodes, the largest in the group. They are also called the Southern Sporades. (Pop. 145,000)

Dodoma the capital (since 1974) of TANZANIA, in its centre. (Pop. 45,700)

Doha (Ad Dawhah) the capital of Qatar. (Pop. 180,000)

Dolomites a range of mountains in northeastern Italy, near the border with Austria. The highest point is Mount Marmolada (3342 m/10,964 ft)

Dominica (*Area* 751 sq km (290 sq miles); *population* 81,200; *capital* Roseau; *form of government* Republic; *religion* RC; *currency* Franc). Dominica is the most northerly of the Windward Islands in the West Indies. The island is very rugged consists of inactive volcanoes. The climate is tropical, and the wettest season is from June to October when hurricanes often occur. The steep slopes are difficult to farm, but agriculture provides almost all Dominica's exports, eg bananas, copra, citrus fruits, cocoa, bay leaves and vanilla. Industry is mostly food processing.

Dominican Republic (*Area* 48,734 sq km (18,816 sq miles); *population* 7,200,000; *capital* Santo Domingo; *other major city* Santiago de los Caballeros; *form of government* Republic; *currency* Dominican peso). The Dominican Republic forms the eastern two-thirds of the island of Hispaniola in the West Indies. Although well endowed with fertile land, only about 30% is cultivated. Sugar is the main crop and mainstay of the country's economy. It is grown mainly on plantations in the southeast plains. Other crops grown are coffee, cocoa and tobacco. The main industries are food processing and the manufacture of consumer goods.

Don, River a river flowing southwards into the Sea of Azov from its source to the south of Moscow. (Length 1870 km/1165 miles)

Donau *see* **Danube, River.**

Donbass *see* **Donets Basin.**

Donegal the northern-most county of the Republic of Ireland, on the west coast.

The county town is also called Donegal. (Pop. county 125,100)

Donets Basin (Donbass) a coal mining region and major industrial area in the eastern Ukraine.

Donetsk the main industrial centre of the Donets Basin. (Pop. 1,064,000)

Dongbei (Manchuria) the northeastern region of China, covering part of the Nei Mongol Autonomous Region and the three provinces, Heilongjiang, Jilin and Liaoning. (1,300,000 sq km/502,000 sq miles; pop. 87,962,000)

Dordogne, River a river of southwestern France which rises in the Massif Central and flows west to the Gironde estuary. (Length 475 km/295 miles)

Dordrecht a river port and industrial city of medieval origin 19 km (12 miles) southeast of Rotterdam in the Netherlands. (Pop. 199,200)

Dorset a county of southwest England; the county town is Dorchester. (2654 sq km/1025 sq miles; pop. 618,000)

Dortmund industrial city in the Ruhr region of Germany. (Pop. 620,000)

Douala the main port of Cameroon, on the Gulf of Guinea. (Pop. 800,000)

Douro (Duero), River a river flowing west from north central Spain across northern Portugal to the Atlantic Ocean. (Length 895 km/555 miles)

Dover (1) a port in the county of Kent, England, overlooking the English Channel at its narrowest point, opposite Calais, France. (Pop. 33,000). (2) The state capital of Delaware, USA. (Pop. 22,500)

Dover, Strait of the stretch of water separating England and France, where the English Channel meets the North Sea. The ports of Dover and Calais are situated on either side of its narrowest point, 34 km (21 miles) across.

Down a county of Northern Ireland, on the east coast; the county town is Downpatrick. (2448 sq km/945 sq miles; pop. 362,100)

Drakensberg Mountains a range of mountains which stretch 1125 km (700 miles) across Lesotho and neighbouring regions of South Africa. The highest point is Thabana Ntlenyana (3482 m/11,424 ft).

Drake Passage the broad strait, some 640 km (400 miles) wide, which separates Cape Horn on the southern tip of South America and Antarctica.

Drava (Drau), River a river flowing from eastern Austria to Croatia and Serbia, where it forms much of the border with Hungary before joining the Danube. (Length 718 km/447 miles)

Dresden a historic city on the River Elbe in the south of eastern Germany. Formerly the capital of Saxony, it was noted particularly for its fine porcelain. (Pop. 522,500)

Duarte, Pico a mountain peak in central Dominican Republic which is the highest point in the West Indies. (3175 m/10,417 ft)

Dubai (Dubayy) the second largest of the United Arab Emirates, at the eastern end of The Gulf. Most of the population lives in the capital, Dubai. (3900 sq km/ 1506 sq miles; pop. emirate 296,000/city 265,700)

Dublin (Baile Atha Cliath) the capital of the Republic of Ireland, on the River Liffey, and also the name of the surrounding county. Its main port area is at Dun Laoghaire. (Pop. county 1,002,000/city 525,400)

Dubrovnik (Ragusa) a pretty medieval port on the Adriatic coast of Croatia, for long a popular tourist destination. (Pop. 31,200)

Duero, River *see* **Douro, River.**

Duisburg a major inland port situated at the confluence of the Rivers Rhine and Ruhr in Germany. (Pop. 541,800)

Duluth a port and industrial centre on Lake Superior, in the state of Michigan, USA. (Pop. city 85,600/ metropolitan area 253,800)

Dumfries and Galloway a region of southwest Scotland created out of the old counties of Dumfriesshire, Kirkudbrightshire and Wigtownshire. The regional capital is Dumfries. (6370 sq km/2459 sq miles; pop. 145,200)

Dunbartonshire *see* **Strathclyde.**

Dundee a port on the east coast of Scotland, on the north side of the Firth of Tay, and the administrative centre of Tayside region. (Pop. 180,000)

Dunfermline *see* **Fife.**

Dunkirk (Dunkerque) a port and industrial town in northeastern France, close to the Belgian border. It was virtually destroyed in 1940 when British, French and Belgian forces were trapped by the advancing German army, but were evacuated to Britain in a fleet of small boats. (Pop. 196,600)

Dun Laoghaire *see* **Dublin.**

Durango a mineral-rich state in northern Mexico, with a capital called (Victoria de) Durango. (Pop. state 1,200,000/city 209,000)

Durban a port on the east coast of South Africa, and the largest city of the province of Natal. (Pop. 960,800)

Durham a city of northeast England, and the name of the county of which it is the county town. (County 2436 sq km/940 sq miles; pop. county 607,000/city 26,000)

Dushanbe an industrial city and the capital of Tajikistan. (Pop. 539,000)

Düsseldorf a major commercial and industrial centre in the Ruhr region of Germany, on the River Rhine north of Cologne. (Pop. 579,800)

Dvina, River the name of two quite separate rivers. The West (Zapadnaya) Dvina flows from its source to the west of Moscow into the Baltic Sea at Riga in Latvia. The North (Severnaya) Dvina flows through the northwest of the Russian Federation to the White Sea at Archangel. (Length West Dvina 1020 km/635 miles; North Dvina 1320 km/820 miles)

Dyfed a county in southwest Wales, created in 1974 out of the old counties of Cardiganshire, Carmarthenshire and Pembrokeshire. Carmarthen is the county town. (5765 sq km/2226 sq miles; pop. 377,000)

Dzungaria *see* **Xinjiang Uygur Autonomous Region.**

East Anglia an old Anglo-Saxon kingdom occupying the bulge of the east coast of England between the Thames estuary and The Wash, and now covered by Norfolk, Suffolk, and parts of Cambridgeshire and Essex.

Easter Island (Isla de Pascua) a remote and tiny island in the South Pacific Ocean annexed by Chile in 1888. About 1000 years ago it was settled by Polynesians who set up over 600 huge stone statues of heads on the island. (120 sq km/46 sq miles; pop. 1300)

Ebro, River a river flowing across northeastern Spain, from near the north coast to the Mediterranean Sea south of Tarragona. (Length 909 km/565 miles)

Ecuador (*Area* 283,561 sq km (109,483 sq miles); *population* 10,490,000; *capital* Quito; *other major cities* Guayaquil, Cuenca; *form of government* Republic; *religion* RC; *currency* Sucre). Ecuador is an Andean country situated in the northwest of South American. It is bounded to the north by Colombia and to the east and south by Peru. The country contains over thirty active volcanos. The climate varies from equatorial through warm temperate to mountain conditions, according to altitude. It is in the coastal plains that plantations of bananas, cocoa, coffee and sugar cane are found. In contrast to this, the highland areas are adapted to grazing, dairying and cereal growing. The fishing industry is important on the Pacific Coast. Oil produced in the tropical eastern region is Ecuador's most important export.

Edinburgh the capital of Scotland, a university city and commercial centre, on the Firth of Forth (the estuary of the River Forth). (Pop. 439,000)

Edmonton the capital of Alberta, Canada. (Pop. 657,000)

Edo *see* **Tokyo.**

Edward (Rutanzige), Lake a lake in the Great Rift Valley, on the border between Uganda and Zaïre. (2135 sq km/820 sq miles)

Egypt (*Area* 1,001,449 sq km (386,659 sq miles); *population* 50,740,000; *capital* Cairo (El Qahira); *other major cities* Alexandria, El Gîza; *form of government* Republic; *religions* Sunni Islam, Christianity; *currency* Egyptian pound). Egypt is situated in northeast Africa, straddling the River Nile and with vast deserts either side. The climate is mainly dry, but there are winter rains along the Mediterranean coast. The temperatures are comfortable in winter but summer temperatures are extremely high, particularly in the south. The rich soils deposited by floodwaters of the Nile can support a large population, and the delta is one of the world's most fertile agricultural regions. Some 96% of the population live in the delta and Nile valley, where the main crops are rice, cotton, sugar cane, maize, tomatoes and wheat. The main industries are food processing and textiles. The economy has been boosted by the discovery of oil. Suez Canal shipping and tourism are also important revenue earners.

Eifel an upland area of western Germany between the Moselle River and the border with Belgium.

Eiger, The a mountain in southern central Switzerland, renowned among climbers for its daunting north face. (3970 m/13,025 ft)

Eilat *see* **Elat.**

Eindhoven an industrial city in south central Netherlands. (Pop. 194,600)

Eire *see* **Ireland, Republic of.**

Ekaterinburg *see* **Yekaterinburg.**

Ekaterinoslav *see* **Dnepropetrovsk.**

Elat (Eilat) a port and tourist resort in the very south of Israel at the tip of the Gulf of Aqaba, an arm of the Red Sea. (Pop. 18,800)

Elba an island lying about 10 km (6 miles) off the coast of Tuscany, Italy. (223 sq km/86 sq miles; pop. 28,400)

Elbe, River a largely navigable river flowing northward from its source in the Czech Republic through Germany to Hamburg, and then into the North Sea. (Length 1160 km/720 miles)

Elbrus, Mount the highest mountain in Europe, situated in the western Caucasus, Russian Federation. (5642 m/18,510 ft)

Elburz Mountains a range of mountains in northern Iran, between Tehran and the Caspian Sea. The highest peak is the extinct volcano, Damavand (5670 m/ 18,600 ft).

El Djazair *see* **Algiers.**

Eleuthera *see* **Bahamas.**

El Faiyum (Fayum) a large and fertile oasis to the west of the River Nile in Egypt. (Pop. 167,080)

El Gezira a major irrigation scheme in Sudan between the Blue Nile and the White Nile.

El Gîza a sprawling suburb of Cairo, Egypt, at the edge of which stand the three most famous pyramids of the Ancient Egyptians. (Pop. 1,230,500)

Elisabethville *see* **Lubumbashi.**

El Khartum *see* **Khartoum.**

El Mansura a city on the Nile delta in northern Egypt. (Pop. 323,000)

El Paso a city in western Texas, USA, close to the border with Mexico. (Pop. city 463,000/metropolitan area 526,500)

El Qahira *see* **Cairo.**

El Salvador (*Area* 21,041 sq km (8123 sq miles); *population* 5,220,000; *capital* San Salvador; *other major cities* Santa Ana, San Miguel; *form of government* Republic; *religion* RC; *currency* Colón). El Salvador is the smallest and most densely populated state in Central America. It is bounded north and east by Honduras and has a Pacific coast to the south. Two volcanic ranges run from east to west across the country. It is predominantly agricultural, and 32% of the land is used for crops such as coffee, cotton, maize, beans, rice and sorghum, and a slightly smaller area is used for grazing cattle, pigs, sheep and goats.

Elsinore (Helsingør) a town of medieval origins on the island of Zealand, Denmark, to the north of Copenhagen. Kronborg Castle, which dominates the town, is the setting for Shakespeare's play Hamlet. (Pop. 65,200)

Emilia-Romagna a region on the east coast of northern central Italy; the capital is Bologna. (22,123 sq km/8542 sq miles; pop. 3,943,000)

Emmenthal the valley of the River Emme, in Switzerland, famous for its distinctive cheese.

Empty Quarter *see* **Rub al-Khali.**

Enewetak *see* **Marshall Islands.**

Engel's an industrial town on the River Volga, in the Russian Federation. (Pop. 175,000)

England the country occupying the greater part of the island of Great Britain, and the largest of the countries that make up the United Kingdom. Scotland lies to the north and Wales to the west. The capital is London. (130,357 sq km/50,331 sq miles; pop. 46,795,000)

English Channel the arm of the eastern Atlantic Ocean which separates the south coast of England from France.

Enschede an industrial town in the eastern part of the Netherlands, close to the border with Germany. (Pop. 144,900)

Entebbe a town with an international airport on Lake Victoria, Uganda. It was the capital until 1962. (Pop. 30,000)

Enugu a coal-mining centre in southern central Nigeria, the capital of Biafra (Iboland) during the Civil War (1967-70). (Pop. 222,600)

Eolian (Lipari) Islands a group of small volcanic islands which lie between the north coast of Sicily and mainland Italy. The main islands are Stromboli, Lipari, Salina, Panarea and Vulcano. (Pop. 12,500)

Eptanisos *see* **Ionian Islands.**

Equatorial Guinea (*Area* 28,051 sq km (10,830 sq miles); *population* 417,000; *capital* Malabo; *other major city* Bata; *form of government* republic; *religion* RC; *currency* Franc CFA). Equatorial Guinea lies about 200 km (124 miles) north of the Equator on the hot humid coast of West Africa. The country consists of a square-shaped mainland area (Mbini) with its few small offshore islets, and the islands of Bioko and Pagalu. Bioko is a very fertile centre of the country's cocoa production.

Ercolano *see* **Herculaneum.**

Erfurt a historic town and tourist centre in central Germany. (Pop. 215,000)

Erie, Lake one of the five Great Lakes (the second smallest after Lake Ontario), on the border between Canada and the USA. (25,670 sq km/9910 sq miles)

Eritrea an autonomous province of northern Ethiopia, bordering the Red Sea. The capital is Asmara. (117,400 sq km/45,316 sq miles; pop. 3,000,000)

Erzurum a market town in western Turkey, and the name of the surrounding province. (Pop. town 252,700)

Esfahan (Isfahan) a city in central Iran noted for its magnificent blue-tiled mosques and other Islamic buildings. (Pop. 926,700)

Eskisehir a spa town in western Turkey and the name of the surrounding province. (Pop. town 367,300)

Espiritu Santo *see* **Vanuatu.**

Esseg *see* **Osijek.**

Essen an industrial city in western Germany, and the largest in the Ruhr region. (Pop. 635,200)

Essex a county in southeast England; the county town is Chelmsford. (3674 sq km/1419 sq miles; pop. 1,492,000)

Estonia (*Area* 45,100 sq km (17,413 sq miles); *population* 1,573,000; *capital* Tallinn; *other major cities* Tartu, Narva; *form of government* Republic; *religion* Eastern Orthodox, Lutheranism; *currency* Rouble). Estonia lies to the northwest of the Russian Federation and is bounded to the north by the Gulf of Finland, to the west by the Baltic Sea and to the south by Latvia. It is the smallest of the three previous Soviet Baltic Republics. Agriculture, especially dairy farming, is the chief occupation. Almost 22% of Estonia is forested and this provides material for sawmills, furniture, match and pulp industries. The country has rich, high-quality shale deposits, and phosphorous has been found near Tallinn.

Ethiopia (*Area* 1,221,900 sq km (471,776 sq miles); *population* 50,000,000; *capital* Addis Ababa (Adis Abeba); *other major cities* Asmara, Dire Dawa; *form of government* People's republic; *religion* Ethiopian Orthodox, Sunni Islam; *currency* : Ethiopian birr). Ethiopia, one of Africa's largest countries, stretches from the shores of the Red Sea to the north of Kenya. Most of the country consists of highlands. Because of the wide range of latitudes, Ethiopia has many climatic variations between the high temperate plateau and the hot humid lowlands. The country is very vulnerable to drought, but in some areas thunderstorms can erode soil from the slopes, reducing the area available for crop planting. Coffee is the main source of rural income, and teff is the main food grain. Droughts have brought much famine.

Etna, Mount the largest volcano in Europe, situated near the east coast of Sicily, Italy, and still highly active. (3323 m/10,902 ft)

Euboea (Evvoia) a large island in the Aegean Sea lying close to the east coast of mainland Greece and joined to the mainland by a bridge. (3655 sq km/1411 sq miles; pop. 188,400)

Euphrates, River (Al Furat) one of the great rivers of the Middle East, flowing from its source in eastern Turkey, across Syria and central Iraq to The Gulf. (Length 2720 km/1690 miles)

Europe a continent that is divided from Asia by a border that runs down the Ural Mountains to the Caspian Sea and then west to the Black Sea. For convenience it is commonly divided into two areas: Eastern Europe (the countries that have or had Communist governments since the Second World War) and Western Europe. (10,498,000 sq km/4,053,300 sq miles; pop. 682,000,000)

Everest, Mount the highest mountain in the world, situated on the border between Nepal and China in the eastern Himalayas. (8848 m/29,028 ft)

Everglades a vast area of subtropical swampland on the western side of southern Florida, USA.

Evvoia *see* **Euboea.**

Eyre, Lake a large salt lake in South Australia. (8900 sq km/3400 sq miles)

Faeroe (Faroe) Islands (Føroyar) a group of 18 islands in the North Atlantic Ocean belonging to Denmark, which lie approximately halfway between Iceland and Scotland. (1399 sq km/540 sq miles; pop. 44,500)

Fair Isle a small island situated between the Orkney and Shetland Islands to the north of Scotland, famous for distinctive, patterned sweaters. (pop. 75)

Faisalabad (Lyallpur) an industrial city and agricultural centre in northeast Pakistan. (Pop. 1,092,000)

Faiyum *see* **El Faiyum.**

Falkland Islands (Islas Malvinas) a British Crown Colony consisting of two large islands and some 200 smaller ones lying about 650 km (410 miles) east of southern Argentina. The capital is Port Stanley. (12,173 sq km/4700 sq miles; pop. 1800)

Fao (Al Faw) a port and oil tanker terminal in Iraq, at the mouth of the Shatt al Arab waterway.

Faro the capital of the Algarve province of Portugal. (Pop. 28,200)

Faroe Islands *see* **Faeroe Islands.**

Fatehpur Sikri a magnificent deserted palace complex some 150 km(93 miles) south of Delhi, India, built as a capital by the Moghul Emperor Akbar in 1580 but abandoned in 1605.

Fayum *see* **El Faiyum.**

Fermanagh a lakeland county in the southwest of Northern Ireland; the county town is Enniskillen. (1676 sq km/647 sq miles; pop. 51,400)

Fernando Póo *see* **Bioko.**

Ferrara a historic city in northeastern Italy in the Po Valley. (Pop. 150,300)

Fès (Fez) a city in northern Morocco, the oldest of that country's four imperial cities. (Pop. 448,823)

Fife a region of eastern Scotland. The administrative centre is Glenrothes. (1308 sq km/505 sq miles; pop. 344,000)

Fiji (*Area* 18,274 sq km (7056 sq miles); *population* 727,104; *capital* Suva; *form of government* Republic; *religion* Christianity, Hinduism; *currency* Fiji dollar). Fiji consists of some 320 islands and atolls, situated around the 180° International Date Line and about 17° south of the Equator. Fiji has high rainfall, high temperatures and plenty of sunshine all year round. The two main islands, Viti Levu and Vanua Levu, are extinct volcanoes. The main cash crop is sugar cane although copra, ginger and fish are also exported. Tourism is now a major industry.

Finistère the department of France occupying the tip of the Brittany peninsula. (Pop. 828,000)

Finisterre, Cape the northwest corner of Spain.

Finland (*Area* 338,127 sq km (130,551 sq miles); *population* 4,970,000; *capital* Helsinki (Helsingfors); *other major cities* Turku, Tampere; *form of government* Republic; *religion* Lutheranism; *currency* Markka). Finland lies in northern Europe, with the Russian Federation to the east and the Gulf of Bothnia to the west. Most of the country is low-lying except for the north, which rises to over 1000 m (3281 ft) in Lappland. It is covered with extensive forests and thousands of lakes. Winter is severe and summer is short. It is largely self-sufficient in food and produces surpluses of dairy produce. Most crops are grown in the southwest. In the north reindeer are herded and forests yield much timber for export. Major industries are timber products, wood pulp and paper, machinery and shipbuilding.

Finland, Gulf of the easternmost arm of the Baltic Sea, with Finland to the north, St Petersburg at its eastern end, and Estonia to the south.

Firenze *see* **Florence.**

Flanders (Vlaanderen, Flandre) A Flemish-speaking coastal region of northern Belgium, now divided into two provinces, East and West Flanders. (6115 sq km/2361 sq miles; pop. 2,400,000)

Flinders Range mountains in the eastern part of South Australia, stretching over 400 km (250 miles). St Mary Peak is the highest.(1188 m/3898 ft).

Flintshire *see* **Clwyd.**

Florence (Firenze) one of the great Renaissance cities of Italy, straddling the River Arno, and the capital of the region of Tuscany. (Pop. 453,300)

Flores a volcanic island in the Sunda group in Indonesia, lying in the chain due east of Java. (17,150 sq km/6622 sq miles; pop. 803,000)

Flores Sea a stretch of the Pacific Ocean between Flores and Sulawesi.

Florida a state occupying the peninsula in the southeastern corner of the USA. The state capital is Tallahassee. (151,670 sq km/58,560 sq miles; pop. 11,366,000)

Florida, Straits of the waterway which separates the southern tip of Florida, USA from Cuba, some 145 km (90 miles) to the south.

Flushing (Vlissingen) a port on the southwest coast of the Netherlands. (Pop. 46,400)

Fly, River a largely navigable river flowing from the central mountains in western Papua New Guinea to its broad estuary on the Gulf of Papua to the south. (Length 1200 km/750 miles)

Foggia a city in the Puglia region of southeastern Italy. (Pop. 158,400)

Fontainebleau a town 55 km (35 miles) southeast of Paris, France, with a 16th-century royal château and a famous forest. (Pop. 39,400)

Formosa *see* **Taiwan.**

Fortaleza a major port on the northeastern coast of Brazil. (Pop. 1,309,000)

Fort-de-France a port and the capital of MARTINIQUE. (Pop. 100,000)

Fort Knox a military reservation in Kentucky, USA, 40 km (25 miles) southwest of Louisville; also the site of the principal depository of the country's gold bullion. (Pop. 37,600)

Fort Lamy *see* **Ndjamena.**

Fort Lauderdale a city and resort on the east coast of Florida, USA, 40 km (25 miles) north of Miami. (Pop. city 149,900/metropolitan area 1,093,300)

Fort Worth a city in northeast Texas, USA, just to the west of Dallas and part of a Dallas-Fort Worth conurbation (the Southwest Metroplex). (Pop. city 414,600/ metropolitan area 1,144,400)

Foshan an industrial city in Guangdong province, China. (Pop. 500,000)

France (*Area* 551,500 sq km (212,934 sq miles); *population* 56,180,000; *capital* Paris; *other major cities* Bordeaux, Lyon, Marseille, Toulouse; *form of government* Republic; *religion* RC; *currency* Franc). France is the largest country in western Europe and has a coastline on the English Channel, the Mediterranean Sea and on the Atlantic Ocean. The lowest parts of the country are the great basins of the north and southwest from which it rises to the Massif Central and the higher Alps, Jura and Pyrénées. Climate ranges from moderate maritime in the northwest to Mediteranneam in the south. Farming is possible in all parts of France. Its vineyards produce some of the world's best wines. The main industrial area of France is in the north and east.

Frankfort the state capital of Kentucky, USA. (Pop. 26,800)

Frankfurt (Frankfurt am Main) a major financial, trade and communications centre in central western Germany, on the River Main. (Pop. 614,700)

Frankfurt an der Oder a town on the River Oder in eastern Germany, on the border with Poland. (Pop. 84,800)

Fraser, River a river flowing through southern British Columbia, Canada, from its source in the Rocky Mountains to the Strait of Georgia by Vancouver. (Length 1370 km/850 miles)

Fredericton the capital of New Brunswick, Canada. (Pop. 43,750)

Freemantle *see* **Perth (Australia).**

Freetown the main port and capital of SIERRA LEONE. (Pop. 316,300)

Freiburg (Freiburg im Breisgau) the largest city in the Black Forest in southwest Germany, close to the border with France. (Pop. 175,000)

French Guiana (Guyane) *see* **Guiana (French).**

French Polynesia a total of about 130 islands in the South Pacific Ocean administered as overseas territories by France.

French Southern and Antarctic Territories a set of remote and widely scattered territories in Antarctica and the Antarctic Ocean administered by France. They include the Crozet Islands and Kerguelen.

Fresno a city in central eastern California. (Pop. city 267,400/metropolitan area 564,900)

Friesian (Frisian) Islands a string of sandy, low-lying islands that line the coasts in the southeastern corner of the North Sea. The West Friesians (including Terchelling and Texel) belong to the Netherlands; the East Friesians (including Borkum and Norderney) belong to Germany; and the North Friesians are divided between Germany and Denmark.

Frunze *see* **Bishkek.**

Fuji, Mount (Fujiyama) the highest peak in Japan, a distinctive volcanic cone 100 km (62 miles) to the southwest of Tokyo. (3776 m/12,389 ft)

Fujian (Fukien) a coastal province in southeast China. The capital is Fuzhou. (120,000 sq km/46,350 sq miles; pop. 24,800,000)

Fukuoka a port and largest city on Kyushu, Japan. (Pop. 1,160,400)

Funafuti the capital of Tuvalu, and the name of the atoll on which it is sited. (2.4 sq km/0.9 sq miles; pop. 2600)

Funchal the capital of Madeira. (Pop. 45,600)

Fundy, Bay of lies between Nova Scotia and New Brunswick, Canada. It has the world's largest tidal range—15 m (50 ft) between low and high tide.

Fünen (Fyn) the second largest of the islands of Denmark, in the centre of the country. (2976 sq km/1048 sq miles; pop. 433,800)

Fushun a mining city in Liaoning province, China, situated on one of the largest coalfields in the world. (Pop. 1,800,000)

Fuzhou a port and capital of Fujian province, China. (Pop. 1,050,000)

Fyn *see* **Fünen**

Gabès, Gulf of a branch of the Mediterranean Sea which, with the Gulf of Sirte to the east, makes a deep indent in the coast of north Africa.

Gabon (*Area* 267,667 sq km (103,346 sq miles); *population* 1,220,000; *capital* Libreville; *other major city* Port Gentile; *form of government* Republic; *religion* RC, Animism; *currency* Franc CFA). Gabon is a small country in west-central Africa which straddles the Equator. It has a low narrow coastal plain, and the rest of the country comprises a low plateau. Three-quarters of Gabon is covered with dense tropical forest. The climate is hot, humid and typically equatorial with little or no seasonal variations. Until the 1960s timber was virtually Gabon's only resource. By the mid 1980s it was Africa's sixth largest oil producer. Much of the earnings from this were squandered, however, and most of the Gabonese people remain subsistence farmers.

Gaborone the capital of Botswana, in the southeast. (Pop. 79,000)

Galapagos Islands a group of 15 islands on the Equator administered by Ecuador, but located some 1100 km (680 miles) to the west of that country. (7812 sq km/3016 sq miles; pop. 6200)

Galati an inland port on the River Danube in eastern Romania, close to the border with the Moldova. (Pop. 261,000)

Galicia a region in the very northwest corner of Spain. (Pop. 2,754,000)

Galilee the most northerly region of Israel, bordering Lebanon and Syria, with the Sea of Galilee (Lake Tiberias) on its eastern side.

Gallipoli (Gelibolu) the peninsula and port on the northern side of the Dardanelles in Turkey.

Galloway *see* **Dumfries and Galloway.**

Galveston a port in Texas, USA, sited on an island in the Gulf of Mexico. (Pop. city 62,400/metropolitan area 215,400)

Galway a county in the central part of the west coast of Ireland. The county town is also called Galway, or Galway City. (5940 sq km/2293 sq miles; pop. county 171,800/city 37,700)

Gambia (*Area* 11,295 sq km (4361 sq miles); *population* 875,000; *capital* Banjul; *form of government* Republic; *religion* Sunni Islam; *currency* Dalasi). Gambia, the smallest country in Africa, pokes like a crooked finger into Senegal. The country is divided along its entire length by the river Gambia. Most Gambians grow enough millet and sorghum to feed themselves. Groundnuts are the main crop and the only export of any significance. The river provides a thriving local fishing industry, and the white sandy beaches on the coast are popular with foreign tourists.

Gambia, River a major river of west Africa, flowing into the Atlantic Ocean from its source in Guinea, through Senegal and Gambia. (Length 483 km/300 miles)

Gand *see* **Ghent.**

Ganges, River (Ganga) the holy river of the Hindus, flowing from its source in the Himalayas, across northern India and forming a delta in Bangladesh as it flows into the Bay of Bengal. (Length 2525 km/1568 miles)

Gansu a mountainous province in northern central China. The capital is Lanzhou. (450,000 sq km/170,000 sq miles; pop. 19,600,000)

Garonne, River a major river of southwestern France, flowing north from the central Pyrénées to the Gironde estuary. (Length 575 km/355 miles)

Gascony (Gascogne) the historic name of an area in the southwestern corner of France bordering Spain.

Gaza Strip a finger of coastal land stretching from the Egyptian border to the Mediterranean port of Gaza. It borders with Israel to its east and north. It was administered by Egypt after the creation of Israel in 1948, and became home to numerous Palestinian refugees. It was taken over by Israel in the Six-Day War of 1967. (Pop. 510,000)

Gaziantep a town in southern central Turkey, close to the border with Syria, and also the name of the surrounding province. (Pop. town 466,300)

Gdansk (Danzig) The main port of Poland, on the Baltic Sea. (Pop. 464,500)

Gdynia (Gdingen) a port on the Baltic coast of Poland 16 km (10 miles) northwest of Gdansk. (Pop. 240,200)

Geelong a port and second city of Victoria, Australia. (Pop. 142,000)

Gelsenkirchen an industrial and coal mining town in the Ruhr region of Germany. (Pop. 290,000)

Geneva (Genève; Genf) a city in the extreme southwest of Switzerland, at the western end of Lake Geneva, and close to the border with France. It is also the name of the surrounding canton. (Pop. city 165,000)

Genoa (Genova) the major seaport of northwest Italy, and the capital of Liguria. (Pop. 760,300)

Gent *see* **Ghent.**

George Town a port and the main city of Penang Island, Malaysia. (Pop. 250,600)

Georgetown (1) the main port and capital of GUYANA. (Pop. 200,000) (2) the capital and main port of the Cayman Islands. (Pop. 12,970)

Georgia (1) a state in the southeast of the USA, named after George II by English colonists in 1733; the state capital is Atlanta. (152,490 sq km/58,876 sq miles; pop. 5,837,000).

Georgia (2) (*Area* 69,700 sq km (26,900 sq miles); *population* 5,976,000; *capital* Tbilisi; *other major cities* Kutaisi, Rustavi, Batumi; *form of government* Republic; *religion* Russian Orthodox; *currency* Rouble). Georgia is a republic in the southwest of the former USSR, occupying the central and western parts of the Caucasus. Almost 40% of the country is covered with forests. Agriculture is the main occupation, especially tea cultivation and fruit growing. It is rich in minerals and has many industries. Georgia declared itself independent in 1991.

Georgia, Strait of the southern part of the stretch of water which separates Vancouver Island from the coast of British Columbia in Canada.

Germany (*Area* 356,910 sq km (137,803 sq miles); population 79,070,000; *capital* Berlin, Bonn (Seat of government); *other major cities* Cologne, Frankfurt, Hamburg, Leipzig, Munich, Stuttgart; *form of government* Republic; *religions* Lutheranism, RC; *currency* Deutsche Mark). Germany is a large industrialized country in northern central Europe, which comprises the former East and West German Republics, reunified in 1990. Its landscapes vary from flat coastal plains in the north, through central plateaux to the Bavarian and Swabian Alps in the south. The main rivers, like the Rhine and Elbe, flow northwards. Generally the country has warm summers and cold winters. Agricultural products include wheat, rye, barley, oats, potatoes and sugar beet. Principal industries are mechanical and electrical engineering, chemicals, textiles and motor vehicles, located in the large provincial cities and concentrated in the Ruhr and Rhine valleys. The country depends heavily on imports.

Gezira *see* **El Gezira.**

Ghana (*Area* 238,533 sq km (92,098 sq miles); *population* 14,900,000; *capital* Accra; *other major cities* Kumasi, Tamale, Sekondi-Takoradi; *form of government* Republic; *religion* Protestant, Animism, RC; *currency* Cedi). Ghana is located in West Africa between Côte d'Ivoire and Togo. It has palm-fringed beaches of white sand along the Gulf of Guinea. The climate on the coast is equatorial, and towards the north there are steamy tropical evergreen forests which give way in the far north to tropical savanna. The landscape becomes harsh and barren near the border with Burkina. In the south, cocoa, rubber, palm oil and coffee are grown. Ghana has important mineral resources such as manganese and bauxite.

Ghats the two ranges of mountains that line the coasts of the Deccan peninsula in India: the Eastern Ghats (rising to about 600 m/2000 ft) and the Western Ghats (1500 m/5000 ft).

Ghent (Gent; Gand) a medieval city spanning the Rivers Lys and Schelde and the capital of the province of East Flanders, Belgium. (Pop. city 235,000/ metropolitan area 490,000)

Gibraltar a self-governing British Crown Colony on the southwestern tip of Spain, where a limestone hill called the Rock of Gibraltar rises to 425 m (1394 ft). Its commanding view over the Strait of Gibraltar has made the territory strategically significant. English is the official language, although Spanish is also spoken. The capital is Gibraltar Town. (6.5 sq km/2.5 sq miles; pop. 32,200; cur. Gibraltar pound)

Gibraltar, Strait of the narrow waterway, 13 km (8 miles) at its narrowest, which connects the Mediterranean Sea to the Atlantic Ocean, with Spain to the north and Morocco to the south.

Gibson Desert a desert of sand and salt marshes in central western Australia.

Gifu a town in central Honshu Island, Japan. (Pop. 411,700)

Gijón a port and industrial town in Austurias, in the centre of the north coast of Spain. (Pop.256,000)

Gilbert Islands *see* **Kiribati.**

Gilgit a mountain district in northern Pakistan, noted for its great beauty. The small town of Gilgit perches startlingly beneath a dramatic rockface.

Gironde the long, thin estuary stretching some 80 km (50 miles) which connects the Rivers Dordogne and Garonne to the Atlantic coast of southwest France.

Giuba, River *see* **Jubba, River.**

Giza *see* **El Gîza**.

Glamorgan a former county of south Wales, which was divided into three in the 1970s: Mid Glamorgan, West Glamorgan and South Glamorgan.

Glasgow a major industrial city and important cultural centre on the River Clyde. It is the largest city in Scotland. (Pop. 751,000)

Gliwice (Gleiwitz) an industrial city in southern Poland. (Pop. 211,000)

Gloucestershire a county in western England; the county town is Gloucester. (2638 sq km/1019 sq miles; pop. 508,000)

Goa a territory on the west coast of India, 400 km (250 miles) south of Bombay, which was captured by the Portuguese in 1510 and remained under the control of Portugal until it was annexed by India in 1961. (3702 sq km/1429 sq miles; pop. 1,007,800)

Gobi Desert a vast expanse of arid land which occupies much of Mongolia and central northern China. (1,295,000 sq km/500,000 sq miles)

Godavari, River a river which runs eastwards across the middle of the Deccan peninsula in India. (Length 1465 km/910 miles)

Godthåb (Nuuk) The capital of Greenland. (Pop. 10,500)

Godwin Austen *see* **K2.**

Golan Heights an area of high ground in southwest Syria on the border with northern Israel. The Heights were captured by Israel in the Arab-Israeli War of 1967 and annexed by Israel in 1981. (2225 m/7300 ft)

Gold Coast (1) the name given to a string of beach resorts on the east coast of Queensland, Australia, to the south of Brisbane. (2) *see* **Ghana**.

Golden Triangle the remote and mountainous region where the borders of Thailand, Burma and Laos meet, noted in particular for its opium cultivation and as one of the world's main sources of the drug heroin.

Gomel an industrial city in southeastern Belarus. (Pop. 452,000)

Gomera *see* **Canary Islands.**

Good Hope, Cape of the tip of the narrow Cape Peninsula which extends from the southwestern corner of South Africa.

Gor'kiy (Gorky) *see* **Nizhniy Novgorod.**

Gothenburg (Göteborg) a major port on the Kattegat and the second largest city in Sweden. (Pop. 425,500)

Gotland an island in the Baltic Sea which forms a county of Sweden. (3140 sq km/1210 sq miles; pop. 56,100)

Göttingen a university town in central Germany and an important trading centre in medieval times. (Pop. 138,000)

Gouda a town in eastern Netherlands, famous for its cheese. (Pop. 59,200)

Gozo *see* **Malta.**

Grampian an administrative region of northeastern Scotland created in 1975 out of the former counties of Aberdeenshire, Kincardineshire, Banffshire and part of Morayshire. The capital is Aberdeen. (8550 sq km/3301 sq miles; pop. 497,000)

Grampian Mountains a range of mountains that stretch across northern Scotland to the south of Loch Ness. The mountains rise to their highest point at Ben Nevis (1344 m/4409 ft), the highest peak in the UK.

Granada a city in the Sierra Nevada of central southern Spain. An administrative centre during the Moorish occupation of Spain, during which its famous Alhambra Palace was built (1248-1345). Granada is also the name of the surrounding province. (Pop. city 262,200)

Gran Canaria *see* **Canary Islands**.

Grand Bahama *see* **Bahamas.**

Grand Canyon the dramatic gorge of the Colorado River, in places over 1.5 km (1 mile) deep, in northwestern Arizona.

Grand Rapids a city 40 km (14 miles) to the east of Lake Michigan in the state of Michigan, USA. (Pop. city 183,000/metropolitan area 626,500)

Graz the second largest city in Austria, in the southeast. (Pop. 243,000)

Great Australian Bight the arm of the Southern Ocean which forms the deep indentation in the centre of the southern coastline of Australia.

Great Australian Desert the collective word for the deserts that occupy much of the centre of Australia. (3,830,000 sq km/1,480,000 sq miles)

Great Barrier Reef the world's most extensive coral reef which lines the coast of Queensland, Australia, stretching some 2000 km (1250 miles).

Great Bear Lake the fourth largest lake in North America, in northwest Canada. It drains into the Mackenzie. (31,153 sq km/12,028 sq miles)

Great Britain the island shared by England, Scotland and Wales, and which forms the principal part of the United Kingdom of Great Britain and Northern Ireland.

Great Dividing Range a range of mountains which runs down the east coast of Australia, from Queensland in the north, across New South Wales to Victoria in the south, some 3600 km (2250 miles) in all. The highest point is Mount Kosciusko. (2230 m/7316 ft)

Greater Manchester *see* **Manchester.**

Greater Sunda Islands *see* **Lesser Sunda Islands.**

Great Lakes the largest group of freshwater lakes in the world, drained by the St Lawrence River. There are five lakes, four of which (Lakes Huron, Superior, Erie and Ontario) are on the border of Canada and the USA; the fifth (Lake Michigan) is in the USA.

Great Plains a vast area in North America of flat and undulating grassland east of the Rocky Mountains and stretching from northern Canada to Texas, USA. It includes the Prairies, most of which are now ploughed for cereal and fodder crops.

Great Rift Valley a series of geological faults which has created a depression stretching 6400 km (4000 miles) from the valley of the River Jordan across the Red Sea and down East Africa to Mozambique.

Great Salt Lake a salt lake in northwest Utah, USA, lying just to the northwest of Salt Lake City. (5200 sq km/2000 sq miles)

Great Sandy Desert the desert region in north Western Australia.

Great Slave Lake a lake drained by the Mackenzie River in the southern part of the Northwest Territories of Canada. (28,570 sq km/11,030 sq miles)

Great Smoky Mountains part of the Appalachian Mountains, running along the border between Tennessee and North Carolina. The highest point is Clingmans Dome (2025 m/6643 ft).

Great Victoria Desert A vast area of sand dunes straddling the border between Western Australia and South Australia.

Greece (*Area* 131,990 sq km (50,961 sq miles); *population*: 10,140,000; *capital* Athens (Athinai); *other major cities* Patras, Piraeus, Thessaloníki; *form of government* Republic; *religion* Greek Orthodox; *currency* Drachma). Greece is a peninsular-shaped country, the most southeasterly extension of Western Europe. About 70% of the land is hilly, with harsh mountain climates and poor soils. The Greek islands and coastal regions have a typical Mediterranean climate while winter in the northern mountains is severe. Agriculture is the chief activity and large scale farming is concentrated on the east coast. Fishing is an important activity around the 2000 islands which lie off the mainland. Tourists visit the country for the sun and its spectacular ancient ruins.

Greenland a huge island to the northeast of North America, most of which lies within the Arctic Circle. A province of Denmark, the island was granted home rule in 1979. The economy is heavily reliant on fishing and most of the population is Eskimo. The capital is Godthåb (Nuuk). (2,175,600 sq km/840,000 sq miles; pop. 54,600; cur. Danish Krone = 100øre)

Greenwich a borough of east London, England, on the south bank of the River Thames. It was the site of the Royal Observatory, and since 1884 has been accepted that Greenwich Mean Time is the time at 0° longitude, against which all world time differences are measured.

Grenada (*Area* 344 sq km (133 sq miles); *population* 110,000; *capital* St. Georges; *form of government* Constitutional Monarchy; *religion* RC, Anglicanism, Methodism; *currency* East Caribbean dollar). Grenada is the most southerly of the Windward Island chain in the Caribbean. It consists of the remains of extinct volcanoes and has an attractive wooded landscape. In the dry season its typical climate is very pleasant with warm days and cool nights, but in the wet season it is hot day and night. Agriculture is the island's main industry and tourism is an important source of foreign revenue.

Grenadines a string of some 600 small islands that lie between St Vincent to the north and Grenada to the south. Most of them belong to St Vincent, but the largest, Carriacou, is divided between St Vincent and Grenada.

Grenoble a manufacturing city in southeast France. (Pop. 396,800)

Groningen the largest city in northeast Netherlands. (Pop. city 205,700)

Guadalajara a major city of central western Mexico. (Pop. 2,300,000)

Guadalcanal an island at the southern end of the archipelago where Honiara, capital of the Solomon Islands, is located.

Guadeloupe a group of islands in the Leeward Islands in the eastern Caribbean which since 1946 has been an overseas department of France. The principal island is Guadeloupe (divided into two parts, Basse Terre and Grande Terre). The capital is Basse Terre. (1779 sq km/687 sq miles; pop. 328,400)

Guam the largest of the Mariana Islands in the western Pacific Ocean. (549 sq km/212 sq miles; pop. 112,000)

Guangdong a province of southeast China. The capital is Guangzhou (Canton). (210,000 sq km/81,000 sq miles; pop. 56,810,000)

Guangxi-Zhuang an autonomous region of southern China on the border with Vietnam. To the south of the city of Guilin, around the Gui Jiang River, is a famous landscape of towering rock hills which rise up from the watery plains. The regional capital is Nanning. (230,000 sq km/89,000 sq miles; pop. 34,700,000)

Guangzhou (Canton) a major port in southeast China, the country's sixth largest city and the capital of Guangdong province. (Pop. 5,350,000)

Guantanamo a city in the southeast of Cuba. The USA has a naval base at nearby Guantanamo Bay. (Pop. 205,000)

Guatemala (*Area* 108,889 sq km (42,042 sq miles); *population* 9,000,000; *capital* Guatemala City; *other major cities* Puerto Barrios, Quezaltenango; *form of government* Republic; *religion* RC; *currency* Quetzal). Guatemala is situated where North America meets Central America. It is a mountainous country with a ridge of volcanoes running parallel to the Pacific coast. It has a tropical climate. The Pacific slopes of the mountains are exceptionally well watered and fertile and it is here that most of the population are settled. Coffee growing on the lower slopes dominates the economy. A small strip on the coast produces sugar, cotton and bananas.

Guatemala City the capital of GUATEMALA, in the southeast of the country. (Pop. 1,329,600)

Guayaquil the main port and the largest city of Ecuador. (Pop. 1,223,500)

Guernica a small town in the Basque country of northeast Spain where the Basque parliament used to assemble. In 1937, during the Spanish Civil War, it was heavy bombed from the air by German forces. (Pop. 17,836)

Guernsey one of the Channel Islands, lying in the centre of the group and some 50 km (30 miles) off the coast of France. The capital is St Peter Port. (78 sq km/30 sq miles; pop. 55,000)

Guiana (French) *or* **Guyane** (*Area* 90,000 sq km (34,749 sq miles); *population* 73,800; *capital* Cayenne; *form of government* French overseas department; *religion* RC; *currency* Franc). Guiana is situated on the northeast coast of South America The climate is tropical with heavy rainfall. Guiana's economy relies almost completely on subsidies from France. It has little to export apart from shrimps and the small area of land which is cultivated produces rice, manioc and sugar cane.

Guinea (*Area* 245,857 sq km (94,925 sq miles); *population* 6,710,000; *capital* Conakry; *other major cities* Kankan, Labé; *form of government* Republic; *religion* :Sunni Islam; *currency* Guinea franc). Guinea, located on the coast at the "bulge" in Africa, is a lush green beautiful country with a tropical climate. Guinea has great agricultural potential, and many of the coastal swamps and forested plains have been cleared for the cultivation of rice, cassava, yams, maize and vegetables. Further inland, on the plateau of Fouta Djallon, dwarf cattle are raised , and in the valleys bananas and pineapples are grown. Coffee and kola nuts are important cash crops grown in the Guinea Highlands to the southwest.

Guinea, Equatorial *see* **Equatorial Guinea**.

Guinea Bissau (*Area* 36,125 sq km (13,948 sq miles); *population* 966,000; *capital* Bissau; *form of government* Republic; *religion*; Animism, Sunni Islam; *currency* Peso). Guinea Bissau, south of Senegal on the Atlantic, is coast of West Africa. It is a country of stunning scenery and rises from a deeply indented and island fringed coastline to a low inland plateau. The climate is tropical but it is one of the poorest West African states. The main crops grown are groundnuts, sugar cane, plantains, coconuts and rice. Fishing is an important export industry.

Guinea, Gulf of the arm of the Atlantic Ocean which creates the deep, right-angled indent in the west coast of Africa.

Guiyang an industrial city in central southern China, and capital of Guizhou province. (Pop. 1,260,000)

Guizhou a province of central southern China. The capital is Guiyang. (170,000 sq km/65,600 sq miles; pop. 27,310,000)

Gujarat a state in northwest India, on the border with Pakistan. The capital is Gandinagar. (196,024 sq km/75,665 sq miles; pop. 34,085,800)

Gujranwala a textile city in the province of Punjab, Pakistan, some 65 km (40 miles) north of Lahore. (Pop. 658,753)

Gulf, The the huge inlet to the south of Iran which is connected to the Arabian Sea by the Strait of Hormuz. It is often referred to as the Persian Gulf, or the Arabian Gulf.

Guyana (*Area* 214,969 sq km (83,000 sq miles); *population* 990,000; *capital* Georgetown; *other major city* New Amsterdam; *form of government* Cooperative Republic; *religion* Hinduism, protestantism, RC; *currency* Guyana dollar). Guyana, situated on the northeast coast of the continent on the Atlantic Ocean, is intersected by many rivers, and the coastal area comprises tidal marshes and mangrove swamps. The jungle in the southwest has potential for the production of minerals, hardwood and hydroelectric power, but 90% of the population live in the coastal area, where the climate is moderated by sea breezes; here rice is grown, and the vast plantations produce sugar.

Guyane *see* **Guiana (French).**

Gwalior a city in central India, southeast of Delhi. (Pop. 555,900)

Gwangju *see* **Kwangju.**

Gwent a county in southeast Wales, bordering the Severn estuary just to the east of Cardiff. The county was created in 1974 and more or less coincides with the old county of Monmouthshire. The county town is Cwmbran. (1376 sq km/532 sq miles; pop. 440,000)

Gwynedd a county in northwest Wales which includes the island of Anglesey. It was created in 1974 out of the former county of Caernarfonshire, and parts of Denbighshire and Merionethshire. The administrative centre is Caernarfon. (3868 sq km/1493 sq miles; pop. 232,000)

Haarlem a city in central western Netherlands. (Pop. 154,300)

Hagen a steel town in the Ruhr region of Germany. (Pop. 210,000)

Hague, The (Den Haag; 's-Gravenhage) the administrative centre of the Netherlands, on the west coast. (Pop. 449,300)

Haifa the main port of Israel. (Pop. 224,700)

Hainan Island a large tropical island in the South China Sea belonging to China, and the southern-most extremity of that country. (33,670 sq km/13,000 sq miles; pop. 5,400,000)

Haiphong a port in the north of Vietnam. It is Vietnam's third largest city after Ho Chi Minh City and Hanoi. (Pop. 1,379,000)

Haiti (*Area* 27,750 sq km (10,714 sq miles); *population* 5,700,000; *capital* Port-au-Prince; *other major cities* Les Cayes, Gonaïves, Jérémie; *form of government* Republic; *religion* RC, Voodooism; *currency* Gourde). Haiti occupies the western third of the large island of Hispaniola in the Caribbean. It is a country of high mountain ranges separated by deep valleys and plains. The climate is tropical but semi-arid conditions can occur in the lee of the central mountains. Hurricanes and severe thunderstorms are a common occurrence. Only a third of the country is arable, yet agriculture is the chief occupation. Many farmers grow only enough to feed their own families and the export crops, coffee, sugar and sisal are grown on large estates. Severe soil erosion caused by extensive forest clearance has resulted in a decline in crop yields. Haiti is the poorest country in the Americas.

Hakodate a port at the southern tip of Hokkaido Island, Japan. (Pop. 319,200)

Halicarnassus *see* **Bodrum**.

Halifax (1) the capital of Nova Scotia, Canada. (Pop. city 114,595/metropolitan area 278,000) (2) a town in West Yorkshire, England. (Pop. 88,000)

Halle an industrial town and inland port served by the Saale River in central Germany. (Pop. 236,500)

Halmahera *see* **Maluku.**

Hamah an industrial city in eastern Syria. (Pop. 514,750)

Hamamatsu a city in southern Honshu Island, Japan. (Pop. 514,100)

Hamburg the main port of Germany, situated on the River Elbe. (Pop. 1,617,800)

Hamelin (Hameln) a town in northern Germany. Famous for its legendary Pied Piper. (Pop. 56,300)

Hamersley Range part of the Pilbara Range in Western Australia. The highest peak is Mount Bruce (1235 m/4052 ft)

Hamhung (Hamheung) A port and industrial city on the east coast of North Korea. (Pop. 420,000)

Hamilton (1) the capital of Bermuda. (Pop. 3000) (2) a port and industrial city at the western end of Lake Ontario, Canada. (Pop. city 306,430/metropolitan area 542,090). (3) a town in the northwestern part of North Island, New Zealand. (Pop. 97,900). (4) a town in the Strathclyde region of Scotland, 17 km (10 miles) southeast of Glasgow. (Pop. 51,700)

Hammerfest a town in the very north of Norway, and one of the world's most northerly settlements. (Pop. 7400)

Hampshire a county of central southern England; the county town is Winchester. (3773 sq km/1456 sq miles; pop. 1,500,000)

Hangzhou (Hangchow) a port and industrial city on the east coast of central China, at the head of an estuary called Hangzhou Wan. Hangzhou is at the southern end of the Grand Canal, which links it to Beijing 1100 km (690 miles) to the north. (Pop. 1,105,000)

Hankow *see* **Wuhan.**

Hannover *see* **Hanover.**

Hanoi the capital of Vietnam, in the north of the country. (Pop. 2,570,900)

Hanover (Hannover) a historic city in central northern Germany. (Pop. 514,000)

Haora (Howrah) an industrial city in West Bengal, India, on the Hugli River, facing Calcutta. (Pop. 744,400)

Harare the capital of Zimbabwe; it was formerly called Salisbury (until 1982). (Pop. 656,000)

Harbin the largest city of northern China, situated in central Dongbei (Manchuria), and capital of Heilongjiang province. (Pop. 2,100,000)

Harrisburg the state capital of Pennsylvania, USA. (Pop. city 52,100/metropolitan area 570,200)

Hartford the state capital of Connecticut, USA. (Pop. city 136,400/metropolitan area 1,030,400)

Haryana a state in northwest India, formed in 1966. (44,212 sq km/17,066 sq miles; pop. 12,922,600)

Harz Mountains a range of mountains, noted for their forests, in central Germany. The highest peak is Brocken (1142 m/3747 ft).

Hastings a historic port and resort on the south coast of England, in the county of East Sussex. (Pop. 77,000)

Hatteras, Cape the tip of a chain of islands lining the coast of North Carolina, USA, notorious for its violent weather.

Havana (La Habana) the capital of Cuba, a port on the northwest coast of the island. It is also the name of the surrounding province. (Pop. 1,925,000)

Hawaii a group of 122 islands just to the south of the Tropic of Cancer, some 3700 km (2300 miles) from the coast of California. Since 1959 they have formed a state of the USA. The main islands are Oahu, Maui and Hawaii Island, which at 10,488 sq km (4049 sq miles) is by far the largest. Honolulu, the state capital, is on Oahu. (16,705 sq km/6450 sq miles; pop. 1,054,000)

Hebei a province in northern China which surrounds (but does not include) Beijing. The capital is Shijiazhuang. (180,000 sq km/70,000 sq miles; pop. 51,046,400)

Hebrides some 500 islands lying off the west coast of Scotland, consisting of the Inner Hebrides to the southeast, whose main islands are Tiree, Jura, Coll, Mull, Eigg and Skye, and the Outer Hebrides to the northwest whose islands include Lewis and Harris, the Uists, Benbecula and Barra.

Hefei an industrial city in central eastern China, capital of Anhui province. (Pop. 1,484,000)

Heidelberg a university town in southwest. (Pop. 130,000)

Heilongjiang a province of Dongbei (Manchuria) in northern China; the capital is Harbin. (464,000 sq km/179,000 sq miles; pop. 32,700,000)

Heilong Jiang, River *see* **Amur, River.**

Hejaz (Hijaz) a mountainous region which lines the Red Sea, formerly an independent kingdom but since 1932 a part of Saudi Arabia.

Helena the state capital of Montana, USA. (Pop. 24,600)

Heligoland (Helgoland) A small island and former naval base in the North Sea off the coast of Germany. (2.1 sq km/0.5 sq miles; pop. 2000)

Hellespont *see* **Dardanelles.**

Helsingfors *see* **Helsinki.**

Helsingør *see* **Elsinore.**

Helsinki (Helsingfors) the capital and chief industrial centre and port of Finland. (Pop. 482,900)

Henan a province of central China; the capital is Zhengzhou. (160,000 sq km/62,000 sq miles; pop. 71,890,000)

Heraklion (Iraklion) the capital and main port of Crete. (Pop. 111,000)

Herat a city in western Afghanistan on the Hari Rud River. (Pop. 150,500)

Hercegovina *see* **Bosnia Herzegovina.**

Hereford and Worcester a county in the west of England, on the border with Wales, which was created in 1974 when the old counties of Herefordshire and Worcestershire were combined. The county town is Worcester. (3927 sq km/1516 sq miles; pop. 648,000)

Herefordshire *see* **Hereford and Worcester.**

Hermon, Mount a mountain in southern Lebanon near the borders with Syria and Israel. It is the source of the River Jordan. (2814 m/9332 ft)

Hertfordshire a county in southeast England, to the north of London. The county town is Hertford. (1634 sq km/631 sq miles; pop. 980,000)

Herzegovina *see* **Bosnia Herzegovina.**

Hessen a state in central western Germany. The capital is Wiesbaden. (21,112 sq km/8151 sq miles; pop. 5,500,000)

Highland Region an administrative region in northern Scotland comprising the most northerly part of the mainland and many of the Inner Hebrides. It is the largest county in the UK. It was created in 1975 out of the old counties of Caithness, Nairnshire, Sutherland, most of Inverness-shire, Ross and Cromarty and parts of Argyll and Morayshire. The capital is Inverness. (26,136 sq km/10,091 sq miles; pop. 196,000)

Highlands the rugged region of northern Scotland, which includes the Grampian mountains and the North West Highlands.

Himachal Pradesh a state in northern India, in mountainous country bordering Tibet. (55,673 sq km/21,490 sq miles; pop. 4,280,000)

Himalayas the massive mountain range stretching some 2400 km (1500 miles) in a broad sweep from the northern tip of India, across Nepal, Bhutan and southern Tibet to Assam in northeastern India. The average height of the mountains is some 6100 m (20,000 ft), rising to the world's tallest peak, Mount Everest (8848 m/29,028 ft).

Himeji an industrial port in southern Honshu, Japan. (Pop. 452,900)

Hims *see* **Homs.**

Hindu Kush a range of mountains which stretches some 600 km (370 miles) at the western end of the Himalayas, straddling the web of borders where Afghanistan, Tajikistan, China, India and Pakistan meet. The highest peak is Tirich Mir (7690 m/25,229 ft) in Pakistan.

Hiroshima an industrial city in southwestern Honshu Island, Japan. Three quarters of the city was destroyed on August 6, 1945 when the world's first atomic bomb was dropped here, killing 78,000 people. (Pop. 899,400)

Hispaniola the name of the large Caribbean island that is shared by Haiti and the Dominican Republic. (76,200 sq km/29,400 sq miles)

Hitachi an industrial city on east Honshu Island, Japan. (Pop. 206,100)

Hobart a port and capital of Tasmania, Australia. (Pop. 173,700)

Ho Chi Minh City (Saigon) the largest city in Vietnam, and the capital of former independent South Vietnam. (Pop. 3,500,000)

Hoggar (Ahaggar) a remote mountain range of southern Algeria noted for its rock formations. The highest peak is Tahat (2918 m/9573 ft).

Hohe Tauern a part of eastern Alps in southern Austria, rising to the highest point at Grossglockner (3797 m/12,460 ft), Austria's highest peak.

Hohhot an industrial city and the capital of the Nei Mongol Autonomous Region

(Inner Mongolia), China. (Pop. 1,130,000)

Hokkaido the most northerly of the main islands of Japan, and the second largest after Honshu. The capital is Sapporo. (78,509 sq km/30,312 sq miles; pop. 5,679,400)

Holland a name generally applied to the Netherlands, but in fact the term really applies to the central coastal region which comprise the two provinces of Noord Holland and Zuid Holland.

Hollywood a suburb in the northern part of Los Angeles in California, USA. It has long served as the base for the USA.'s powerful film industry.

Homs (Hims) an industrial city of ancient origins in Syria. (Pop. 414,401)

Honduras (*Area* 112,088 sq km (43,277 sq miles); *population* 4,440,000; *capital* Tegucigalpa; form of government *republic*; *religion* RC; *currency* Lempira). Honduras is a fan-shaped country in Central America which spreads out toward the Caribbean Sea. Four fifths of the country is covered in mountains, which are indented with river valleys running toward the very short Pacific coast. There is little change in temperatures throughout the year and rainfall is heavy. The country is sparsely populated and although agricultural, only about 25% of the land is cultivated.Bananas, grains, coffee and sugar are now important crops and these are grown mainly on the coastal plains.

Hong Kong (*Area* 1045 sq km (403 sq miles); *population* 5,760,000; *form of government* Colony under British administration until 1997 when China will take over.; *religion* Buddhism, Taoism, Christianity; *currency* Hong Kong dollar). Hong Kong is located in the South China Sea and consists of Hong Kong Island, the peninsula of Kowloon and about 1000 sq km (386 sq miles) of adjacent land known as the New Territories, situated at the mouth of the Pearl River about 130 km (81 miles) southeast of Guangzhou (Canton). The climate is warm subtropical with cool dry winters and hot humid summers. Hong Kong has no natural resources. Its main assets are its magnificent natural harbour and its position close to the main trading routes of the Pacific. Hong Kong's main industry is textiles and clothing which accounts for 38% of its domestic exports.

Honiara the capital of the Solomon Islands, situated on Guadalcanal. (Pop. 23,500)

Honolulu the state capital of Hawaii, USA, on the south coast of the island of Oahu. (Pop. city 373,000/ metropolitan area 805,300)

Honshu the central and largest of the islands of Japan. (230,988 sq km/89,185 sq miles; pop. 96,685,000)

Hooghly, River *see* **Hugli, River.**

Hormuz (Ormuz), Strait of the narrow strait at the mouth of The Gulf between the Musandam peninsula of Oman to the south, and Iran to the north.

Horn, Cape (Cabo de Hornos) The southern tip of South America, represented by a spattering of remote islands belonging to Chile off Tierra del Fuego.

Houston the largest city in Texas, USA. (Pop. city 1,705,700/metropolitan area 3,164,400)

Howrah *see* **Haora**.

Hrvatska *see* **Croatia.**

Huang He (Hwang Ho; Yellow River) the second longest river in China, flowing from the Qinghai mountains across northern central China to the Yellow Sea, south of Beijing. (Length 5464 km/3395 miles)

Huascaran a peak in the Andes in central Peru, and that country's highest mountain. (6768 m/22,205 ft)

Hubei a landlocked province of central China. (180,000 sq km/69,500 sq miles; pop. 46,320,000)

Hudson Bay a huge bay in northeastern Canada, hemmed in to the north by Baffin Island, and connected to the Atlantic Ocean by the Hudson Strait.

Hudson River a river flowing from its source in the Adirondack Mountains in New York State, USA, to the Atlantic Ocean at New York City. The Erie Canal joins the Hudson River to link New York to the Great Lakes. (Length 492 km/ 306 miles)

Hué the capital of the rulers of Vietnam from 200BC to the 19th century, located in the central coastal region of the country. (Pop. 190,100)

Hugli (Hoogly) a major branch of the River Ganges which forms at its delta and flows through Calcutta and the surrounding industrial conurbations into the Bay of Bengal. (Length 193 km/120 miles)

Hull *see* **Kingston upon Hull.**

Humber the estuary of the Rivers Ouse and Trent which cuts deep into the east coast of England to the north of the Wash. (Length 60 km/35 miles)

Humberside a county on the northeast coast of England, centreing upon the Humber estuary. It was created in 1974 out of parts of the East and West Ridings of Yorkshire and Lincolnshire. The county town is Beverley. (3512 sq km/1356 sq miles; pop. 854,000)

Hunan an inland province of southeast China. The capital is Changsha. (210,000 sq km/81,000 sq miles; pop. 52,320,000)

Hungary (*Area* 93,032 sq km (35,920 sq miles); *population* 10,590,000; *capital* Budapest; *other major cities* Debrecen, Miskolc, Pécs, Szeged; *form of government* Republic; *religion* RC, Calvinism, Lutheranism; *currency* Forint). Landlocked in the heartland of Europe, Hungary is dominated by the great plain to the east of the river Danube, which runs northsouth across the country. In the west lies the largest lake in Central Europe, Lake Balaton. Winters are severe, but the summers are warm. Hungary experienced a modest boom in its economy in the 1970s and 1980s. Yields of cereals for breadmaking and rice have since soared and large areas between the Danube and Tisza rivers are now used to grow vegetables. Industries have been carefully expanded where adequate natural resources exist and tourism is fast developing.

Hunter Valley the valley of the Hunter River, lying 100 km (60 miles) northwest of Sydney, Australia. It is particularly noted for its wine.

Huntingdonshire *see* **Cambridgeshire.**

Huron, Lake one of the Great Lakes, lying at the centre of the group on the border between Canada and the state of Michigan in the USA. (59,570 sq km/23,000 sq miles)

Hwang Ho *see* **Huang He.**

Hyderabad (1) the capital of the state of Andhra Pradesh in eastern south India. (Pop. 2,093,500). (2) a city on the Indus delta 160 km (100 miles) northeast of Karachi, Pakistan. (Pop. 795,000)

Hydra (Idhra) a small island in the Aegean Sea, off the east coast of the Peloponnese, Greece, noted as a haven where motor traffic is prohibited.

Iasi a historic city in northeastern Romania. (Pop. 271,400)

Ibadan the second largest city in Nigeria, some 120 km (75 miles) north of Lagos. It is a busy market and university town. (Pop. 1,009,000)

Ibiza (Iviza) *see* **Balearic Islands.**

Iboland a densely populated region of southeastern Nigeria inhabited by the Ibo people. The attempt by the region to break away from Nigeria (1967-70) under the name of Biafra caused a civil war that led to a famine which killed over a million people. (Pop. 10,000,000)

Ica, River *see* **Putumayo, River.**

Içel *see* **Mersin.**

Iceland (*Area* 103,000 sq km (39,768 sq miles); *population* 253,500; capital Reykjavík; *form of government* Republic; *religion* Lutheranism; *currency* Icelandic krónais). Iceland is a large island situated in the North Atlantic Ocean, just south of the Arctic Circle. The island has over 100 volcanoes, at least one of which erupts every five years. One ninth of the country is covered with ice and snowfields and there are about seven hundred hot springs which are an important source of central heating. The climate is cool temperate. Only 1% of the land is cultivated. The island's economy is based on its sea fishing industry which accounts for 70% of exports.

Idaho a inland state in the northwest of the USA. The state capital is Boise. (216,413 sq km/83,557 sq miles; pop. 1,005,000)

Idhra *see* **Hydra**.

Idlib a large commercial centre in northwestern Syria. (Pop. 428,000)

Ieper *see* **Ypres.**

IJsselmeer formerly a large inlet of the North Sea known as the Zuiderzee on the northeastern coast of the Netherlands, but after the creation of the dam called the Afsluitdijk across its mouth, it has filled with water from the River IJssel and is now a freshwater lake, bordered by fertile areas of reclaimed land (polders).

Ile de France a region and former province of France with Paris at its centre, now consisting of eight separate departments. (12,012 sq km/4638 sq miles; pop. 10,073,000)

Illinois a state in the Midwest of the USA, bordering Lake Michigan to the north. The capital is Springfield, but Chicago is its main city. (146,075 sq km/56,400 sq miles; pop. 11,535,000)

Inagua *see* **Bahamas.**

Inch'on (Incheon) a port and industrial city on the western (Yellow Sea) coast of South Korea, 39 km (24 miles) west of Seoul. (Pop. 1,083,900)

India (*Area* 3,287,590 sq km (1,269,338 sq miles); population 843,930,000; *capital* New Delhi; *other major cities* Bangalore, Bombay, Calcutta, Delhi, Hyderabad, Madras; *form of government* Federal Republic; *religion* Hinduism, Sunni Islam, Christianity; *currency* Rupee). India is a vast country in South Asia, which is dominated in the extreme north by the world's youngest and highest mountains, the Himalayas. At their foot, a huge plain, drained by the Indus and Ganges rivers, is one of the most fertile areas in the world and the most densely populated part of India. Further south, the ancient Deccan plateau extends to the southern tip of the country. India generally has four seasons, the cool, the hot, the rainy and the dry. Rainfall varies from 100 mm (3.94 inches) in the northwest desert to 10,000 mm (394 inches) in Assam. About 70% of the population depend on agriculture for their living. Much rice, sugar cane and wheat are grown.

Indiana a state in the Midwest of the USA to the southeast of Lake Michigan. The state capital is Indianapolis. (93,994 sq km/36,291 sq miles; pop. 5,499,000)

Indianapolis the state capital of Indiana. (Pop. city 710,300/metropolitan area 1,194,600)

Indian Desert *see* **Thar Desert.**

Indian Ocean the third largest ocean, bounded by Asia to the north, Africa to the west and Australia to the east. The southern waters merge with the Antarctic Ocean. (73,481,000 sq km/28,364,000 sq miles)

Indonesia (*Area* 1,904,569 sq km (735,354 sq miles); *population* 179,100,000; Capital Jakarta; *other major cities* Badung, Medan, Semarang, Surabaya; *form of government* Republic; *religion* Sunni Islam, Christianity, Hinduism; *currency* Rupiah). Indonesia is made up of 13,667 islands which are scattered across the Indian and Pacific Oceans in a huge crescent. Its largest landmass is the province of Kalimantan which is part of the island of Borneo. Sumatra is the largest individual island. Java, however, is the dominant and most densely populated island. The climate is generally tropical monsoon. The country has one hundred volcanoes, and earthquakes are frequent. Rice, maize and cassava are the main crops grown. Indonesia has the largest reserves of tin in the world and is one of the world's leading rubber producers.

Indore a textile-manufacturing city, and once the capital of the princely state of Indore, in western Madhya Pradesh, central India. (Pop. 829,300)

Indus, River one of the great rivers of Asia, whose valleys supported some of the world's earliest civilizations, notably at Mohenjo Daro. It flows from its source in Tibet and across the northern tip of India before turning south to run through the entire length of Pakistan to its estuary on the Arabian Sea, south of Karachi. (Length 3059 km/1900 miles)

Inner Mongolia *see* **Nei Mongol Autonomous Region.**

Inverness a town in northeastern Scotland at the head of the Moray Firth and at the eastern end of Loch Ness. (Pop. 40,000)

Iona a small island off the southwestern tip of Mull, Scotland where the Irish monk St Columba founded a monastery in AD563. (8 sq km/3 sq miles)

Ionian Islands (Eptanisos) the seven largest of the islands which lie scattered along the west coast of Greece in the Ionian Sea. They are Corfu, Paxoí, Cephalonia, Levkás, Ithaca, Zákinthos and Kíthira. (Pop. 182,700)

Ionian Sea that part of the Mediterranean Sea between southern Italy and Greece. It is named after Io, a mistress of the Ancient Greek god Zeus.

Ios (Nios) *see* **Cyclades.**

Iowa a state in the Midwest of the USA bounded on the east and west by the upper reaches of the Mississippi and Missouri rivers. The capital is Des Moines. (145,791 sq km/56,290 sq miles; pop. 2,884,000)

Iran (*Area* 1,648,000 sq km (636,293,sq miles); *population* 53,920,000; *capital* Tehran; *other major cities* Esfahan, Mashhad, Tabriz; *form of government* Islamic Republic; *religion* Shia Islam; *currency* Rial). Iran lies across The Gulf from the Arabian peninsula and stretches from the Caspian Sea to the Arabian Sea. It is a land dominated by mountains in the north and west, with a huge expanse of desert in its centre. The climate is mainly hot and dry, although more temperate conditions are found on the shores of the Caspian Sea. Most of the population live in the north and west, where Tehran is situated. The only good agricultural land is on the Caspian coastal plains, and here rice is grown. Most of Iran's oil is in the southwest of The Gulf. The main exports are petrochemicals, carpets and rugs, textiles, raw cotton and leather goods.

Iraq (*Area* 438,317 sq km (169,234 sq miles); *population* 17,060,000; *capital* Baghdad; *other major cities* Al-Basrah, Al Mawsil; *form of government* Republic; *religion* ; *currency* : Iraqi dinar). Iraq is located in southwest Asia, wedged between The Gulf and Syria. It is almost landlocked except for its outlet to The Gulf at Shatt al Arab. Its two great rivers, the Tigris and the Euphrates, flow from the northwest into The Gulf at this point. The climate is arid with very hot summers and cold winters. The high mountains on the border with Turkey are snow covered for six months of the year, and desert in the southwest covers nearly half the country. The only fertile land in Iraq is in the basins of the Tigris and Euphrates where wheat, barley, rice, tobacco and cotton are grown.

Ireland an island off the west coast of Great Britain, almost four fifths of which is the independent Republic of Ireland, while the remainder is Northern Ireland, which is a province of the UK. (80,400 sq km/32,588 sq miles, pop. 5,202,000)

Ireland, Republic (*Area* 70,284 sq km (27,137 sq miles); *population* 3,540,000; *capital* Dublin (Baile Atha Cliath); *other major cities* Cork, Galway, Limerick, Waterford; *form of government*: Republicp; *religion* RC; *currency* Punt = 100 pighne). The Republic of Ireland is one of Europe's most westerly countries, situated in the Atlantic Ocean and separated from Great Britain by the Irish Sea. It has an equable mild climate. The Republic extends over four-fifths of the island of Ireland, and the west and southwest are mountainous. The central plain is largely limestone covered in boulder clay which provides good farmland and pasture. Despite the fertile land, the Republic of Ireland remains one of the poorest countries in western Europe. The rural population tend to migrate to the cities, mainly Dublin, which is the main industrial centre.

Irian Jaya the western half of the island of New Guinea, which has been part of Indonesia since 1963. (410,660 sq km/158,556 sq miles; pop. 2,584,000)

Irish Sea the arm of the Atlantic that separates Ireland and Great Britain.

Irkutsk an industrial city on the Trans-Siberian Railway lying near the southern end of Lake Baikal in the Russian Federation. (Pop. 590,000)

Irrawaddy, River the central focus of Burma (Myanmar), flowing from its two primary sources in the north of the country to Mandalay and then south to its delta in the Bay of Bengal. (Length 2000 km/1250 miles)

Irtysh, River a largely navigable river flowing northwards from its source near the border between northwest China and Mongolia across the centre of Kazakhstan and through Omsk to join the River Ob' on its journey to the Arctic Ocean. (Length 4440 km/2760 miles)

Isfahan *see* **Esfahan.**

Iskenderun a port of ancient origin in southern Turkey, in the northeastern corner of the Mediterranean Sea. (Pop. 173,600)

Islamabad the capital of Pakistan since 1967, in the north of the country. (Pop. 201,000)

Israel (*Area* 20,770 sq km (8019 sq miles); *population* 4,820,000; *capital* Jerusalem; *other major cities* Tel Aviv-Jaffa, Haifa; *form of government* Republic; *religion* Judaism, Sunni Islam, Christianity; *currency* Shekel). Isreal occupies a long narrow stretch of land in the southeast of the Mediterranean. Its eastern boundary is formed by the River Jordan into the Dead Sea. The south of the country is made up of a triangular wedge of the Negev Desert which ends at the Gulf of Aqaba. The climate in summer is hot and dry, in winter it is mild with some rain. Most of the population live on the coastal plain bordering the Mediterranean where Tel Aviv-Jaffa is the main commercial city. The country is virtually self-sufficient in foodstuffs and a major exporter of its produce. Main exports include finished diamonds, textiles, fruit, vegetables, chemicals, machinery and fertilizers.

Issyk-Kul' a lake in southern central Kazakhstan, set in the high mountains that line the border with China. (6280 sq km/2424 sq miles)

Istanbul the largest city in Turkey, built mainly on the western bank of the Bosphorous, with a commanding view of shipping entering the Black Sea. It was founded by the Greeks in 660BC and was known as Byzantium; between AD330 and 1930 it was called Constantinople. (Pop. 5,858,600)

Italy (*Area* 301,268 sq km (116,320 sq miles); *population* 57,600,000; *capital* Rome (Roma); *other major cities* Milan, Naples, Turin, Genoa, Palermo; *form of government* Republic; *religion* RC; *currency* Lira). Italy is a republic in southern Europe, which comprises a large peninsula and the two main islands of Sicily and Sardinia. The Alps form a natural boundary to the north. The

Apennine Mountains form the backbone of peninsular Italy. Between the Alps and the Apennines lies the Po valley, a great fertile lowland. Sicily and Sardinia are largely mountainous. Italy has four active volcanoes, including Etna and Vesuvius. It enjoys warm dry summers and mild winters. The north is the main industrial centre and agriculture is well mechanized. In the south farms are small and traditional. Industries include motor vehicles, textiles, clothing, leather goods, glass and ceramics.

Ivanovo a textile manufacturing city in the Russian Federation, 240 km (150 miles) northeast of Moscow. (Pop. 476,000)

Iviza *see* **Balearic Islands.**

Ivory Coast *see* **Côte d'Ivoire.**

Iwo Jima the largest in the group of islands called the Volcano Islands belonging to Japan, which lie some 1200 km (745 miles) south of Tokyo in the Pacific Ocean. (21 sq km/8 sq miles)

Ixtacihuatl a volcanic peak south of Mexico City, which is twinned with neighbouring Popocatépetl. (5286 m/17,342 ft)

Izmir (Smyrna) a port of ancient Greek origin on the Aegean coast of Turkey, to the south of Istanbul. (Pop. 1,489,800)

Izmit (Kocaeli) a port and naval base on the Sea of Marmara, 90 km (55 miles) southeast of Istanbul. (Pop. 236,100)

Jackson the state capital of Mississippi. (Pop. city 208,800/metropolitan area 382,400)

Jacksonville a port on the northeast coast of Florida, USA. (Pop. city 578,000/ metropolitan area 795,300)

Jaffna a port on the tip of the northern peninsula of Sri Lanka, and the main centre for the Tamil population of the island. (Pop. 118,200)

Jaipur the capital of the state of Rajasthan, India. (Pop. 1,015,200)

Jakarta the capital of INDONESIA, a port on the northwestern tip of Java. (Pop. 6,503,000)

Jamaica (*Area* 10,990 sq km (4243 sq miles); *population* 2,400,000; *capital* Kingston; *other major cities* Montego Bay, Spanish Town; *form of government* Constitutional Monarchy; *religion* Anglicanism, RC, other Protestantism; *currency* Jamaican dollar). Jamaica is an island state in the Caribbean Sea about 150 km (93 miles) south of Cuba. The centre of the island comprises a limestone plateau, and this is surrounded by narrow coastal flatlands and palm-fringed beaches. The climate is tropical with frequent hurricanes. The traditional crops grown are sugar cane, bananas, peppers, ginger, cocoa and coffee. The decline in the principal export products, bauxite and alumina, has resulted in near economic stagnation. Tourism is an important industry.

James Bay the southern arm of the Hudson Bay, Canada, which extends 440 km (273 miles) into Ontario and Quebec.

Jammu and Kashmir the state in the very north of India, bordering China and Pakistan. The total size of the state is 222,236 sq km (85,783 sq miles), but its borders are disputed, and following wars with Pakistan (1947–49, 1967 and 1971) and annexation by China in the 1950s, India occupies only about a half of what it claims. (Pop. 5,987,400)

Jamshedpur an industrial city in northeast India. (Pop. 669,600)

Jamuna, River the name given to the river formed by the Brahmaputra and the Tista as it flows through Bangladesh to join the Ganges.

Japan (*Area* 377,801 sq km (145,869 sq miles); *population* 123,260,000p; capital Tokyo; *other major cities* Osaka, Nagoya, Sapporo, Kobe, Kyoto, Yokohama; *form of government* Constitutional Monarchy; *religion* Shintoism, Buddhism, Christianity; *currency* Yen). Japan is located on the eastern margin of Asia and consists of four major islands, Honshu, Hokkaido, Kyushu and Shikoku, and many small islands. The country is made up of six chains of steep serrated mountains, which contain about 60 active volcanoes. Earthquakes are frequent and widespread. Summers are warm and humid, and winters mainly mild. Japan's agriculture is highly advanced. Fishing is important. Japan is the second largest industrial economy in the world. It is very dependent on imported raw materials.

Japan, Sea of a part of the Pacific Ocean between Japan and Korea.

Java (Jawa) the central island in the southern chain of islands of Indonesia. The capital is Jakarta. (130,987 sq km/50,574 sq miles; pop. 91,269,600)

Java Sea an arm of the Pacific Ocean that separates Java and Borneo.

Jedda *see* **Jiddah.**

Jefferson City the state capital of Missouri, USA. (Pop. 35,000)

Jena a university town in southern central Germany. (Pop. 107,700)

Jerez de la Frontera (Jerez) a town in southwest Spain, just inland from Cadiz, famous for the sweet wine to which it has given its name, sherry. (Pop. 176,200)

Jericho a town in the West Bank area occupied by Israel since 1967, on the site of a city that dates back to about 7000bc. (Pop. 15,000)

Jersey the largest of the British Channel Islands. The capital is St Helier. (117 sq km/45 sq miles; pop. 77,000)

Jerusalem the capital of ISRAEL, and a historic city considered holy by Muslims, Christians and Jews. (Pop. 446,500)

Jiangsu a heavily populated but highly productive province on the central east coast of China. The capital is Nanjing. (100,000 sq km/38,600 sq miles; pop. 60,521,000)

Jiangxi an inland province of southeastern China. Its capital is Nanchang. (164,800 sq km/64,300 sq miles; pop. 32,290,000)

Jiddah (Jedda) a port on the Red Sea coast of Saudi Arabia, and one of the country's main centres of population. (Pop. 750,000)

Jilin (Kirin) a province of central Dongbei (Manchuria) in northern China. The capital is Changchun. (180,000 sq km/69,500 sq miles; pop. 22,502,000)

Jinan the capital of Shandong province, situated close to the Huang He River, 360 km (225 miles) to the south of Beijing. (Pop. 3,200,000)

Jodhpur a city in central Rajasthan, India, on the perimeter of the Thar Desert. The city has given its name to the riding breeches that first became popular here. (Pop. 506,300)

Jogjakarta *see* **Yogyakarta.**

Johannesburg the centre of the Rand goldmining area of South Africa and now that country's largest town. (Pop. 1,536,500)

John o'Groats the village traditionally held to be on the most northerly point of mainland Scotland and Great Britain.

Johor Bahru (Johore) a port and growing city in Malaysia situated on the southern tip of the Malay Peninsula opposite Singapore, to which it is connected by a causeway. It is also the capital of the state of Johor. (Pop. city 246,400)

Jordan (*Area* 97,740 sq km (37,737 sq miles); *population* 3,170,000; *capital* Amman; *other major cities* Irbid, Zarga; *form of government* Constitutional Monarchy; *religion* Sunni Islam; *currency* Jordan dinar). Jordan is almost landlocked except for a short coastline on the Gulf of Aqaba. It is bounded by Saudi Arabia, Syria, Iraq and Israel. Almost 80% of the country is desert and the rest comprises the East Bank Uplands and Jordan Valley. In general summers are hot and dry, and winters cool and wet, with variations related to altitude. The east has a desert climate. Only one fifth of the country is fertile, but it is self-sufficient in potatoes, onions and poultry meat. Amman is the capital and main industrial centre.

Jordan, River a river flowing southwards from Mount Hermon in southern Lebanon, through northern Israel to Lake Tiberias (Sea of Galilee) and then on through Jordan into the Dead Sea, where it evaporates. The West Bank to the north of the Dead Sea is disputed territory which has been occupied by Israel since the Six Day War in 1967. (Length 256 km/159 miles)

Juan de Fuca Strait the channel to the south of Vancouver Island on the border between Canada and the USA, through which ships from Victoria, Vancouver and Seattle can pass to reach the Pacific Ocean.

Juan Fernández Islands a group of three remote islands in the Pacific Ocean belonging to Chile and some 650 km (400 miles) due west of Santiago. (181 sq km/62 sq miles; pop. 550)

Judaea the southern part of ancient Palestine, occupying the area of modern Israel between the Mediterranean coast to the west and the Dead Sea and River Jordan to the east.

Jumna, River *see* **Yamuna, River.**

Juneau The state capital of Alaska. (Pop. 23,800)

Jura a large upland band of limestone in eastern central France which lines the border with Switzerland, giving its name to a department in France and a canton in Switzerland. A further extension continues across southern Germany as far as Nuremberg (the Swabian and Franconian Jura).

Jutland (Jylland) a large peninsula stretching some 400 km (250 miles) northwards from Germany to separate the North Sea from the Baltic Sea. Most of it is occupied by the mainland part of Denmark, while the southern part belongs to the German state of Schleswig-Holstein.

K2 (Godwin Austen) the second highest mountain in the world after Mount Everest, situated in the Karakoram mountain range on the disputed border between Pakistan and China. (8611 m/28,250 ft)

Kabul the capital and main city of AFGHANISTAN, in the northeast of the country on the Kabul River. (Pop. 1,036,400)

Kachchh *see* **Kutch.**

Kagoshima a port on the south coast of Kyushu Island, Japan. (Pop. 530,500)

Kaifeng a city of ancient origins in Henan province, China. (Pop. 500,000)

Kairouan a city in northern Tunisia, to Muslims the most holy city of the Maghreb. (Pop. 72,300)

Kalahari a region of semi-desert occupying much of southern Botswana and straddling the border with South Africa and Namibia.

Kalgoorlie a town in southern Western Australia which has grown up around its gold and nickel reserves. (Pop. 19,800)

Kalimantan the greater part of Borneo, which is governed by Indonesia. (538,718 sq km/208,000 sq miles; pop. 6,724,000)

Kalimnos (Calino) *see* **Dodecanese.**

Kalinin *see* **Tver.**

Kaliningrad (Königsberg) a port and industrial city on the Baltic coast belonging to the Russian Federation, in an enclave between Lithuania and Poland. Founded in the 13th century, it was called Königsberg and was the capital of the former East Prussia. (Pop. 380,000)

Kalmyk (Kalmuck) Republic an autonomous republic of the Russian Federation, lying to the northwest of the Caspian Sea. (75,900 sq km/29,300 sq miles; pop. 315,000)

Kamchatka a peninsula, some 1200 km (750 miles) long, which drops south from eastern Siberia into the north Pacific Ocean. (Pop. 422,000)

Kampala the capital and main city of Uganda, situated on Lake Victoria. (Pop. 500,000)

Kampuchea *see* **Cambodia.**

Kananga a city in central southern Zaïre, founded in 1894 as Luluabourg. (Pop. 704,000)

Kanazawa a historic port on the central northern coast of Honshu Island, Japan. (Pop. 430,500)

Kandahar the second largest city in Afghanistan, situated in the southeastern part of the country, near the border with Pakistan. (Pop. 191,400)

Kandy a town in the central mountains of Sri Lanka, which was once the capital of the Sinhalese kings and is sacred to Buddhists. (Pop. 101,300)

Kangchenjunga the world's third highest mountain (after Mount Everest and K2), situated in the eastern Himalayas, on the borders between Nepal, China and the Indian state of Sikkim. (8585 m/28,165 ft)

Ka-Ngwane a small state, formerly a Bantu homeland, in east Transvaal, South Africa. (3910 sq km/1510 sq miles; pop. 458,000)

Kano a historic trading city of the Hausa people of northern Nigeria, the third largest city in Nigeria after Lagos and Ibadan. (Pop. city 475,000)

Kanpur (Cawnpore) an industrial city in northern central India. (Pop. 1,639,100)

Kansas a state in the Great Plains of the USA. The state capital is Topeka. (213,064 sq km/82,264 sq miles; pop. 2,450,000)

Kansas City an industrial city on the Missouri River which straddles the border between the states of Missouri and Kansas. (Pop. city 603,600/metropolitan area 1,476,700)

Kao-hsiung the second largest city in Taiwan and a major port, situated in the southwest of the island. (Pop. 1,269,000)

Karachi a port and industrial centre, and the largest city in Pakistan. (Pop. 5,103,000)

Karaganda an industrial city in the mining region of Kazakhstan. (Pop. 608,000)

Karakoram a range of mountains at the western end of the Himalayas on the borders between Pakistan, China and India.

Kara Kum (Karakumy) a sand desert in southern Turkmenistan, to the east of the Caspian Sea, and on the borders with Iran and Afghanistan.

Kara Sea a branch of the Arctic Ocean off the central northern coast of the Russian Federation.

Karbala a town in central Iraq, 90 km (55 miles) south of Baghdad. As the site of the tomb of Hussein bin Ali and his brother Abbas, grandsons of the prophet Mohammad, it is held sacred by the Shia Muslims. (Pop. 107,500)

Karelia a region which straddles the Finnish-Russian border.

Kariba Dam a hydroelectric dam on the River Zambezi on the border between Zambia and Zimbabwe.

Karl-Marx-Stadt *see* **Chemnitz.**

Karlovy Vary (Carlsbad; Karlsbad) a spa town in the Czech Republic. (Pop. 59,200)

Karlsruhe (Carlsruhe) an industrial city in the valley of the River Rhine, in southwestern Germany. (Pop. 275,000)

Karnataka a state in southwest India. The capital is Bangalore. (191,791 sq km/74,031 sq miles; pop. 37,135,700)

Kärnten *see* **Carinthia.**

Karoo (Karroo) two separate regions of semi-desert, the Great Karoo and the Little Karoo, lying between the mountain ranges of southern Cape Province, South Africa.

Kasai (Cassai), River a major river of Zaïre. (Length 2150 km/1350 miles)

Kashmir a mountainous region straddling the border between India and Pakistan and subject to dispute since the partition of India and Pakistan in 1947. About half of the former princely state of Jammu and Kashmir is now ruled by Pakistan and is known as Azad (Free) Kashmir.

Kassel (Cassel) an industrial city in central Germany. (Pop. 190,400)

Kasvin *see* **Qazvin.**

Kathmandu (Katmandu) the capital and principal city of Nepal. (Pop. 195,260)

Katowice (Kattowitz) an industrial city in central southern Poland. (Pop. 361,300)

Kattegat (Cattegat) the strait, 34 km (21 miles) at its narrowest, at the entrance to the Baltic Sea which separates Sweden from Jutland.

Kaunas (Kovno) an industrial city and former capital of Lithuania. (Pop. 400,000)

Kavango (Cubango), River a river, known formerly as the Okavango, which flows southeast from central Angola to form the border with Namibia before petering out in the swampy inland Okavango Delta in northern Botswana. (Length 1600 km/1000 miles)

Kaveri (Caveri, Cauvery), River a holy river of southern India, flowing southeast from the Deccan plateau to the coast on the Bay of Bengal. (Length 800 km/497 miles)

Kavkaz *see* **Caucasus.**

Kawasaki an industrial city on the east coast of Honshu Island, Japan, forming part of the Tokyo-Yokohama conurbation. (Pop. 1,088,600)

Kazakhstan (*Area* 2,717,000 sq km (1,050,000 sq miles); *population* 15,654,000; *capital* Alma Ata; *other major city* Karaganda; *form of government* Republic; *religion* Sunni Islam; *currency* Rouble). Kazakhstan, the second largest republic of the former USSR, extends from the Caspian Sea to Mongolia. The west of the country is low-lying, the east hilly, and the southeast mountainous. The climate is continental and very dry with great extremes of temperature. Much of the country is semi-desert. Crops can only be grown in the wetter northwest regions or where irrigated. Extensive pastoral farming is carried out. The country is rich in minerals. Kazakhstan declared itself independent in 1991.

Kazan' an industrial city and capital of the Tatar Republic in central Russian Federation. (Pop. 1,039,000)

Keeling Islands *see* **Cocos Islands.**

Kefallinia *see* **Ionian Islands.**

Kells a market town in County Meath, Ireland. It was the site of a monastery founded in the 6th century by St Columba, which was the source of the illuminated Book of Kells.

Kelsty *see* **Kielce.**

Kemerovo an industrial city in southern Siberia. (Pop. 505,000)

Kennedy, Cape *see* **Canaveral, Cape.**

Kent a county in the extreme southeast of England. The county town is Maidstone. (3732 sq km/1441 sq miles; pop. 1,494,000)

Kentucky a state in east central USA. The state capital is Frankfort. (104,623 sq km/40,395 sq miles; pop. 3,726,000)

Kenya (*Area* 580,367 sq km (224,080 sq miles); *population* 24,080,000; *capital* Nairobi; *other major cities* Mombasa, Kisumu; *form of government* Republic; *religions* RC, Protestantism, other Christianity, Animism; *currency* Kenya shilling). Located in east Africa, Kenya straddles the Equator and extends from Lake Victoria in the west, to the Indian Ocean in the east. Highlands run north to south through central Kenya and are divided by the steep-sided Great Rift Valley. The coastal lowlands have a hot humid climate, but in the highlands it is cooler and rainfall heavier. In the east it is very arid. The fertile southwestern region accounts for almost all its economic production. The main crops include wheat, maize, tea, coffee, sisal, sugar cane and cotton. Tourism is an important source of foreign revenue.

Kenya, Mount a towering extinct volcano in central Kenya, the second highest mountain in Africa after Mount Kilimanjaro. (5200 m/17,058 ft)

Kerala a state occupying the western coast of the southern tip of India. The capital is Trivandrum. (38,863 sq km/15,005 sq miles; pop. 25,453,000)

Kerguelen the largest in a remote group of some 300 islands in the southern Indian Ocean forming part of the French Southern and Antarctic Territories, now occupied only by scientists. (3414 sq km/1318 sq miles)

Kérkira *see* **Corfu.**

Kermanshah *see* **Bakhtaran.**

Kerry a county in the southwest of the Republic of Ireland, noted for the rugged beauty of its peninsulas and its green dairy pastures. The county town is Tralee. (4701 sq km/1815 sq miles; pop. 122,800)

Key West a port and resort at the southern end of Florida Keys, a chain of coral islands off the southern tip of Florida, USA. (Pop. 24,900)

Khabarovsk a major industrial city in southeastern Siberia, lying just 35 km(22 miles) north of the border with China. (Pop. 569,000)

Kharg Island a small island in the northern Gulf where Iran has constructed a major oil terminal.

Khar'kov a major industrial and commercial centre of the Ukraine. (Pop. 1,536,000)

Khartoum (El Khartum) the capital of Sudan, situated at the confluence of the Blue Nile and White Nile. (Pop. 561,000)

Khios *see* **Chios.**

Khone Falls a massive set of waterfalls on the River Mekong in southern Laos. With a maximum width of 10.8 km (6.7 miles), these are the widest falls in the world.

Khorasan the northeastern province of Iran, bordering Afghanistan and Turkmenistan. The capital is Mashhad. (Pop. 3,267,000)

Khulna a port and district in southwest Bangladesh. (Pop. town 646,400)

Khuzestan (Khuzistan) a province in southwestern Iran, and the country's main oil-producing area. The capital is Ahvaz. (Pop. 2,177,000)

Khyber Pass a strategic route (1072 m/3518 ft) over the Safed Koh mountains connecting Peshawar in Pakistan with Kabul in Afghanistan.

Kiel a port and shipbuilding city on the Baltic coast of northern Germany. It stands at the mouth of the Kiel Ship Canal which permits ocean-going ships to cross the Jutland peninsula from the Baltic to Hamburg and the North Sea. (Pop. 248,400)

Kielce (Kelsty) an industrial city in central southern Poland. (Pop. 197,000)

Kiev (Kiyev) the capital of UKRAINE, situated on the Dnieper. Founded in the 6th century, it is now a major industrial city. (Pop. 2,411,000)

Kigali the capital of RWANDA. (Pop. 170,000)

Kikládhes *see* **Cyclades.**

Kildare a county in the southeast of the Republic of Ireland, famous for its racehorses and the racecourse, The Curragh. The county town is Naas. (1694 sq km/654 sq miles; pop. 104,100)

Kilimanjaro, Mount Africa's highest mountain, in northeastern Tanzania. (5895 m/19,340 ft)

Kilkenny a county and county town in the southeast of the Republic of Ireland. (2062 sq km/769 sq miles; pop. county 70,800/city 10,100)

Killarney a market town in county Kerry, Republic of Ireland, which is at the centre of a much admired landscape of lakes and mountains. (Pop. 7700)

Kimberley a town in the north of Cape Province, South Africa, which is at the centre of South Africa's diamond mining industry. (Pop. 153,900)

Kimberleys, The a vast plateau of hills and gorges in the north of Western Australia. (420,000 sq km/162,000 sq miles)

Kincardineshire *see* **Grampian.**

Kingston the capital and main port of Jamaica. (Pop. 700,000)

Kingston upon Hull (Hull) a port in the county of Humberside in eastern England, situated on the north side of the Humber estuary. (Pop. 270,000)

Kingstown the capital of ST VINCENT and a port. (Pop. 22,800)

Kinshasa the capital of ZAÏRE, on the banks of the River Zaïre. It is the largest city in Central Africa. (Pop. 2,444,000)

Kirghizia (Kirgizia) *see* **Kyrgyzstan.**

Kirin *see* **Jilin.**

Kiribati (*Area* 726 sq km (280 sq miles); *population* 66,250; *capital* Tarawa; *form of government* Republic; *religions* RC, Protestantism; *currency* Australian dollar). Kiribati comprises three groups of coral atolls and one isolated volcanic island spread over a large expanse of the central Pacific. The climate is maritime equatorial with a high rainfall. Most islanders are involved in subsistence agriculture. The principal tree is the coconut. Soil is negligible, and the only vegetable which can be grown is calladium. Tuna fishing is an important industry. The country is heavily dependent on overseas aid.

Kiritimati *see* **Christmas Island.**

Kircudbrightshire *see* **Dumfries and Galloway.**

Kirkuk an industrial city and regional capital in the Kurdish north of Iraq. (Pop. 650,000)

Kirov an industrial city in east central Russian Federation, founded in the 12th century. (Pop. 407,000)

Kisangani a commercial centre and regional capital in northern Zaïre, on the River Zaïre. It was originally called Stanleyville. (Pop. 339,000)

Kishinev (Chisinau) the capital of MOLDOVA. (Pop. 605,000)

Kistna, River *see* **Krishna, River.**

Kita-Kyushu a major industrial city situated in the north of Kyushu Island, Japan. (Pop. 1,056,400)

Kitchener-Waterloo two towns in southern Ontario, Canada, which have become twin cities, 100 km (62 miles) west of Toronto. (Pop. 288,000)

Kíthira (Cerigo) *see* **Ionian Islands.**

Kivu, Lake a lake in the Great Rift Valley on the border between Rwanda and Zaïre. (2850 sq km/1100 sq miles)

Kiyev *see* **Kiev.**

Kizil Irmak the longest river in Turkey, flowing westwards from the centre, before curling north to the Black Sea. (Length 1130 km/700 miles)

Klaipeda a major port and shipbuilding centre on the Baltic coast of Lithuania. (Pop. 181,000)

Knock a village in County Mayo, in the west of the Republic of Ireland, where a group of villagers witnessed a vision of the Virgin Mary in 1879. It has now become a Marian shrine of world importance. (Pop. 1400)

Knossos the site of an excavated royal palace of the Minoan civilization, 5 km (3 miles) southeast of Heraklion, the capital of Crete. The palace was built in about 1950bc and destroyed in 1380bc.

Knoxville an industrial city in eastern Tennessee, USA, and a port on the Tennessee River. (Pop. city 174,000/metropolitan area 589,400)

Kobe a major container port and shipbuilding centre at the southern end of Honshu Island, Japan. (Pop. 1,410,800)

København *see* **Copenhagen.**

Koblenz (Coblenz) a city at the confluence of the Rivers Rhine and Moselle in western Germany, and a centre for the German winemaking industry. (Pop. 113,000)

Kola Peninsula a bulging peninsula in the Barents Sea in the extreme northwest of the Russian Federation, to the east of Murmansk.

Köln *see* **Cologne.**

Kolonia the capital of the Federated States of Micronesia, on the island of Pohnpei. (Pop. 22,000).

Kolyma, River a river in northeastern Siberia, flowing north from the gold-rich Kolyma mountains into the East Siberian Sea. (Length 2600 km/1600 miles)

Komi Republic an autonomous republic in the north of the Russian Federation, which produces timber, coal, oil and natural gas. (415,900 sq km/160,600 sq miles; pop. 1,197,000)

Komodo a small island of Indonesia in the Lesser Sunda group, between Sumbawa and Flores, noted above all as the home of the giant monitor lizard, the Komodo Dragon. (520 sq km/200 sq miles)

Königsberg *see* **Kaliningrad.**

Konya a carpet-making town and capital of the province of the same name in central southern Turkey. (Pop. town 438,900)

Korcula *see* **Dalmatia.**

Korea, North (*Area* 120,538 sq km (46,540 sq miles); *population* 22,420,000; *capital* Pyongyang; *other major cities* Chongjin, Nampo; *form of government* Socialist Republic; *religions* Chondoism, Buddhism; *currency* North Korean won). North Korea occupies just over half of the Korean peninsula in east Asia. It is a mountainous country, three-quarters of which is forested highland or scrubland. The climate is warm temperate, although winters can be cold in the north. Most rain falls during the summer. Nearly 90% of its arable land is farmed by cooperatives, on which rice is the main crop grown. North Korea is quite well endowed with fuel and minerals, including iron ore. Some 60% of the labour force are employed in industry, the most important of which are metallurgical, building, cement and chemicals.

Korea, South (*Area* 99,016 sq km (38,230 sq miles); *population* 42,800,000; *capital* Seoul (Soul); *other major cities* Pusan, Taegu, Inch'on; *form of government* Republic; *religions* Buddhism, Christianity; *currency* South Korean won). South Korea occupies the southern half of the Korean peninsula. It is predominantly mountainous with the highest ranges running north to south along the east coast. The west is lowland, which is extremely densely populated. The extreme south has a humid warm temperate climate, while farther north it is more continental. Cultivated land represents only 23% of the country's total area and the main crop is rice. The country has a flourishing manufacturing industry and is the world's leading supplier of ships and footwear. Other important industries are electronic equipment, electrical goods, steel, petrochemicals, motor vehicles and toys.

Korea Strait the stretch of water, 64 km (40 miles) at its narrowest), which separates the southern tip of South Korea from Japan. It is also sometimes known as the Tsushima Strait, after the island of that name.

Korinthos *see* **Corinth.**

Koror the capital of Belau. (Pop. 8000)

Kos (Cos) one of the Dodecanese Islands, belonging to Greece, in the Aegean Sea. (290 sq km/112 sq miles; pop. 20,300)

Kosciusko, Mount the highest mountain in Australia, a peak in the Snowy Mountains range in southern New South Wales. (2230 m/7316 ft)

Kosice a rapidly growing industrial city, and the regional capital of eastern Slovakia. (Pop. 214,300)

Kosovo an autonomous province in the southwest of Serbia. About 75% of the population are ethnic Albanians. The capital is Pristina. (10,887 sq km/4202 sq miles; pop. 1,584,000)

Kovno *see* **Kaunas.**

Kowloon *see* **Hong Kong.**

Kra, Isthmus of the narrow neck of land, only some 50 km (30 miles) wide and shared by Burma and Thailand, which joins Peninsular Malaysia to the mainland of Southeast Asia.

Krakatau (Krakatoa) a volcano which erupted out of the sea between Java and Sumatra in Indonesia in 1883 in an explosion that was heard 5000 km (3100 miles) away, and which killed 36,000 people. Today the site is marked by a more recent volcano called Anak Krakatau (Son of Krakatau).

Krakow *see* **Cracow.**

Krasnodar an agricultural centre and industrial city in the Russian Federation near the Black Sea. (Pop. 604,000)

Krasnoyarsk a mining city on the Trans-Siberian Railway in central southern Siberia. (Pop. 860,000)

Krefeld a textile town specializing in silk in western Germany, near the border with the Netherlands. (Pop. 224,000)

Krishna (Kistna) a river that flows through southern India from its source in the Western Ghats to the Bay of Bengal. (Length 1401 km/871 miles)

Kristiania *see* **Oslo.**

Krití *see* **Crete.**

Krivoy Rog a city in the Donets Basin region of Ukraine. (Pop. 680,000)

Krk (Veglia) a richly fertile island belonging to Croatia, in the northern Adriatic Sea. (408 sq km/158 sq miles; pop. 1500)

Krung Thep *see* **Bangkok.**

Krym *see* **Crimea.**

Kuala Lumpur the capital of Malaysia, sited on the banks of the Kelang and Gombak Rivers. (Pop. 937,900)

Kuanza, River *see* **Cuanza, River.**

Kumamoto a city in the west of Kyushu Island, Japan, noted for its electronics industries. (Pop. 555,700)

Kumasi a town in central southern Ghana, and the capital of the Ashanti people. (Pop. 415,300)

Kunming an industrial and trading city, and capital of Yunnan province in southern, central China. (Pop. 1,930,000)

Kurashiki a city in southwestern Honshu Island, Japan. Although now a major industrial centre, it still preserves much of its medieval heritage. (Pop. 411,400)

Kurdistan a region of the Middle East occupied by the Kurdish people spanning the borders of Iraq, Iran and Turkey.

Kuril (Kurile) Islands a long chain of some 56 volcanic islands stretching between the southern coast of the Kamchatka peninsula in eastern Russian Federation and Hokkaido Island, northern Japan. The archipelago was taken from Japan by the former USSR. in 1945; this remains an issue of contention between the Russian Federation and Japan. (15,600 sq km/6020 sq miles)

Kursk a major industrial city in the Russian Federation, 450 km (280 miles) south of Moscow. (Pop. 423,000)

Kurukshetra a sacred Hindu city in northern India, 140 km (87 miles) north of Delhi. (Pop. 186,100)

Kutch (Kachchh) an inhospitable coastal region on the border between Pakistan and India, which floods in the monsoon season and then dries out into a baking, salty desert. (44,185 sq km/17,060 sq miles)

Kuwait (*Area* 17,818 sq km (6880 sq miles); *population* 2,040,000; *capital* Kuwait (Al Kuwayt); *form of government* Constitutional Monarchy; *religion* Sunni Islam, Shia Islam; *currency* Kuwait dinar). Kuwait is a tiny state on The Gulf, wedged between Iraq and Saudi Arabia. It has a dry desert climate that is cool in winter but very hot and humid in summer. There is little agriculture due to lack of water. Shrimp fishing is becoming an important industry. Large reserves of petroleum and natural gas are the mainstay of the economy. Apart from oil, industry includes boat building, food production, petrochemicals, gases and construction.

Kuybyshev *see* **Samara.**

Kuznetsk *see* **Novokuznetsk.**

Kwai, River two tributaries of the Mae Khlong River in western Thailand, the Kwai Yai (Big Kwai) and the Kwai Noi (Little Kwai).

Kwajalein one of the largest atolls in the world, with a lagoon covering some 2800 sq km (1100 sq miles). The island forms part of the Marshall Islands in the Pacific Ocean, and is leased to the USA as a missile target.

KwaNdebele a semi-autonomus black homeland in central Transvaal province, northeastern South Africa. (3410 sq km/1317 sq miles)

Kwangju (Gwangju; Chonnam) an industrial city and regional capital in the southwestern corner of South Korea. (Pop. 727,600)

Kwango (Cuango), River a river which rises in northern Angola and flows northwards to join the River Kasai in Zaïre. (Length 110 km/68 miles)

KwaZulu a self-governing black homeland consisting of 10 separate territories in Natal, South Africa. (32,390 sq km/12,503 sq miles; pop. 4,186,000)

Kyongju an ancient city in the southeast of South Korea which was the capital of the Silla kingdom from 57bc to ad935. (Pop. 108,000)

Kyoto situated in central southern Honshu Island, this was the old imperial capital of Japan from ad794 to 1868. (Pop. 1,479,100)

Kyrgyzstan (*Area* 198,500 sq km (76,600 sq miles); *population* 3,886,000; *capital* Bishkek (formerly Frunze); *form of government* Republic; *religion* Sunni Islam; *currency* Rouble). Kyrgyzstan, a central Asian republic of the former USSR., declared itself independent in 1991. It is located on the border with northwest China. Much of the country is occupied by the Tian Shan Mountains which rise to spectacular peaks. Most of the country is semi-arid or desert, but climate is greatly influenced by altitude. Soils are poor except in the valleys, where wheat and other grains can be grown. Grazing of sheep, horses and cattle is carried out extensively. In the west the raising of silkworms is important. Other industries include non-ferrous metallurgy, machine building, coal mining, tobacco, food processing, textiles and gold mining.

Kyushu the most southerly of Japan's main islands, and the third largest after

Honshu and Hokkaido. (43,065 sq km/16,627 sq miles; pop. 13,276,000)

Laatokka, Lake *see* **Ladoga, Lake.**

Labrador the mainland part of the province of Newfoundland, on the east coast of Canada. (295,800 sq km/112,826 sq miles)

Laccadive Islands *see* **Lakshadweep.**

Ladakh a remote and mountainous district in the northeastern part of the state of Jammu and Kashmir, India, noted for its numerous monasteries which preserve the traditions of Tibetan-style Buddhism. The capital is Leh. (Pop. 70,000)

Ladoga (Ladozhskoye; Laatokka), Lake Europe's largest lake, in the Russian Federation, northeast of St Petersburg. (18,390 sq km/7100 sq miles)

Lagos the principal port and former capital (until 1992) of Nigeria, situated on the Bight of Benin. (Pop. 1,477,000)

Lahore a city in east central Pakistan. (Pop. 2,922,000)

Lake District a region of lakes and mountains in the county of Cumbria, in northwest England famed for their beauty. It includes England's highest peak, Scafell Pike (978 m/3208 ft).

Lake of the Woods a lake spattered with some 17,000 islands in southwestern Ontario, Canada, on the USA border. (4390 sq km/1695 sq miles)

Lakshadweep a territory of India consisting of 27 small islands (the Amindivi Islands, Laccadive Islands and Minicoy Islands) lying 300 km (186 miles) off the southwest coast of mainland India. (32 sq km/12 sq miles; pop. 40,250)

La Mancha a high, arid plateau in central Spain, some 160 km (100 miles) south of Madrid, the setting for Don Quixote, a 17th-century novel by Miguel de Cervantes.

Lambaréné a provincial capital in eastern central Gabon, famous as the site of the hospital founded by Albert Schweitzer (1875–1965). (Pop. 28,000)

Lanarkshire *see* **Strathclyde.**

Lancashire a county of northwest England, once the heart of industrial Britain. The county town is Preston. (3043 sq km/1175 sq miles; pop. 1,378,000)

Landes a department of the Aquitaine region on the coast of southwest France. (Pop. 297,400)

Land's End the tip of the peninsula formed by Cornwall in southwest England, and the most westerly point of mainland England.

Languedoc-Rousillon a region of France which lines the Mediterranean coast from the River Rhone to the border with Spain. (27,376 sq km/10,567 sq miles; pop. 1,927,000)

Lansing the state capital of Michigan, USA. (Pop. city 128,000/metropolitan area 416,200)

Lantau the largest of the islands which form part of the New Territories of Hong Kong. (150 sq km/58 sq miles; pop. 17,000)

Lanzarote *see* **Canary Islands.**

Lanzhou a major industrial city and the capital of Gansu province, central China. (Pop. 2,260,000)

Laois a county in the centre of the Republic of Ireland. The county town is Portlaoise. (1718 sq km/664 sq miles; pop. 51,200)

Laos (*Area* 236,800 sq km (91,428 sq miles); *population* 4,050,000; *capital* Vientiane; *form of government* People's Republic; *religion* Buddhism; *currency* Kip). Laos is a landlocked country in southeast Asia, which is ruggedly mountainous apart from the Mekong river plains along its border with Thailand. The Annam mountains form a natural border with Vietnam. It has a tropical monsoon climate. Laos is one of the poorest countries in the world, and its development has been retarded by war, drought and floods. The principal crop is rice, grown on small peasant plots.

La Paz a city set high in the Andes of Bolivia, and the capital and seat of government. (Pop. 900,000)

La Plata a port on the estuary of the River Plate (Rio de la Plata) in northeastern Argentina, southeast of Buenos Aires. (Pop. 455,000)

Lappland (Lapland) the region of northern Scandinavia and the adjoining territory of the Russian Federation, traditionally inhabited by the nomadic Lapp people; also a province of northern Finland, called Lappi.

Laptev Sea part of the Arctic Ocean bordering central northern Siberia.

Larnaca a port, with an international airport, on the southeast coast of Cyprus. (Pop. 48,400)

Lascaux a set of caves in the Dordogne department of southwest France with Paleolithic wall paintings dating back to about 15,000BC.

Las Palmas de Gran Canaria the main port and largest city of the Canary Islands, on the island of Gran Canaria. (Pop. 366,500)

Las Vegas a city in the southeast of the state of Nevada, USA. This state's liberal gaming laws has allowed it to develop as a centre for gambling and entertainment. (Pop. city 183,200/metropolitan area 536,500)

Latakia (Al Ladhiqiyah) a city on the Mediterranean coast of Syria, founded by the Romans, and now that country's main port. (Pop. 204,000)

Latium *see* **Lazio.**

Latvia (*Area* 63,700 sq km (24,595 sq miles); *population* 2,681,000; *capital* Riga; *other major cities* Daugavpils, Jurmala, Liepaja; *form of government* Republic; *religion* Lutheranism; *currency* Rouble). Latvia, a Baltic state that regained its independence in 1991 with the break-up of the USSR, is sandwiched between Estonia and Lithuania. The chief agricultural occupations are cattle and dairy farming, and the main crops grown are oats, barley, rye, potatoes and flax. Latvia's population is now 70% urban, and its cities produce high-quality textiles, machinery, electrical appliances, paper, chemicals, furniture and foodstuffs. Latvia has extensive deposits of peat and gypsum.

Lausanne a city on the north shore of Lake Geneva, Switzerland, and capital of the French-speaking canton of Vaud. (Pop. 140,000)

Laval a city in Quebec province of Canada which effectively forms a northern surburb of Montreal. (Pop. 238,300)

Lazio (Latium) a region occupying the central western coast of Italy around Rome, the regional capital. (17,203 sq km/6642 sq miles; pop. 3,076,000)

Lebanon (*Area* 10,400 sq km (4015 sq miles); *population* 2,800,000; *capital* Beirut (Beyrouth); *other important cities* Tripoli, Zahle; *form of government* Republic; *religions* Shia Islam, Sunni Islam, Christianity; *currency* Lebanese pound). Lebanon is a mountainous country in the eastern Mediterranean. There is a fertile narrow coastal plain, and between the two main ranges lies the Beqa'a Valley. The climate is Mediterranean but rainfall can be torrential in winter and snow falls on high ground. Lebanon is an agricultural country, and its main products include olives, grapes, citrus fruits, apples, cotton, tobacco and sugar beet. Industry is small scale.

Lebowa a self-governing homeland created for the North Sotho people, made up of several unconnected areas, in the north of the province of Transvaal, South Africa. (Pop. 2,246,000)

Lecce a historic city in the Puglia region of Italy. (Pop. 97,200)

Leeds an important industrial town on the River Aire in West Yorkshire, in northern England. (Pop. 450,000)

Leeward and Windward Islands (1) the Lesser Antilles in the southern Caribbean are divided into two groups. The northern islands in the chain, from the Virgin Islands to Guadeloupe are the Leeward Islands; the islands further south, from Dominica to Grenada, form the Windward Islands. (2) the Society Islands of French Polynesia are also divided into Leeward and Windward Islands.

Leghorn *see* **Livorno.**

Le Havre the largest port on the north coast of France. (Pop. 255,900)

Leicester a historic cathedral city, and the county town of Leicestershire. (Pop. 280,000)

Leicestershire a county in central England. Since 1974 it has included the former county of Rutland. (2553 sq km/986 sq miles; pop. 864,000)

Leiden (Leyden) a university city in western Netherlands. (Pop. 103,800)

Leinster one of the four ancient provinces into which Ireland was divided, covering the southeastern quarter of the country.

Leipzig an industrial city and important cultural centre in southeastern Germany. (Pop. 559,000)

Leitrim a county in the northwest of the Republic of Ireland, with a small strip of coast and a border with Northern Ireland. The county town is Carrick-on-Shannon. (1525 sq km/589 sq miles; pop. 27,600)

Léman, Lake another name for Lake Geneva.

Le Mans a university city in north western France, famous for the 24-hour car race held annually at a circuit nearby. (Pop. 194,000)

Lemberg *see* **L'vov.**

Lena a river which flows north across eastern Siberia, from its source close to Lake Baikal to the Laptev Sea. (Length 4270 km/2650 miles)

Leningrad *see* **St Petersburg.**

Lens a sprawling industrial city in the coal-mining region of northern France. (Pop. 327,400)

Léon (1) a major manufacturing city in central Mexico. (Pop. 675,000) (2) a historic city, founded by the Romans, in northwest Spain, and capital of the province of the same name. (Pop. city 131,200)

Léopoldville *see* **Kinshasa.**

Lesbos a large, fertile island in the Aegean, belonging to Greece, but only 10 km (6 miles) from Turkey. (1630 sq km/630 sq miles; pop. 41,900)

Lesotho (*Area* 30,355 sq km (11,720 sq miles); *population* 1,720,000; *capital* Maseru; *form of government* Monarchy; *religions* RC, other Christianity; *currency* Loti). Lesotho is a small landlocked kingdom entirely surrounded by the Republic of South Africa. Snow-capped mountains and treeless uplands, cut by spectacular gorges, cover two thirds of the country. The climate is pleasant with variable rainfall but frequent snow in the highlands. Due to the mountainous terrain, only one eighth of the land can be cultivated, and the main crop is maize. Wool, mohair and diamonds are exported but most foreign exchange comes from money sent home by Lesotho workers in South Africa. Tourism is beginning to flourish.

Lesser Sunda Islands (Nusa Tenggara) a chain of islands to the east of Java, Indonesia, stretching from Bali to Timor. (The Greater Sunda Islands comprise Borneo, Sumatra, Java and Sulawesi.)

Levkas *see* **Ionian Islands**

Lexington a city in central Kentucky, USA. (Pop. city 210,200/metropolitan area 327,200)

Leyden *see* **Leiden**

Leyte an island of the Visayan group in the central Philippines. The main town is Tacloban. (7213 sq km/ 2785 sq miles; pop. 1,480,000)

Lhasa the capital of Tibet, an autonomous region of China. It lies 3606 m (11,830 ft) above sea level. (Pop. 120,000)

Liaoning a coastal province of Dongbei (Manchuria), northeast China, bordering North Korea. The capital is Shenyang. (140,000 sq km/54,000 sq miles; pop. 34,426,000)

Liberia (*Area* 111,369 sq km (43,000 sq miles); *population* 2,440,000; *capital* Monrovia; *form of government* Republic; *religion* Animism, Sunni Islam, Christianity; *currency* Liberian dollar). Liberia is located in West Africa between Sierra Leone and Côte d'Ivoire. It has a treacherous coast with rocky cliffs and lagoons enclosed by sand bars. Inland the land rises to a densely forested plateau dissected by deep, narrow valleys. Farther inland still, there are beautiful waterfalls and the Nimba Mountains rise to over 1700 m (5577 ft). Agriculture employs three-quarters of the labour force and produces cassava and rice as subsistence crops and rubber, coffee and cocoa for export. The Nimba Mountains are rich in Iron Ore which accounts for 70% of export earnings.

Libreville the capital and main port of GABON. It is so called ("Freetown") because it was originally a settlement for freed slaves. (Pop. 308,000)

Libya (*Area* 1,759,540 sq km (679,358 sq miles); *population* 4,000,000; *capital* Tripoli (Tarabulus); *other major cities* Benghazi, Misurata; *form of government* Socialist People's Republic; *religion* Sunni Islam; *currency* Libyan dinar). Libya is a large north African country that stretches from the Mediterranean to, and in some parts beyond, the Tropic of Cancer. The Sahara Desert covers much of the country. The only green areas are the scrublands found in the northwest and the forested hills near Benghazi. The coastal area has mild wet winters and hot dry summers, but the interior has had some of the highest recorded temperatures of anywhere in the world. Only 14% of the people work on the land. Many sheep, goats and cattle are reared and there is an export trade in skins, hides and hairs. Libya is one of the world's largest producers of oil and natural gas.

Liechtenstein (*Area* 160 sq km (62 sq miles); *population* 28,181; *capital* Vaduz; *form of government* Constitutional Monarchy; *religion* RC; *currency* Swiss franc). The principality of Liechtenstein is a tiny central European mountainous state situated on the River Rhine between Austria and Switzerland. The climate is mild alpine. Once an agricultural country, it now has a great variety of light industries such as textiles, high-quality metal goods, precision instruments, pharmaceuticals and ceramics. Tourism is also big business, beautiful scenery and good skiing being the main attractions.

Liège (Luik) a historic city in eastern Belgium, and capital of the province of Liège, built on the confluence of the Rivers Meuse and Ourthe. (Pop. city 203,000/metropolitan area 609,000)

Liffey, River the river upon which Dublin, the capital of the Republic of Ireland, is set. (Length 80 km/49 miles)

Liguria the region of northwestern Italy which fronts the Gulf of Genoa; it has a border with France. (5415 sq km/2091 sq miles; pop. 1,772,000)

Ligurian Sea the northern arm of the Mediterranean Sea to the west of Italy, which includes the Gulf of Genoa.

Lille-Roubaix-Tourcoing a conurbation of industrial towns in northeastern France. (Pop. 945,600)

Lilongwe the capital of Malawi, and the second largest city in the country after Blantyre. (Pop. 172,000)

Lima the capital of Peru, situated on the banks of the River Rimac, 13 km (8 miles) from the coast. (Pop. 5,500,000)

Limassol the main port of Cyprus, in the south. (Pop. 107,200)

Limerick a city and port on the River Shannon, and the county town of the county of Limerick, in the southwest of the Republic of Ireland. (County 2686 sq km/ 1037 sq miles; pop. county 161,700; pop. city 60,700)

Limoges a city in eastern central France, famous for its richly decorated porcelain. It is the capital of the Limousin region. (Pop. 144,100)

Limousin a region of east-central France in the foothills of the Massif Central, famous in particular for its Limousin cattle. (Pop. 737,000)

Limpopo a river which flows northwards in the Transvaal to form part of the border between South Africa and Botswana before crossing southern Mozambique to the Indian Ocean. (Length 1610 km/1000 miles)

Lincoln (1) a historic city, with a fine cathedral dating from the 11th century, and the county town of Lincolnshire, England. (Pop. 77,000). (2) The state capital of Nebraska, USA. (Pop. city 180,400/metropolitan area 203,000)

Lincolnshire a county on the east coast of central England. The county town is Lincoln. (5885 sq km/2272 sq miles; pop. 558,000)

Lindisfarne a small island, also known as Holy Island, just off the coast of Northumberland in northeast England. It has an 11th-century priory built on the site of a monastery founded in the 7th century.

Linz a city and port on the River Danube in northern Austria. (Pop. 201,500)

Lion, Golfe de (Gulf of Lions) the arm of the Mediterranean Sea which forms a deep indent in the southern coast of France.

Lisbon (Lisboa) the capital and principal port of Portugal, situated on the broad River Tagus, near the Atlantic coast. (Pop. 817,600)

Lithuania (*Area* 65,200 sq km (25,174 sq miles); *population* 3,690,000; *capital* Vilnius; *other major cities* Kaunas, Klaipeda, Siauliai; *form of government* Republic; *religion* RC; *currency* Rouble). Lithuania, lying to the northwest of the Russian Federation and Belarus, is the largest of the three former Soviet Baltic Republics. Before 1940 Lithuania was a mainly agricultural country but has since been considerably industrialized. Most of the land is lowland covered by forest and swamp, and the main products are rye, barley, sugar beet, flax, meat, milk and potatoes. Industry includes heavy engineering and shipbuilding.

Little Rock the state capital of Arkansas, USA. (Pop. city 170,100/metropolitan area 492,700)

Liverpool a major port on the estuary of the River Mersey in northwest England; it is the administrative centre of Merseyside. (Pop. 497,000)

Livorno (Leghorn) a port and industrial city on the coast of Tuscany, northern Italy. (Pop. 175,300)

Ljubljana an industrial city on the River Sava, and the capital of SLOVENIA. (Pop. 305,200)

Lodz an industrial city and the second largest city in Poland, located in the centre of the country. (Pop. 848,500)

Logan, Mount the highest mountain in Canada, and the second highest in North America after Mount McKinley. It is situated in southwest Yukon, on the border with Alaska. (5951 m/19,524 ft)

Loire, River the longest river in France, flowing northwards from the southeastern Massif Central and then to the west to meet the Atlantic Ocean just to the west of Nantes. Its middle reaches are famous for their spectacular châteaux. (Length: 1020 km/635 miles)

Lombardy (Lombardia) the central northern region of Italy, which drops down from the Alps to the plain of the River Po, one of the country's most productive areas in both agriculture and industry. Milan is the regional capital. (23,854 sq km/9210 sq miles; pop. 898,700)

Lombok an island of the Lesser Sunda group, east of Bali. (5435 sq km/2098 sq miles; pop. 1,300,200)

Lomé the capital and main port of Togo, situated close to the border with Ghana. (Pop. 283,000)

London (1) the capital of the United Kingdom, which straddles both banks of the River Thames near its estuary. It consists of 33 boroughs, including the City, an international centre for trade and commerce. (Pop. 6,755,000). (2) an industrial city in southwestern Ontario, Canada. (Pop. 284,000)

Londonderry (Derry) the second largest city in Northern Ireland after Belfast, and the county town of the county of Londonderry. (County 2076 sq km/801 sq miles; pop. county 84,000; pop. city 62,000)

Longford a county in the centre of the Republic of Ireland, with a county town of the same name. (1044 sq km/403 sq miles; pop. 31,100)

Long Island an island off the coast of New Yory State, stretching some 190 km (118 miles) to the northeast away from the city of New York. Its western end forms part of the city of New York (the boroughs of Brooklyn and Queens) but the rest is a mixture of residential suburbs, farmland and resort beaches. (3685 sq km/1423 sq miles)

Lord Howe Island a small island lying some 600 km (375 miles) to the east of the coast of New South Wales, Australia, now a popular resort. (16 sq km/6 sq miles; pop. 300)

Lorraine a region of northeast France, with a border shared by Belgium, Luxembourg and Germany. The regional capital is Metz. (Pop. 2,320,000)

Los Angeles a vast, sprawling city on the Pacific Ocean in southern California, USA, the second largest city in the USA after New York. (Pop. city 3,096,700/ conurbation 12,372,600)

Lothian a local government region in southeast central Scotland, with Edinburgh as its administrative centre. It was created in 1975 out of the former counties of Midlothian, and East and West Lothian. (1756 sq km/678 sq miles; pop. 745,000)

Louisiana a state in central southern USA, on the lower reaches of the Mississippi River, and with a coastline on the Gulf of Mexico. The state capital is Baton Rouge. (125,675 sq km/48,523 sq miles; pop. 4,481,000)

Louisville a city and commercial centre, in northern Kentucky, USA, on the Ohio River. (Pop. city 289,800/metropolitan area 962,600)

Lourdes one of the world's most important Marian shrines, in the foothills of the central Pyrénées, France. (Pop. 17,600)

Lourenço Marques *see* **Maputo.**

Louth a county on the east coast of the Republic of Ireland, bordering Northern Ireland. The county town is Dundalk. (823 sq km/318 sq miles; pop. 88,500)

Lualaba, River a river that flows northwards across the eastern part of Zaïre from the border with Zambia before joining the River Lomami to form the River Zaïre. (Length 1800 km/1120 miles)

Luanda the capital of Angola, and a major port on the Atlantic Ocean. (Pop. 700,000)

Lübeck a Baltic port in northern Germany, lying some 20 km (12 miles) from the coast on the River Trave. (Pop. 80,000)

Lublin (Lyublin) a city and agricultural centre in southeastern Poland. (Pop. 320,000)

Lubumbashi the principal mining town of Zaïre, and the capital of the Shaba region in the southeast of the country. It was founded in 1910 and known as Elisabethville until 1966. (Pop. 600,000)

Lucca a town in northwestern Tuscany, Italy. (Pop. 89,100)

Lucerne (Luzern) a city set on the beautiful Lake Lucerne in central Switzerland, retaining much of its medieval past; also the name of the surrounding canton. (Pop. city 67,500)

Lucknow the capital of the state of Uttar Pradesh in central northern India. (Pop. 1,007,600)

Lüda (Dalian) an industrial city and port in Liaoning province, northeastern China. (Pop. 4,000,000)

Ludhiana a town in central Punjab, India, home of the respected Punjab Agricultural University. (Pop. 607,000)

Ludwigshafen a town, industrial centre and river port on the River Rhine in southwestern Germany. (Pop. 163,000)

Lugansk a major industrial city of the eastern Ukraine in the Donets Basin. (Pop. 491,000)

Luik *see* **Liège.**

Luluabourg *see* **Kananga.**

Lumbini the birthplace of Buddha in central southern Nepal.

Luoyang a city of ancient origins, founded in about 2100bc, in Henan province in eastern central China. As a principal centre of the Shang dynasty (18th-12th centuries bc), the area is rich in archaeological remains. (Pop. 500,000)

Lusaka the capital of Zambia, situated in the southeast of the country. (Pop. 538,500)

Luton an industrial town in Bedfordshire, England, 50 km (30 miles) north of London. (Pop. 165,000)

Luxembourg (*Area* 2586 sq km (998 sq miles); *population* 378,400; *capital* Luxembourg; *form of government* Constitutional Monarchy; *religion* RC; *currency* Luxembourg franc). Luxembourg is a small country bounded by Belgium on the west, France on the south and Germany on the east. In the north is a wooded plateau, and in the south a fertile lowland area of valleys and ridges. Northern winters are cold and raw with snow covering the ground for almost a month, but in the south winters are mild and summers cool. In the south crops grown include maize, roots, tubers and potatoes. Dairy farming is also important. It is in the south, also, that iron ore is mined as the basis of the country's iron and steel industry.

Luxor a town that has grown up around one of the great archaeological sites of ancient Egypt, on the east bank of the River Nile in the centre of the country, just south of the ancient capital, Thebes, and 3 km (2 miles) from Karnak. (Pop. 78,000)

Luzern *see* **Lucerne.**

Luzon the largest island of the Philippines, in the north of the group, with the nation's capital, Manila, at its centre. (104,688 sq km/40,420 sq miles; pop. 29,400,000)

L'vov (Lemberg) a major industial city of medieval origins in the western Ukraine. (Pop. 688,000)

Lyallpur *see* **Faisalabad.**

Lyons (Lyon) the second largest city in France, at the confluence of the Rhône and Saone in the southeast of the country. (Pop. 1,236,100)

Lyublin *see* **Lublin.**

Maas, River *see* **Meuse.**

Macáu (Macao) a tiny Portuguese province on the south coast of China and due to be handed back to China in 1999. (15.5 sq km/6 sq miles; pop. 406,000; cur. Pataca = 100 avos)

Macdonnell Ranges the parallel ranges of mountains of central Australia, in the southern part of the Northern Territory, near to Alice Springs. The highest peak is Mount Ziel (1510 m/4954 ft).

Macedonia (1) the largest region of Greece, occupying most of the northern part of the mainland, and with northern borders with Albania, former Yugoslavia and Bulgaria. (Pop. 2,122,000). (2) the most southerly of the republics of former Yugoslavia, with Skopje as its capital. (25,713 sq km/9928 sq miles; pop. 1,912,200)

Maceió a port on the central east coast of Brazil. (Pop. 401,000)

Macgillicuddy's Reeks a range of mountains in the southwest of the Republic of Ireland which includes the country's highest peak at Carrauntoohil (1040 m/ 3414 ft).

Mackenzie, River a river flowing northwards through the western part of the Northwest Territories of Canada from the Great Slave Lake to the Arctic Ocean. (Length 4250 km/2640 miles)

McKinley, Mount the highest mountain in North America, located in the Denali National Park in southern Alaska, USA. (6194 m/20,320 ft)

MacMurdo Sound an arm of the Ross Sea off Antarctica.

Madagascar (*Area* 587,041 sq km (226,657 sq miles); *population* 11,440,000; *capital* Antananarivo; *other major cities* Fianarantsoa, Mahajanga, Toamasina; *form of government* Republic; *religions* Animism, RC, Protestantism; *currency* Malagasy franc). Madagascar is an island state situated off the southeast coast of Africa. It is the fourth largest island in the world, and the centre of it is made up of high savanna-covered plateaux. In the east, forested mountains fall steeply to the coast and in the southwest, the land falls gradually through dry grassland and scrub. The staple food crop is rice and 80% of the population grow enough to feed themselves. Some 58% of the land is pasture and there are more cattle than people. The main export earners are coffee, vanilla, cloves and sugar.

Madeira the main island in a small group in the eastern Atlantic Ocean which have belonged to Portugal since the the 16th century, lying some 1000 km (620 miles) due west of Casablanca in Morocco. The capital is Funchal. (740 sq km/ 286 sq miles; pop. 248,500)

Madhya Pradesh the largest state in India, in the centre of the country. The capital is Bhopal. (443,446 sq km/171,170 sq miles; pop. 52,178,800)

Madison the state capital of Wisconsin, USA. (Pop. city 170,700/metropolitan area 333,000)

Madras the main port on the east coast of India, and the capital of the state of Tamil Nadu. (Pop. 4,289,300)

Madrid the capital of Spain, situated in the middle of the country, and also the name of the surrounding province. (Pop. city 3,188,300/province 4,727,000)

Madura an island off the northeastern coast of Java. (5290 sq km/2042 sq miles; pop. 1,860,000)

Madurai a textile city in Tamil Nadu, in the southern tip of India. (Pop. 907,700)

Mae Nam Khong, River *see* **Salween, River.**

Mafikeng (Mafeking) a town in the black state of Bophuthatswana, South Africa. (Pop. 29,400)

Magdalena, River a river which flows northwards through western Colombia and into the Caribbean at Barranquila. (Length 1550 km/965 miles)

Magdeburg a city and inland port on the River Elbe in eastern Germany, 120 km (75 miles) southwest of Berlin. (Pop. 289,000)

Magellan, Strait of the waterway, 3 km (2 miles) across at its narrowest, which separates the island of Tierra Del Fuego from the southern tip of mainland South America. It was discovered by the Portuguese navigator Ferdinand Magellan (?1480–1521) in 1520.

Maghreb (Maghrib) the name by which the countries of northwest Africa, Morocco, Algeria and Tunisia are often called collectively.

Magnitogorsk a steel-making town, in the southern Ural Mountains in the Russian Federation, founded in 1930. (Pop. 421,000)

Maharashtra a state in the centre of the west coast of India, with Bombay as its capital. (307,690 sq km/118,768 sq miles; pop. 62,784,200)

Mahore *see* **Mayotte.**

Main, River a river that snakes its way westwards from its source near Bayreuth in central Germany, passing through Frankfurt am Main before joining the River Rhine at Mainz. (Length 524 km/325 miles)

Maine a state in the northeastern corner of the USA, bordering Canada. The state capital is Augusta. (86,027 sq km/33,215 sq miles; pop. 1,164,000)

Mainz a city and inland port on the confluence of the Rivers Rhine and Main in western central Germany. (Pop. 185,000)

Majorca (Mallorca) the largest of the Balearic Islands, in the western Mediterranean. The capital is Palma. (3639 sq km/1405 sq miles; pop. 460,000)

Majuro an atoll of three islands (Dalap, Uliga and Darrit) which together form the capital of the Marshall Islands. (Pop. 8700)

Makassar *see* **Ujung Padang.**

Makassar Strait the broad stretch of water, 130 km(81 miles) across at its narrowest, which separates Borneo and Sulawesi in Indonesia.

Makeyevka an industrial city in the Donets Basin in the southern Ukraine. (Pop. 448,000)

Makhachkala a port and industrial city on the west coast of the Caspian Sea, and the capital of the republic of Dagestan. (Pop. 269,000)

Makkah *see* **Mecca.**

Malabar Coast the name given to the coastal region of the state of Kerala in southwestern India.

Malabo a port and the capital of Equatorial Guinea, situated on the north coast of Bioko Island. (Pop. 37,200)

Malacca *see* **Melaka.**

Malacca, Strait of the busy waterway, just 50 km (31 miles) wide at its narrowest, which separates the island of Sumatra in Indonesia from the southern tip of Malaysia, with Singapore at its eastern end.

Malaga a port, manufacturing city, and tourist resort on the Mediterranean coast of Andalucia, southern Spain. Also the name of the province of which it is the capital. (Pop. town 503,300)

Malagasy Republic *see* **Madagascar.**

Malawi (*Area* 118,484 sq km (45,747 sq miles); *population* 7,980,000; *capital* Lilongwe; *other major cities* Blantyre, Mzuzu, Zomba; *form of government* Republic; *religions* Animism, RC, Presbyterianism; *currency* Kwacha). Malawi lies along the southern and western shores of the third largest lake in Africa, Lake Malawi. To the south of the lake the Shire river flows through a valley, overlooked by wooded, towering mountains. The tropical climate has a dry season from May to October and a wet season for the remaining months. Agriculture is the predominant occupation, and many Malawians live off their own crops. Plantation farming is used for export crops of tea and tobacco. Hydroelectricity is now being used for industry, but imports of manufactured goods remain high.

Malawi (Nyasa), Lake a long, narrow lake which runs down most of the eastern side of Malawi and forms Malawi's border with Tanzania and Mozambique. (23,300 sq km/9000 sq miles)

Malaysia (*Area* 329,749 sq km (127,316 sq miles); *population* 17,810,000; *capital* Kuala Lumpur; *other major cities* Ipoh, Georgetown, Johor Baharu; *form of government* Federal Constitutional Monarchy; *religion* Sunni Islam; *currency* Malaysian ringgit). The Federation of Malaysia lies in southeast Asia, and comprises Peninsular Malaysia and the states of Sabah and Sarawak on the island of Borneo. The country is affected by a tropical monsoon climate. Peninsular Malaysia has always had thriving rubber-growing and tin-dredging industries, and now oil palm growing is also important on the east coast. Sabah and Sarawak have grown rich by exploiting their forests. There is also some offshore oil, and around the capital, Kuala Lumpur, new industries such as electronics are expanding.

Maldives (*Area* 298 sq km (115 sq miles); *population* 214,139; capital : Malé; *form of government* Republic; religion : Sunni Islam; currency : Rufiyaa). The Republic of Maldives lies in the Indian Ocean and comprises 1200 low-lying coral islands grouped into 12 atolls. The climate is hot and humid. The islands are covered with coconut palms, and some millet, cassava, yams and tropical fruit are grown. Rice, however, the staple diet of its islanders, has to be imported. Fishing is an important occupation and the chief export is now canned or frozen tuna. Tourism is developing fast.

Malé the main atoll of the Maldives, and the town which is the country's capital. (2.6 sq km/1 sq mile; pop. 29,000)

Mali (*Area* 1,240,192 sq km (478,838 sq miles); *population* 9,090,000; *capital* Bamako; other major cities Segou, Mopti; *form of government* Republic; *religions* Sunni Islam, Animism; *currency* Franc CFA). Mali is a landlocked state in West Africa. The country mainly comprises vast and monotonous plains and plateaux. The Sahara, in the north of the country, is encroaching southwards, and the country is one of the poorest in the world. In the south there is some rain, and plains are covered by grassy savanna and a few scattered trees. The River Niger runs through the south of the country, and small steamboats use it for shipping. Only one-fifth of the land can be cultivated. Rice, cassava and millet are grown for domestic consumption and cotton for export.

Mallorca *see* **Majorca.**

Malmö a port in southwest Sweden, on the narrow channel which separates Sweden from Copenhagen in Denmark. (Pop. 229,900)

Malta (*Area* 316 sq km (122 sq miles); *population* 354,900; *capital* Valletta; *form of government* Republic; *religion* RC; *currency* Maltese pound). Malta, a small republic in the middle of the Mediterranean Sea, lies just south of Sicily. It comprises three islands, Malta, Gozo and Comino, which are made up of low limestone plateaux with little surface water. The climate is Mediterranean. Malta is virtually self-sufficient in agricultural products and exports potatoes, vegetables, wine and cut flowers. Commercial shipbuilding and repairing is one of the leading industries. Tourism has also boomed.

Maluku (Moluccas) a group of some 1000 islands in eastern Indonesia, known as the Spice Islands, for they were once the only source of cloves and nutmegs. The principal islands are Halmahera, Seram and Buru. The capital is Ambon. (74,505 sq km/28,766 sq miles; pop. 1,411,000)

Man, Isle of an island of the British Isles, in the Irish Sea, halfway between

England and Ireland. It is a British Crown possession, not a part of the UK, and has its own parliament, the Court of Tynwald. The capital is Douglas. (585 sq km/226 sq miles; pop. 66,000)

Managua the capital of NICARAGUA, situated on the edge of Lake Managua. (Pop. 630,000)

Manaus a major port on the River Amazon in Brazil, lying 1600 km (1000 miles) from the sea. (Pop. 635,000)

Manchester a major industrial and commercial city in northwest England, and the administrative centre for the metropolitan county of Greater Manchester. It is connected to the estuary of the River Mersey by the Manchester Ship Canal. (County 1286 sq km/497 sq miles; pop. city 448,000/county 2,594,778)

Manchuria *see* **Dongbei.**

Mandalay the principal city of central Burma, and a port on the River Irrawaddy. (Pop. 417,300)

Manila the capital of the PHILIPPINES. The city is an important port and commercial centre, and is sited on Luzon island. (Pop. city 6,000,000)

Manipur a small state of India in the far northeast, on the border with Burma. The capital is Imphal. (22,327 sq km/8618 sq miles; pop. 1,421,000)

Manitoba the most easterly of the prairie provinces of Canada. The capital is Winnipeg. (650,087 sq km/250,998 sq miles; pop. 1,026,000)

Mannheim an inland port and industrial city on the confluence of the Rivers Rhine and Neckar. (Pop. 300,000)

Mansura *see* **El Mansura.**

Mantua (Mantova) a city in the valley of the River Po, in the Lombardy region of Italy, retaining much of its medieval heritage. (Pop. 60,400)

Maputo the capital and main port of MOZAMBIQUE. It was formerly known as Lourenço Marques. (Pop. 785,500)

Maracaibo the second largest city in Venezuela, in the northwest. (Pop. 1,100,000)

Maracaibo, Lake a shallow lake in northwest Venezuela, containing one of the richest oil fields in the world. (13,280 sq km/5127 sq miles)

Marbella a popular resort on the Mediterranean coast of southern Spain, in the province of Malaga. (Pop. 67,900)

Marburg *see* **Maribor.**

Marche (Marches) a region of central eastern Italy, lining the Adriatic coast. The capital is Ancona. (9694 sq km/3743 sq miles; pop. 1,424,000)

Mar del Plata a coastal city and beach resort on the northeast coast of Argentina, 400 km (250 miles) south of Buenos Aires. (Pop. 424,000)

Maribor (Marburg) an industrial city in Slovenia. (Pop. 185,700)

Marie Galante *see* **Guadeloupe.**

Marigot *see* **St Martin.**

Marmara, Sea of a small sea lying between the Dardanelles and the Bosphorus, providing a vital link in the route between the Mediterranean Sea and the Black Sea. The surrounding coasts all belong to Turkey.

Marmolada, Mount *see* **Dolomites.**

Marquesas Islands a group of a dozen or so fertile, volcanic islands in the northeastern sector of French Polynesia, lying about 1400 km (875 miles) northeast of Tahiti. (1189 sq km/459 sq miles; pop. 6500)

Marrakech (Marrakesh) a historic oasis city in central western Morocco, founded in the 11th century and formerly the country's capital. (Pop. 440,000)

Marseilles (Marseille) the largest port in France, on the Mediterranean coast, and France's third largest city after Paris and Lyons. (Pop. 1,110,500)

Marshall Islands a scattered group of some 1250 islands in Micronesia, in the western Pacific Ocean. They form a self-governing republic which remains in free association with the USA. Copra is the main export. The principal languages are Marshallese and English, and the capital is Majuro. (181 sq km/70 sq miles; pop. 37,000; cur. US dollar = 100cents)

Martinique one of the larger of the islands in the Windward Islands group in the southern Caribbean, lying between Dominica and St Lucia. It is administered as a department of France. Fort-de-France is the capital. (1079 sq km/417 sq miles; pop. 330,000)

Maryland a state on the central east coast of the USA, virtually divided in two by Chesapeake Bay. The state capital is Annapolis. (27,394 sq km/10,577 sq miles; pop. 4,392,000)

Masbate *see* **Visayan Islands.**

Maseru the capital of LESOTHO. (Pop. 45,000)

Mashhad (Meshed) a major trading centre and the capital of Khorasan province in northeastern Iran. (Pop. 1,120,000)

Masqat *see* **Muscat.**

Massachusetts one of the New England states on the northeastern coast of the USA. The capital is Boston. (21,386 sq km/8257 sq miles; pop. 5,822,000)

Massif Central the rugged upland region which occupies much of southern central France to the west of the River Rhone. The highest point is at Puy de Sancy (1885 m/6184 ft).

Matsuyama a port and industrial city on the north coast of Shikoku Island, Japan. (Pop. 426,600)

Matterhorn (Monte Cervino) a distinctive, pyramid-shaped peak on the border between Italy and Switzerland, 5 km (3 miles) south of Zermatt. (4477 m/14,688 ft)

Maui the second largest island of Hawaii, USA. (1885 sq km/727 sq miles; pop. 63,000)

Mauna Kea a dormant volcano in the north of the island of Hawaii, USA. (4205 m/13,796 ft)

Mauna Loa an active volcano in the centre of the island of Hawaii. (4169 m/13,677 ft)

Mauritania (*Area* 1,025,520 sq km (395,953 sq miles); *population* 1,970,000; *capital* Nouakchott; *form of government* Republic; *religion* Sunni Islam; *currency* Ouguiya). Mauritania is located on the west coast of Africa. About 47% of the country is desert, the Sahara covering much of the north. The main agricultural regions are in the Senegal river valley in the south. The rest of the country is made up of the drought-stricken Sahel grasslands, from which the traditionally nomadic herdsmen have moved to shanty towns in the south. Deposits of iron ore and copper provide the country's main exports, and development of these and the fishing industry on the coast is the only hope for a brighter future.

Mauritius (*Area* 2040 sq km (788 sq miles); *population* 1,081,669; *capital* Port Louis; *form of government* Constitutional Monarchy; *religions* Hinduism, RC, Sunni Islam; *currency* Mauritius rupee). Mauritius is a beautiful island with tropical beaches, which lies in the Indian Ocean east of Madagascar. The climate is hot and humid. The island has well-watered fertile soil, ideal for the sugar plantations that cover 45% of the island. Although the export of sugar still dominates the economy, diversification is being encouraged. The clothing and electronic equipment industries are becoming increasingly important, and tourism is now the third largest source of foreign exchange.

Mayo a county on the west coast of the Republic of Ireland. The county town is Castlebar. (4831 sq km/1865 sq miles; pop. 114,700)

Mayotte (Mahore) part of the Comoros Island group, lying between Madagascar and the mainland of Africa. Unlike the other three islands in the group, Mayotte voted to remain under the administration of France when the Comoros Islands became independent in 1974. (373 sq km/144 sq miles; pop. 60,000)

Mbabane the capital of SWAZILAND. (Pop. 36,000)

Meath a county on the east coast of the Republic of Ireland, to the north of Dublin. The county town is Navan. (2336 sq km/902 sq miles; pop. 95,400)

Mecca (Makkah) a city in central western Saudi Arabia, 64 km (40 miles) east of the Red Sea port of Jiddah. An important trading city on caravan routes in ancient times, it was the birthplace of the Prophet Mohammed, and as such is the holiest city of Islam. (Pop. 375,000)

Medan a major city in northern Sumatra, Indonesia. (Pop. 2,378,000)

Medellín the second largest city in Colombia after the capital Bogota, situated in the centre of the country, 240 km (150 miles) northwest of the capital. (Pop. 1,998,000)

Medina (Al Madinah) the second holiest city of Islam after Mecca. The Prophet Mohammed fled from Mecca to Medina, 350 km (217 miles) to the north, to escape persecution in AD622 (year 0 in the Islamic lunar calendar). (Pop. 210,000)

Mediterranean Sea a large sea bounded by southern Europe, North Africa and southwest Asia. It is connected to the Atlantic Ocean by the Strait of Gibraltar.

Médoc one of the prime wine-producing regions of France, a flat, triangular-shaped piece of land between the Gironde estuary and the Atlantic Ocean.

Meerut an industrial town of northern India, 60 km (40 miles) northeast of Delhi.

The Indian Mutiny began here in 1857. (Pop. 536,600)

Meghalaya a predominantly rural state in the hills of northeastern India, with Bangladesh to the south. (22,429 sq km/8658 sq miles; pop. 1,335,800)

Meissen a historic town on the River Elbe, 20 km (12 miles) to the northwest of Dresden, in southeastern Germany. It is famous above all for its fine porcelain, produced here since 1710. (Pop. 38,200)

Meknès a former capital, with a fine 17th-century royal palace, in northern Morocco. (Pop. 320,000)

Mekong, River the great river of Southeast Asia, flowing from Tibet, through southern China, Laos and Cambodia before forming a massive and highly fertile delta in southern Vietnam and flowing into the South China Sea. (Length 4184 km/2562 miles)

Melaka (Malacca) a port on the southwest coast of Malaysia, overlooking the Straits of Malacca, once a key port in Far Eastern trade. (Pop. 87,500)

Melanesia the central and southern group of islands in the South Pacific Ocean, including the Solomon Islands, Vanuatu, Fiji and New Caledonia.

Melbourne the second largest city in Australia after Sydney and the capital of the state of Victoria. (Pop. 2,700,000)

Melos *see* **Cyclades.**

Memel *see* **Klaipeda.**

Memphis a city on the River Mississippi in the southwest corner of Tennessee, USA, on the border with and extending into Arkansas. (Pop. city 648,000/ metropolitan area 934,600)

Menai Strait the narrow strait, 180 m (590 ft) across at its narrowest, separating mainland Wales from the island of Anglesey, spanned by road and rail bridges.

Mendoza a trading, processing and wine-producing centre in the foothills of the Andes, in western Argentina. (Pop. 600,000)

Menorca *see* **Minorca.**

Merida the historic capital of the Yucatan province of eastern Mexico. (Pop. 424,500)

Merionethshire *see* **Gwynedd.**

Mersey, River a river in northwest England. It forms an estuary to the south of Liverpool which is deep and wide enough to permit access for ocean-going ships to Liverpool and Manchester (via the Manchester Ship Canal. (Length 110 km/70 miles)

Merseyside a metropolitan county created in 1974 out of parts of Lancashire and Cheshire, centring on River Mersey, with Liverpool as its administrative centre. (652 sq km/252 sq miles; pop. 1,501,000)

Mersin (Içel) the principal Mediterranean port of Turkey, in the central south of the country, to the north of Cyprus. (Pop. 314,100)

Meshed *see* **Mashhad.**

Messina a historic port, founded in the 8th century BC, in northeast Sicily, overlooking the narrow Strait of Messina (6 km/4 miles wide at its narrowest) which separates Sicily from mainland Italy. (Pop. 266,300)

Metz the capital of the industrial Lorraine region in eastern France, situated on the River Moselle, close to the border with Germany. (Pop. 194,800)

Meuse (Maas), River a river which flows northwest from its source in the Lorraine region of France, across central Belgium and into the Netherlands, where it joins part of the delta of the River Rhine before entering the North Sea. (Length 935 km/580 miles)

Mexico (*Area* 1,958,201 sq km (756,061 sq miles); *population* 81,140,000; *capital* México City; *other major cities* Guadalajara, Monterrey, Puebla de Zaragoza; *form of government* Federal Republic; *religion* RC; *currency* : Mexican peso). Mexico is the most southerly country in North America. It is a land of volcanic mountain ranges and high plateaux, with coastal lowlands along the Pacific and the Gulf of Mexico. In the north there are arid and semi-arid conditions, while in the south there is a humid tropical climate. Some 30% of the labour force are involved in agriculture growing maize, wheat, kidney beans and rice for subsistence and coffee, cotton, fruit and vegetables for export. Mexico is the world's largest producer of silver and has large reserves of oil and natural gas. Developing industries are petrochemicals, textiles, motor vehicles and food processing.

Mexico, Gulf of an arm of the Atlantic Ocean, bounded by the Florida peninsula in the southeast USA and the Yucatan peninsula in Mexico, with the island of Cuba placed in the middle of its entrance.

México City the capital of MEXICO, and the most populous city in the world. It lies in the south of the country on a high plateau 2200 m (7350 ft) above sea level. (Pop. 17,000,000)

Miami a major city and resort on the Atlantic coast of southeast Florida, USA. (Pop. city 372,600/metropolitan area 1,706,000)

Michigan a state in north central USA, formed out of two peninsulas between the Great Lakes, with Lake Michigan in the middle. The capital is Lansing. (150,780 sq km/58,216 sq miles; pop. 9,088,000)

Michigan, Lake one of the Great Lakes, and the only one to lie entirely within the USA. (57,750 sq km/22,300 sq miles)

Micronesia one of the three main groupings of islands of the Pacific Ocean, lying to the northwest of the other two main groupings, Melanesia and Polynesia. They stretch from Belau to Kiribati.

Micronesia, Federated States of a group of some 600 tropical islands in the west Pacific, which became a self-governing republic in 1982 while remaining in free association with the USA, which considers it strategically important. Heavily dependent on US aid, the country exports copra and fish. The principal language is English, and the capital is Kolonia. (701 sq km/271 sq miles; pop. 89,000; cur. US dollar = 100cents)

Middle East a non-specific term used to describe an area of southwest Asia, which is mainly Islamic and/or Arabic-speaking. Countries included are: Turkey, Iran, Iraq, Syria, Jordan, Israel, Saudi Arabia, Lebanon, Yemen, Oman, the United Arab Emirates, Qatar, Bahrain and Kuwait.

Middlesbrough the county town of Cleveland, England. (Pop. 149,800)

Middle West *see* **Midwest.**

Mid Glamorgan a county in central southern Wales, which was formed in 1974 out of part of the former counties of Breconshire, Glamorgan and Monmouthshire. The administrative centre is in Cardiff. (1000 sq km/393 sq miles; pop. 538,000)

Midlands, The a term used to describe the central industrial counties of England: Debyshire, Northamptonshire, Nottinghamshire, Staffordshire, Warwickshire, Leicestershire, and West Midlands.

Midlothian *see* **Lothian.**

Midway Islands two atolls belonging to the USA, in the north Pacific Ocean, some 2000 km (1242 miles) northwest of Hawaii. (3 sq km/2 sq miles; pop. 2200)

Midwest (Middle West) a term used to describe the fertile north-central part of the USA. States in the Midwest include Ohio, Michigan, Indiana, Illinois, Wisconsin, Minnesota, Iowa and Missouri, but others, such as Kansas, are also often included.

Mikinai *see* **Mycenae.**

Míkinos *see* **Cyclades.**

Milan (Milano) the major industrial and commercial centre of northern Italy, and the country's second largest city after Rome, situated in central Lombardy. (Pop. 1,605,000)

Milos *see* **Cyclades.**

Milwaukee a port on the west side of Lake Michigan, and the main industrial centre of Wisconsin, USA. (Pop. city 620,800/metropolitan area 1,393,800)

Minch, The the broad channel separating northwest Scotland from the Outer Hebrides or Western Isles.

Mindanao the second largest island of the Philippines. (94,631 sq km/36,537 sq miles; pop. 11,100,000)

Mindoro an island in west central Philippines. (9736 sq km/3759 sq miles)

Minicoy Islands *see* **Lakshadweep.**

Minneapolis a major agricultural and commercial centre in southeast Minnesota, USA, on the River Mississippi, and adjoining St Paul. (Pop. city 258,300/ metropolitan area 2,230,900)

Minnesota a state in north central USA. The state capital is St Paul. (217,736 sq km/84,068 sq miles; pop. 4,193,000)

Minorca (Menorca) the second largest of the Balearic Islands (after Majorca). The capital is Mahon. (702 sq km/271 sq miles; pop. 50,200)

Minsk a major industrial city, and the capital of BELARUS. (Pop. 1,442,000)

Miquelon *see* **St Pierre and Miquelon.**

Miskolc a city in the northeast of Hungary, and the country's second largest city after Budapest. (Pop. 210,000)

Mississippi a state in central southern USA with a small coastline on the Gulf of

Mexico. The state capital is Jackson. (123,585 sq km/47,716 sq miles; pop. 2,613,000)

Mississippi, River the second longest river in the USA. It rises in Minnesota and runs south the length of the country to the Gulf of Mexico. (Length 3779 km/ 2348 miles)

Missolonghi *see* **Mesolóngion.**

Missouri a state in the Midwest of the USA. The state capital is Jefferson City. (180,487 sq km/69,686 sq miles; pop. 5,029,000)

Missouri, River the main tributary of the Mississippi with which it is the longest river in North America. It rises in Montana, flows north, east and southeast to join the Mississippi at St Louis. (Length 3969 km/2466 miles)

Mizoram a union territory of India, in the hilly northeast, on the border with Burma. The capital is Aijal. (21,081 sq km/8137 sq miles; pop. 493,800)

Mobile a port on the coast of Alabama, USA, on the Gulf of Mexico. (Pop. city 204,900/metropolitan area 465,700)

Mobutu Sese Seko, Lake *see* **Albert, Lake.**

Modena an industrial city retaining many vestiges of its medieval past, in northeastern Italy. (Pop. 178,300)

Mogadishu (Muqdisho) the capital and main port of of Somalia. (Pop. 400,000)

Mohave Desert *see* **Mojave Desert.**

Mojave (Mohave) Desert a desert in southern California, stretching from Death Valley to Los Angeles. (38,850 sq km/15,000 sq miles)

Moldova a region of northeast Romania.

Moldova (Moldavia) (*Area* 33,700 sq km (13,000 sq miles); *population* 4,052,000; *capital* Kishinev; *other major cities* Tiraspol, Bendery; *form of government* Republic; *religion* Russian Orthodox; *currency* Rouble). Moldova was a Soviet socialist republic from 1940 until 1991 when it became independent of the former USSR. It is bounded to the west by Romania and to the north, east and south by Ukraine. It consists of a hilly plain of fertile soils, and crops grown include wheat, corn, barley, tobacco, sugar beet, soybeans and sunflowers. There are also extensive fruit orchards, vineyards and walnut groves. Beekeeping and silkworm breeding are widespread. Food processing is the main industry.

Molise a region of eastern Italy, on the Adriatic coast, between Abruzzi and Puglia. (4438 sq km/1714 sq miles; pop. 332,900)

Molotov *see* **Perm'.**

Moluccas *see* **Maluku.**

Mombasa the second city of Kenya and an important port on the Indian Ocean. (Pop. 500,000)

Monaco (*Area* 195 hectares (48 acres); *population* 29,876; *capital* Monaco-Ville; *form of government* Constitutional Monarchy; *religion* RC; currency : Franc). Monaco is a tiny principality on the Mediterranean, surrounded landwards by France. It comprises a rocky peninsula and a narrow stretch of coast. The old town of Monaco-Ville houses the royal palace and the cathedral. The Monte Carlo district has its world-famous casino, and Fontvieille is an area reclaimed from the sea where now marinas and light industry are located. Tourism is the main revenue earner.

Monaghan a county in the central north of the Republic of Ireland, with a county town of the same name. (1291 sq km/498 sq miles; pop. county 51,200)

Mönchengladbach an industrial city in the southwest of the Ruhr region of western Germany, 25 km (16 miles) west of Dusseldorf. (Pop. 257,000)

Mongolia (*Area* 1,566,500 sq km (604,826 sq miles); *population* 2,095,000; *capital* Ulan Bator (Ulaanbaatar); *other major cities* Darhan, Erdenet; *form of government* Republic; *religion* Previously Buddhism but religion is now suppressed; *currency* Tugrik). Mongolia is a landlocked country in northeast Asia, which is bounded to the north by the Russian Federation and by China to the south, west and east. Most of Mongolia is mountainous. In the south there are grass-covered steppes and desert wastes of the Gobi. The climate is very extreme and dry. For six months the temperatures are below freezing. Mongolia has had a traditional nomadic pastoral economy for centuries, and cereals including fodder crops are grown on a large scale on state farms. The mining of copper accounts for 40% of all exports.

Monmouthshire *see* **Gwent.**

Monrovia the capital and principal port of Liberia. (Pop. 425,000)

Mons (Bergen) a town in southwest Belgium. (Pop. 94,000)

Montana a state in northwest USA, on the border with Canada. The state capital is Helena. (381,087 sq km/147,138 sq miles; pop. 826,000)

Monte Carlo an elegant coastal town and resort in Monaco, famed in particular for its casinos. (Pop. 13,200)

Montenegro (Crna Gora) the smallest of the republics of former Yugoslavia, in the southwest on the Adriatic Sea and bordering Albania. The capital is Titograd. (13,812 sq km/5331 sq miles; pop. 584,300)

Monterey a resort town on the Pacific coast of central California, USA, 135 km (85 miles) southeast of San Francisco. It is well known for its annual jazz festival. (Pop. 28,700)

Monterrey an industrial city in northeast Mexico, the country's third largest city after Mexico City and Guadaljara. (Pop. 1,916,500)

Montevideo the capital of Uruguay, and an important port on the River Plate estuary. (Pop. 1,500,000)

Montgomery the state capital of Alabama, USA. (Pop. city 185,000/metropolitan area 284,800)

Montgomeryshire *see* **Powys.**

Montpelier the state capital of Vermont, USA. (Pop. 8200)

Montpellier a university and trading city in central southern France, the capital of the Languedoc-Roussillon region. (Pop. 225,300)

Montréal the second largest city in Canada after Toronto, on the St Lawrence River, in the south of the province of Quebec. Two-thirds of the population are French-speaking Québecois. (Pop. 2,828,250)

Montserrat a British Crown colony in the Leeward Islands, in the southeastern Caribbean. The capital is called Plymouth. (102 sq km/39 sq miles)

Monza a city in northern Italy, northeast of Milan. (Pop. 122,500)

Moravia a historical region of the Czech Republic, east of Bohemia, west of Slovakia, with Poland to the north and Austria to the south.

Moray Firth an inlet of the North Sea cutting some 56 km (35 miles) into the eastern coast of northeast Scotland, with Inverness at its head.

Morayshire *see* **Grampian.**

Morocco (*Area* 446,550 sq km (172,413 sq miles); *population* 24,500,000; *capital* Rabat; *other major cities* Casablanca, Fez, Marrakech; *form of government* Constitutional Monarchy; *religion* Sunni Islam; *currency* Dirham). Morocco, in northwest Africa, is a land of great contrasts, with the high rugged Atlas mountains in the north, the arid Sahara in the south, and its green Atlantic and Mediterranean coasts. The north has a pleasant Mediterranean climate. Farther south, winters are warmer and summers even hotter. Morocco is largely a farming country, wheat, barley and maize being the main food crops, and it is one of the world's chief exporters of citrus fruit. Morocco's main wealth comes from phosphates. Industries include textiles, car assembly, soap and cement, and fishing. Tourism is also a major source of revenue.

Moroni the capital of the Comoros islands. (Pop. 20,000)

Moscow (Moskva) the capital of the Russian Federation, sited on the Moskva River. It is an ancient city with a rich heritage, and is the political, industrial and cultural focus of the country. (Pop. 8,600,000)

Moselle (Mosel), River a river which flows northwards from the southeastern Lorraine region of eastern France to form part of the border between Luxembourg and Germany before flowing eastwards to meet the River Rhine at Koblenz. (Length 550 km/340 miles)

Mosul (Al Mawsil) a historic trading city on the banks of the River Tigris in northwest Iraq, and an important centre for the surrounding oil-producing region. (Pop. 1,500,000)

Mourne Mountains a range of noted beauty in the south of County Down, Northern Ireland. The highest point is Slieve Donard (852 m /2795 ft).

Mozambique (*Area* 801,590 sq km (309,494 sq miles); *population* 14,900,000; *capital* Maputo; *other major cities* Beira, Nampula; *form of government* Republic; *religions* Animism, RC, Sunni Islam; *currency* Metical). Mozambique is a republic located in southeast Africa. The Zambezi river separates the high plateaux in the north from the lowlands in the south. The country has a humid tropical climate. Normally, conditions are reasonably good for agriculture, but a drought in the early 1980s followed a few years later by severe flooding resulted in famine and more than 100,000 deaths. A lot of industry was abandoned when the Portuguese left the country in 1975. There is little incentive to produce surplus agricultural products for cash, and food rationing has now been introduced. A black market accounts for a sizable part of the economy.

Mozambique Channel the broad strait, some 400 km (250 miles) across at its narrowest, which separates Madagascar from mainland Africa.

Mühlheim an der Ruhr an industrial city and port on the River Ruhr, in the Ruhr region of western Germany. (Pop. 174,000)

Mulhouse an industrial city in Alsace, eastern France. (Pop. 222,700)

Mull an island off the central west coast of Scotland. (925 sq km/357 sq miles)

Multan an industrial city in the Punjab, Pakistan. (Pop. 730,000)

Munich (München) a historic and industrial city in southern Germany, and capital of Bavaria. (Pop. 1,300,000)

Munster one of the four historic provinces of Ireland, covering the southwest quarter of the country.

Münster an inland port and industrial centre on the Dortmund-Ems Canal in northwestern Germany. (Pop. 260,000)

Muqdisho *see* **Mogadishu.**

Murcia a trading and manufacturing city in southeastern Spain, and capital of the province of the same name. (Pop. city 288,600)

Murmansk the largest city north of the Arctic Circle, a major port and industrial centre on the Kola Peninsula in the far northwestern corner of the Russian Federation. (Pop. 412,000)

Murray, River a major river of southeast Australia, which flows westwards from the Snowy Mountains to form much of the boundary between the states of New South Wales and Victoria. It is joined by the River Darling before flowing across the southeastern corner of South Australia and into the Southern Ocean. (Length 2570 km/1600 miles)

Mururoa an atoll in the southeastern sector of French Polynesia, used by France since 1966 as a testing ground for nuclear weapons.

Musandam a rocky, horn-shaped peninsula which juts out into The Gulf to form the southern side of the Strait of Hormuz. It belongs to Oman, but is separated from it by part of the United Arab Emirates.

Muscat (Masqat) the historic capital of Oman. The neighbouring port of Muttrah has developed rapidly in recent decades to form the commercial centre of Muscat. (Pop. (with Muttrah) 80,000)

Mustique a privately owned island in the Grenadines, to the south of St Vincent, in the southeastern Caribbean. (Pop. 200)

Muttrah *see* **Muscat.**

Myanmar *see* **Burma.**

Mysore an industrial city in the state of Karnataka, southern India. (Pop. 470,000)

Naberezhnyye Chelny an industrial town in the Russian Federation. (Pop. 414,000)

Nablus the largest town on the Israeli-occupied West Bank. (Pop. 44,000)

Nagaland a primarily agricultural state in the hilly far northeastern corner of India, bordering Burma. (16,579 sq km/6399 sq miles; pop. 774,900)

Nagasaki a port and industrial city on the west coast of Kyushu Island, Japan. A second atomic bomb was dropped on Nagasaki (August 9, 1945), killing 40,000 people. (Pop. 446,300)

Nagorny Karabakh a disputed autonomous enclave in Azerbaijan, which is claimed by Armenia. Three quarters of the population are Armenian.

Nagoya a port and industrial centre on the southeastern coast of Honshu, Japan. (Pop. 2,065,800)

Nagpur a commercial centre and textile manufacturing city on the Deccan plateau of Maharashtra state, central India. (Pop. 1,302,100)

Nairobi the capital of Kenya and a commercial centre, in the southwest highland region. (Pop. 1,250,000)

Nakhichevan an autonomous republic, enclaved by Armenia, but a part of Azerbaijan. The capital is also called Nakhichevan. (5500 sq km/2120 sq miles; pop. republic 252,000/capital 37,000)

Namib Desert a sand desert lining the coast of Namibia.

Namibia (*Area* 824,292 sq km (318,259 sq miles); *population* 1,290,000; *capital* Windhoek; *form of government* Republic; *religions* Lutheranism, RC, other Christianity; *currency* Rand). Namibia is situated on the Atlantic coast of southwest Africa. There are three main regions in the country. Running down the entire Atlantic coastline is the Namib Desert, east of which is the Central Plateau of mountains, rugged outcrops, sandy valleys and poor grasslands. East again and north is the Kalahari Desert. Namibia has a poor rainfall, the highest falling at Windhoek. Even here it only amounts to 200–250 mm (8–10 inches) per year. It is essentially a stock-rearing country with sheep and goats raised in the south, and cattle in the central and northern areas. Diamonds are mined just north of the River Orange, and the largest open groove uranium mine in the world is located near Swakopmund. One of Africa's richest fishing grounds lies off the coast, and mackerel, tuna and pilchards are an important export.

Nanchang an industrial city and commercial centre in central southeastern China, and the capital of Jiangxi province. (Pop. 2,390,000)

Nancy a manufacturing city in northeast France, and former capital of Lorraine. (Pop. 314,200)

Nanjing (Nanking) a major industrial and trading city built on the lower reaches of the Chang Jiang (Yangtze) river, and the capital of Jiangsu province, central eastern China. (Pop. 3,551,000)

Nanning the capital of the Guangxi-Zhuang autonomous region in the extreme southeast of China. (Pop. 607,000)

Nansei-shoto *see* **Ryukyu Islands.**

Nantes a port and commercial centre in northwestern France and capital of the Loire Atlantique department. (Pop. 474,100)

Naples (Napoli) the third largest city in Italy after Rome and Milan, is a port situated on the spectacular Bay of Naples. (Pop. 1,203,900)

Nara a historic city in south Honshu Island, Japan, the capital of Japan in the 8th century. (Pop. 327,000)

Nashville the state capital of Tennessee, USA, an industrial city famous as the traditional home of Country and Western music. (Pop. city 462,500/ metropolitan area 890,300)

Nassau the capital of the Bahamas, on the north side of New Providence Island. (Pop. 120,000)

Nasser, Lake a massive artificial lake on the River Nile in southern Egypt, created when the Aswan High Dam was completed in 1971. (5000 sq km/1930 sq miles)

Natal (1) a port city on the northeast tip of Brazil, and capital of the state of Rio Grande do Norte. (Pop. 417,000) **(2)** a province on the eastern coast of South Africa. The capital is Pietermaritzburg, but the main city is Durban. (86,976 sq km/33,573 sq miles; pop. 2,841,700)

Nauru (*Area* 21 sq km (8 sq miles); *population* 8100; *capital* Yaren; *form of government* Republic; *religions* Protestantism, RC; *currency* Australian dollar). Nauru, the world's smallest republic, is a coral island situated just south of the Equator, halfway between Australia and Hawaii. The climate is tropical with a high and irregular rainfall. The country is rich, due entirely to the deposits of high quality phosphate rock in the central plateau, which is sold for fertilizer. However, these deposits are likely to be exhausted by 1995, but the government is investing overseas.

Navarra (Navarre) a province in the mountainous northeastern part of Spain. The capital is Pamplona. (10,420 sq km/4023 sq miles; pop. 507,400)

Naxos a fertile island in the southern Aegean Sea, the largest of the Cyclades. (428 sq km/165 sq miles)

Nazareth a town in northern Israel, and the childhood home of Jesus. (Pop. 46,300)

Ndjamena (N'Djamena) the capital of Chad, in the southeast of the country. It was founded by the French in 1900 and named Fort Lamy. (Pop. 303,000)

Neagh, Lough the largest freshwater lake in the British Isles, in the east of Northern Ireland. (381 sq km/147 sq miles)

Nebraska a state in the Midwest of the USA. The capital is Lincoln. (200,018 sq km/77,227 sq miles; pop. 1,606,000)

Neckar, River a tributary of the River Rhine, rising in the Black Forest in the southwest of Germany. (365 km/227 miles)

Negev a desert in southern Israel.

Negros the fourth largest island of the Philippines. (12,704 sq km/4905 sq miles; pop. 2,750,000)

Nei Mongol Autonomous Region (Inner Mongolia) a region of northeastern China, bordering Mongolia. The capital is Hohhot. (1,200,000 sq km/460,000 sq miles; pop. 18,510,000)

Neisse, River a tributary of the Oder, which flows north from its source in the Czech Republic to form part of the border between Germany and Poland. (Length 256 km/159 miles)

Nepal (*Area* 140,797 sq km (54,362 sq miles); *population* 18,000,000; *capital* Kathmandu; *form of government* Constitutional Monarchy; *religion* Hinduism, Buddhism; *currency* Nepalese rupee). Nepal is a long narrow rectangular country, landlocked between China and India on the flanks of the eastern Himalayas. On its northern border is Everest, the highest mountain in the world. The climate is subtropical in the south, and all regions are affected by the monsoon. Nepal is one of the world's least developed countries, with most of the population trying to survive as peasant farmers.

Netherlands, The (*Area* 40,844 sq km (15,770 sq miles); *population* 14,890,000; *capital* Amsterdam; *seat of government* The Hague (Den Haag, 's-Gravenhage); *other major cities* Eindhoven, Rotterdam; *form of government* Constitutional Monarchy; *religions* RC, Dutch reformed, Calvinism; *currency* Guilder). Situated in northwest Europe, the Netherlands is bounded to the north and west by the North Sea. Over one-quarter of the country is below sea level, and the Dutch have tackled some huge reclamation schemes including the IJsselmeer. The Netherlands has mild winters and cool summers. Agriculture and horticulture are highly mechanized, with salad vegetables, fruit and flowers grown under glass. Industries include chemicals, machinery, petroleum, refining, metallurgy and electrical engineering. The main port, Rotterdam, is the largest in the world.

Netherlands Antilles an overseas division of the Netherlands, spread over the southern Caribbean. The principal islands are: Curacao, St Martin, St Eustatius, and Bonaire. Aruba was part of the group until 1986.

Neusatz *see* **Novi Sad.**

Neva, River the river which flows through St Petersburg. (Length 74 km/45 miles)

Nevada a state in the west of the USA, consisting mostly of desert. The state capital is Carson City. (286,298 sq km/110,540 sq miles; pop. 936,000)

Nevis *see* **St Kitts and Nevis.**

Newark a major port city in New Jersey. (Pop. 314,400/metropolitan area 1,875,300)

New Britain the largest offshore island belonging to Papua New Guinea, in the Bismarck Archipelago. (36,500 sq km/14,100 sq miles; pop. 237,000)

New Brunswick a state on the coast in southeast Canada, bordering the USA. The state capital is Fredericton. (73,436 sq km/28,354 sq miles; pop. 696,000)

New Caledonia the main island of a group called by the same name in the South Pacific, which form an overseas territory of France. The capital is Noumea. (19,103 sq km/7376 sq miles; pop. 155,000)

Newcastle a port and industrial city in New South Wales, Australia. (Pop. 259,000)

Newcastle-under-Lyme a town in the Potteries region of Staffordshire, central England. (Pop. 74,600)

Newcastle upon Tyne a historic and industrial city in the county of Tyne and Wear, northeast England. (Pop. 280,000)

New Delhi the official capital of India as of 1931. (Pop. 273,000)

New England the name given to northeastern states of the USA: Maine, Vermont, New Hampshire, Connecticut, Massachusetts and Rhode Island.

Newfoundland the province in the extreme east of Canada. The capital is St John's. (372,000 sq km/143,634 sq miles; pop. 568,000)

New Guinea one of the world's largest islands, divided into two parts: independent Papua New Guinea in the east and Irian Jaya, a state of Indonesia, in the west.

New Hampshire a state of New England, in the northwest of the USA. The state capital is Concord. (24,097 sq km/9304 sq miles; pop. 998,000)

New Haven a port in Connecticut, USA. (Pop. city 124,200/metropolitan area 506,000)

New Hebrides *see* **Vanuatu.**

New Jersey a state on the Atlantic coast in the northeast of the USA. The state capital is Trenton. (20,295 sq km/7836 sq miles; pop. 7,562,000)

New Mexico a state in the southwest of the USA, bordering Mexico. The state capital is Santa Fe. (315,115 sq km/121,666 sq miles; pop. 1,450,000)

New Orleans an important and historic port in southern Louisiana, on the Mississippi delta. (Pop. city 559,100/metropolitan area 1,318,800)

Newport a port and naval base in Rhode Island, USA. (Pop. 29,900)

Newport News a major eastern seaboard port in Virginia, USA. (Pop. city 154,600/metropolitan area (with Norfolk) 1,261,200)

New Providence *see* **Bahamas.**

New South Wales the most populous of the states of Australia, situated in the southeast of the country. The capital is Sydney. (801,430 sq km/309,433 sq miles; pop. 5,379,000)

New Territories *see* **Hong Kong.**

New York (City) the most populous city in the USA, its most important port, and a major financial centre. It is sited on the mouth of the Hudson River, and comprises five boroughs: Manhattan, the Bronx, Queens, Brooklyn and Staten Island. (Pop. city 7,322,600/metropolitan area 8,376,900)

New York (State) a populous state in the northeast of the USA, on the Atlantic coast. The state capital is Albany (128,402 sq km/49,576 sq miles; pop. 17,783,000)

New Zealand (*Area* 270,986 sq km (104,629 sq miles); *population* 3,390,000; *capital* Wellington; *other major cities* Auckland, Christchurch, Dunedin, Hamilton; *form of government* Constitutional Monarchy; *religions* Anglicanism, RC, Presbyterianism; *currency* New Zealand dollar). New Zealand, lying southeast of Australia in the South Pacific, comprises two large main islands. North Island is hilly with isolated mountains and active volcanoes. On South Island the Southern Alps run north to south, with the Canterbury Plains to their east. It enjoys very mild winters with regular rainfall. Two-thirds of New Zealand is suitable for agriculture and grazing, meat, wool and dairy goods being the main products. Forestry supports the pulp and paper industry, and cheap hydroelectricity the manufacturing industry, which now accounts for 30% of New Zealand's exports.

Ngaliema, Mount *see* **Ruwenzori.**

Niagara Falls spectacular waterfalls on the Niagara River, situated on the Canada-USA border between Lakes Erie and Ontario.

Niamey the capital of Niger. (Pop. 400,000)

Nicaragua (*Area* 130,000 sq km (50,193 sq miles); *population* 3,750,000; *capital* Managua; *form of government* Republic; *religion* RC; *currency* : Córdoba). Nicaragua is the largest of the countries situated on the isthmus of Central America and lies between Honduras and Costa Rica. The east coast contains forested lowland and is the wettest part of the country. The western mountainous region, which contains the two huge lakes, Nicaragua and Managua, is where most of the population live. The whole country is subject to devastating earthquakes. Nicaragua is primarily an agricultural country. The main export crops are coffee, cotton and sugar cane. It enjoys very mild winters with regular rainfall.

Nicaragua, Lake a large lake in the southwest of Nicaragua. (8264 sq km/3191 sq miles)

Nice a city, port and famous resort town of the Côte D'Azur, southeastern France. (Pop. 451,500)

Nicosia the capital of Cyprus, situated in the centre of the island. (Pop. 161,100)

Niger (*Area* 1,267,000 sq km (489,189 sq miles); *population* 7,450,000; *capital* Niamey; *form of government* Republic; *religion* Sunni Islam; *currency* Franc CFA). Niger is a landlocked republic in West Africa. Over half of the country is covered by the encroaching Sahara Desert in the north, and the south lies in the drought-stricken Sahel. In the extreme southwest corner, the River Niger flows through the country, and in the extreme southeast lies Lake Chad, but the rest of the country is extremely short of water. Basic subsistence farming and herding are the main occupations. Uranium mined in the Aïr mountains is Niger's main export.

Niger, River a river in West Africa flowing through Guinea, Mali, Niger and Nigeria to the Gulf of Guinea. (Length 4170 km/2590 miles)

Nigeria (*Area* 923,768 sq km (356,667 sq miles); *population* 118,700,000; *capital* Abuja (New Federal Capital) Lagos (Capital until 1992); *other major cities* Ibadan, Kano, Ogbomsho; *form of government* Federal republic; *religions* Sunni Islam, Christianity; *currency* Nairais). Nigeria is a large and populous country in West Africa, and from the Gulf of Guinea it extends north to the border with Niger. It has a variable landscape and climate, from the hot and humid swampy coastal areas and tropical forest belts of the interior, to the arid mountains and savanna of the north. The two main rivers are the Niger and the Benue. The main agricultural products are cocoa, rubber, groundnuts and cotton. Only cocoa, however, is of any significance for export. The country depends on a fluctuating revenue from petroleum exports.

Nijmegen a city of eastern central Netherlands, close to the border with Germany. (Pop. 234,000)

Nikolayev a port and industrial city on the north coast of the Black Sea, in the Ukraine. (Pop. 480,000)

Nile, River (An Nil) a major river of Africa and the longest river in the world. It rises in Burundi, flows into Lake Victoria and then flows northwards through Uganda, Sudan and Egypt to its delta on the Mediterranean. The river is called the White Nile (Bahr el Abiad) until it reaches Khartoum, where it is joined by its main tributary, the Blue Nile (Bahr el Azraq), which rises in Ethiopia. (Length 6695 km/4160 miles)

Nîmes a city in southern France, overlooking the River Rhone. (Pop. 138,000)

Ningbo a port and industrial city in Zhejiang province, in central eastern China. (Pop. 900,000)

Ningxia-Hui Autonomous Region a region of central northern China, south of Inner Mongolia. The capital is Yinchuan. (60,000 sq km/23,000 sq miles; pop. 3,640,000)

Nis (Nish) a historic city in the east of Serbia. (Pop. 230,000)

Nizhniy Novgorod an industrial city in the Russian Federation on the River Volga, formerly known as Gor'kiy (Gorky). (Pop. 1,392,000)

Nizhniy Tagil an industrial city in the central Ural Mountains, Russian Federation. (Pop. 415,000)

Nordkapp *see* **North Cape.**

Norfolk (1) a county of East Anglia, England. The county town is Norwich. (5355 sq km/2068 sq miles; pop. 714,000) (2) a port and naval base in the state of Virginia, USA. (Pop. city 279,700/metropolitan area (with Newport News) 1,261,200)

Normandy an area of central northern France, now divided into two regions, Haute Normandie and Basse Normandie. (Pop. 3,006,000)

Northampton the county town of Northamptonshire. (Pop. 164,000)

Northamptonshire a county in central England. The county town is Northampton. (2367 sq km/914 sq miles; pop. 547,000)

North Cape (Nordkapp) one of Europe's most northerly points—500 km (310 miles) north of the Arctic Circle in Norway.

North Carolina a state on the southeastern coast of the USA. The state capital is Raleigh. (136,198 sq km/52,586 sq miles; pop. 6,255,000)

North Dakota a state in the west of the USA. The state capital is Bismarck. (183,022 sq km/70,665 sq miles; pop. 685,000)

Northern Ireland a province of the UK, occupying most of the northern part of the island of Ireland. It is divided into six counties. The capital is Belfast. (14,121 sq km/5452 sq miles; pop. 1,572,000)

Northern Marianas a group of 14 islands in the western Pacific which in 1978 became a commonwealth of the USA. The capital is Susepe, on the island of Saipan.

Northern Territory a territory of northern Australia. The capital is Darwin. (1,346,200 sq km/519,770 sq miles; pop. 136,800)

North Island *see* **New Zealand.**

North Korea *see* **Korea.**

North Pole the northernmost point on the earth's axis.

North Sea a comparatively shallow branch of the Atlantic Ocean that separates the British Isles from the European mainland.

Northumberland a county in northeastern England. The county town is Morpeth. (5033 sq km/1943 sq miles; pop. 302,000)

Northwest Territories a vast area of northern Canada, occupying almost a third of the country's whole land area. The capital is Yellowknife. (3,246,000 sq km/ 1,253,400 sq miles; pop. 45,740)

Norway (*Area* 323,895 sq km (125,056 sq miles); *population* 4,200,000; *capital* Oslo; *other major cities* Bergen, Trondheim, Stavanger; *form of government* Constitutional Monarchy; *religion* Lutheranism; *currency* Norwegian krone). Norway occupies the western half of the Scandinavian peninsula in northern Europe, and is surrounded to the north, west and south by water. It is a country of spectacular scenery of fjords, cliffs, rugged uplands and forested valleys. The climate is temperate as a result of the warming effect of the Gulf Stream, and although the winters are long and cold, the waters off the west coast remain ice-free. Agriculture is chiefly concerned with dairying and fodder crops. Fishing is an important industry, and the large reserves of forest provide timber for export. Industry is now dominated by oil from the North Sea.

Norwegian Sea a sea lying between Norway, Greenland and Iceland; to the north it joins the Arctic Ocean, and to the south, the Atlantic.

Norwich the county town of Norfolk, in eastern England. (Pop. 122,000)

Nottingham the historic county town of Nottinghamshire, situated on the River Trent. (Pop. 277,000)

Nottinghamshire a county in the Midlands of England. The county town is Nottingham,. (2164 sq km/836 sq miles; pop. 1,000,000)

Nouakchott the capital city of Mauritania, near the Atlantic coast. (Pop. 135,000)

Nouméa the capital and chief port of New Caledonia. (Pop. 85,000)

Nova Scotia a province on the eastern coast of Canada. The capital is Halifax. (52,841 sq km/20,401 sq miles; pop. 847,000)

Novi Sad (Ujvidek; Neusatz) a city on the River Danube and the capital of Vojvodina, an autonomous province of Serbia. (Pop. 257,700)

Novokuznetsk an industrial city in central southern Siberia. (Pop. 572,000)

Novosibirsk a major industrial city in central Russian Federation. (Pop. 1,386,000)

Nuku'alofa the capital and main port of Tonga. (Pop. 21,000)

Nullarbor Plain a huge, dry and treeless (the name is from the Latin for "no trees") plain which borders the Great Australian Bight, in Western and Southern Australia.

Nuremberg (Nürnberg) a city in Bavaria, central southern Germany. (Pop. 486,000)

Nusa Tenggara *see* **Lesser Sunda Islands.**

Nuuk *see* **Godthåb.**

Nyasa, Lake *see* **Malawi, Lake.**

Nyasaland *see* **Malawi.**

Oahu the third largest of the islands of Hawaii, where the state capital, Honolulu, and Pearl Harbor are located. (1549 sq km/598 sq miles; pop. 797,400)

Oakland a port on San Francisco Bay in central western California, USA. (Pop. city 351,900/metropolitan area 1,871,400)

Ob' a river in the Russian Federation which rises near the border with Mongolia and flows northwards to the Kara Sea. (Length 5570 km/3460 miles)

Oberammergau a village in Bavaria in southwest Germany, famed for the Passion play which it puts on every ten years. (Pop. 4800)

Oceania a general term used to describe the central and southern islands of the Pacific Ocean including those of Australia and New Zealand. (8,900,000 sq km/ 3,400,000 sq miles; pop. 25,800,000)

Oder, River a river in central Europe rising in the Czech Republic and flowing north and west to the Baltic Sea; it forms part of the border between Germany and Poland. (Length 912 km/567 miles)

Odessa a major Black Sea port in the Ukraine. (Pop. 1,113,000)

Offaly a county in the centre of the Republic of Ireland. The county town is Tullamore. (1998 sq km/771 sq miles; pop. 58,300)

Ogaden a desert region of southeastern Ethiopia, claimed by Somalia.

Ohio a Midwest state of the USA, with a shoreline on Lake Erie. The capital is Columbus. (106,765 sq km/41,220 sq miles; pop. 10,744,00)

Ohio River a river in the eastern USA, formed at the confluence of the Allegheny and Monongahela Rivers. It flows west and south and joins the Mississippi at Cairo, Illinois. (Length 1575 km/980 miles)

Okavango, River *see* Kavango (Cubango), River.

Okayama a commercial city in southwest Honshu Island, Japan. (Pop. 572,400)

Okhotsk, Sea of a part of the northwestern Pacific Ocean bounded by the Kamchatka peninsula, the Kuril islands, and the east coast of Siberia.

Oklahoma a state in the southwest of the USA. The state capital is Oklahoma City. (173,320 sq km/66,919 sq miles; pop. 3,301,000)

Oklahoma City the state capital of Oklahoma. (Pop. city 443,200/metropolitan area 962,600)

Olympia a port and the state capital of Washington, on the west coast of the USA. (Pop. city 29,200/metropolitan area 138,300)

Olympus, Mount a range in central mainland Greece, the home of the gods of ancient Greek myth. The highest peak is Mytikas (2917 m/9570 ft).

Omaha a city in eastern Nebraska, USA. (Pop. city 334,000/metropolitan area 607,400)

Oman (*Area* 212,457 sq km (82,030 sq miles); *population* 2,000,000; *capital*

Muscat (Musqat); *form of government* Monarchy (sultanate); *religion* Ibadi Islam, Sunni Islam; *currency* Rial Omani). Situated in the southeast of the Arabian peninsula, Oman is a small country in two parts. It comprises a small mountainous area overlooking the Strait of Hormuz, which controls the entrance to The Gulf, and the main part of the country, consisting of barren hills rising sharply behind a narrow coastal plain. Oman has a desert climate. Only 0.1% of the country is cultivated, the main produce being dates. The economy is almost entirely dependent on oil, which provides 90% of its exports.

Oman, Gulf of a branch of the Arabian sea leading to the Strait of Hormuz.

Omdurman a city situated across the River Nile from Khartoum, the capital of Sudan. (Pop. 526,300)

Omsk an industrial city in central western Siberia, on the Trans-Siberian Railway. (Pop. 1,094,000)

Ontario a province of central Canada. The capital is Toronto. (1,068,582 sq km/ 412,580 sq miles; pop. 8,625,000)

Ontario, Lake the smallest and most easterly of the Great Lakes; it drains into the St Lawrence River. (19,550 sq km/7550 sq miles)

Oporto (Porto) a port in northwest Portugal, and the country's second largest city after Lisbon. (Pop. 330,200)

Oran (Wahran) a Mediterranean port and the second largest city of Algeria. (Pop. 670,000)

Orange, River the longest river in southern Africa, rising in Lesotho and flowing west to the Atlantic. (Length 2090 km/1299 miles)

Orange Free State a landlocked province in central South Africa, with its capital at Bloemfontein. (127,993 sq km/49,405 sq miles; pop. 2,080,000)

Oranjestad (1) the capital of Aruba, and an important port. (Pop. 10,100) (2) the capital of St Eustatius, and a port. (Pop. 1200)

Oregon a state in the northwest of the USA, on the Pacific. The state capital is Salem. (251,180 sq km/96,981 sq miles; pop. 2,687,000)

Orinoco, River a river in northern South America. It rises in southern Venezuela and flows west, then north and finally east to its delta on the Atlantic. It forms part of the border between Colombia and Venezuela. (Length 2200 km/1370 miles)

Orissa an eastern state of India. The capital is Bhubaneswar. (155,707 sq km/ 60,103 sq miles; pop. 26,370,300)

Orkney Islands a group of some 90 islands off the northeast coast of Scotland. The capital is Kirkwall. (976 sq km/377 sq miles; pop. 19,000)

Orlando a city in central Florida, and the focus for visitors to Disney World and Cape Canaveral. (Pop. city 137,100/metropolitan area 824,100)

Orléans a city in north central France, on the River Loire. (Pop. 225,000)

Osaka a port on south Honshu Island, and the third largest city in Japan after Tokyo and Yokohama. (Pop. 2,636,300)

Osijek a city in eastern Croatia, on the Drava River. It was formerly called Esseg. (Pop. 158,800)

Oslo the capital of Norway, and its main port, in the southeast of the country. From 1624 to 1925 it was called Christiania (or Kristiania). (Pop. city 448,800/ metropolitan area 566,500)

Otranto, Strait of the waterway separating the heel of Italy from Albania.

Ottawa the capital of Canada, in eastern Ontario, on the Ottawa River. (Pop. 718,000)

Ottawa, River a river of central Canada which flows into the St Lawrence at Montreal. (Length 1271 km/790 miles)

Ouagadougou the capital of Burkina, situated in the centre of the country. (Pop. 286,500)

Oviedo a steel making city in northern Spain, capital of the province of Asturias. (Pop. 190,100)

Oxford an old university city, and county town of Oxfordshire, England. (Pop. 117,000)

Oxfordshire a county in southern central England. (2611 sq km/1008 sq miles; pop. 558,000)

Oxus, River *see* **Amudar'ya, River.**

Pacific Ocean the largest and deepest ocean on Earth, situated between Asia and Australia to the west and the Americas to the east. (165,384,000 sq km/ 63,838,000 sq miles)

Padang a port and the capital of West Sumatra, Indonesia. (Pop. 480,900)

Padua a historic city in Veneto, northeast Italy. (Pop. 228,700)

Painted Desert a desert of colorful rocks in northern Arizona, USA. (19,400 sq km/7500 sq miles)

Pakistan (*Area* 796,095 sq km (307,372 sq miles); *population* 105,400,000; *capital* Islamabad; *other major cities* Faisalabad, Hyderabad, Karachi, Lahore; *form of government* Federal Islamic Republic; *religion* Sunni Islam, Shia Islam; *currency* Pakistan rupee). Pakistan lies just north of the Tropic of Cancer and the Arabian Sea. The valley of the Indus river splits the country into a highland region in the west, and a lowland region in the east. In the north are some of the world's highest mountains. A weak form of tropical monsoon climate occurs over most of the country, and conditions in the north and west are arid. Most agriculture is subsistence, with wheat and rice as the main crops. Cotton is the main cash crop. Industry concentrates on food processing, textiles and consumer goods.

Palau *see* **Belau.**

Palembang a port and the capital of South Sumatra, on the southeast coast. (Pop. 787,200)

Palermo the capital of Sicily, Italy, on the northwest coast. (Pop. 718,900)

Palestine a disputed area of the Middle East which encompassed the modern countries of Israel and parts of Jordan and Egypt.

Palma (Palma de Mallorca) The capital of Majorca and of the Balearic Islands. (Pop. 304,400)

Palma, La *see* **Canary Islands.**

Palm Beach a resort on an island off the east coast of Florida, USA, with the manufacturing centre of West Palm Beach on the mainland opposite. (Pop. Palm Beach 10,700/metropolitan area 692,200)

Pamir a region of high plateaux in central Asia which straddles the borders of Tajikistan, Afghanistan and China.

Pampas the flat grasslands of central Argentina.

Pamplona a city in northeastern Spain, famous for its bull-running festival in July. (Pop. 183,100)

Panama (*Area* 77,082 sq km (29,761 sq miles); *population* 2,320,000; *capital* Panama City; *other major cities* San Miguelito, Colón; *form of government* Republic; *religion* RC; *currency* Balboa). Panama is located at the narrowest point in Central America, where only 58 km (36 miles) of land separates the Caribbean Sea from the Pacific Ocean, and the Panama Canal provides a major shipping route. The climate is tropical, with high temperatures throughout the year. The country is heavily forested, and very little is cultivated. Rice is the staple food, and hardwoods a main export. The economy is heavily dependent on the Canal as a major foreign currency earner.

Panama Canal a canal 64 km (40 miles) long that runs through the centre of Panama, linking the Caribbean to the Pacific. It was completed in 1914.

Panama City the capital of Panama, situated at the Pacific end of the Panama Canal. (Pop. 502,000)

Panay *see* **Visayan Islands.**

Papeete the capital of French Polynesia, on the northwest coast of Tahiti. (Pop. 62,700)

Papua New Guinea (*Area* 462,840 sq km (178,703 sq miles); population 3,800,000; *capital* Port Moresby; *form of government* Constitutional Monarchy; *religion* Protestantism, RC; *currency* Kina). Papua New Guinea, in the southwest Pacific, comprises the eastern half of the island of New Guinea, together with hundreds of islands, of which New Britain, Bougainville and New Ireland are the largest. The country has a mountainous interior surrounded by broad swampy plains. The climate is tropical, with high temperatures and heavy rainfall. Subsistence farming is the main economic activity. Timber is cut for export. Minerals such as copper, gold, silver and oil form the mainstay of the economy.

Paracel Islands a group of islands lying some 300 km (185 miles) east of Vietnam, owned by China but claimed by Vietnam.

Paraguay (*Area* 406,752 sq km (157,047 sq miles); *population* 4,160,000; *capital* Asunción; *other major city* Ciudad Alfredo Stroessner; *form of government* Republic; *religion* RC; *currency* Guaraní). Paraguay, landlocked in central South America, is bordered by Bolivia, Brazil and Argentina. The climate is tropical, with abundant rain and a short dry season. The River Paraguay splits the country into the Chaco, a flat semi-arid plain of huge meat-exporting cattle ranches on the west, and a partly forested undulating plateau on the east where almost 95% of the population live. Crops grown on the fertile plains include cassava, sugar cane, maize, cotton and soya beans. The world's largest hydroelectric dam has been built at Itaipú and cheap power from this has stimulated industry.

Paraguay, River a major river of South America. It flows south from Brazil through Paraguay to join the Parana. (Length 1920 km/1190 miles)

Paramaribo the capital and main port of SURINAME. (Pop. 180,000)

Parana, River the second longest river in South America. It rises in Brazil and flows south to join the River Plate. (Length 4200 km/2610 miles)

Paris the capital of France, in the north of the country, on the River Seine. (Pop. city 2,188,900/ Greater Paris 8,761,700)

Parma a historic city in northern Italy, in Emilia-Romagna. (Pop. 176,800)

Páros an island in the Cyclades, Greece. (194 sq km/75 sq miles; pop. 7400)

Pasadena a city in southwest California, USA. (Pop. 125,000)

Pascua, Isla de *see* **Easter Island.**

Patagonia a cold desert in southern Argentina and Chile.

Patna the capital of the state of Bihar, in northeast India, on the River Ganges. (Pop. 918,900)

Patras a port and the main city of the Peloponnese, Greece. (Pop. 154,000)

Peace River a river in western Canada, a tributary of the Slave/Mackenzie River, rising in British Columbia. (Length 1923 km/1195 miles)

Pearl Harbor a harbour and naval base on Oahu, Hawaii; the Japanese attack on the US fleet in 1941 drew the USA into World War II.

Pécs the main city of southwest Hungary. (Pop. 174,500)

Peeblesshire *see* **Borders.**

Peking *see* **Beijing.**

Pelée, Mount an active volcano on Martinique, which destroyed the town of St Pierre in 1902. (1397 m/4583 ft)

Peloponnese a broad peninsula of southern Greece, joined to the northern part of the country by the isthmus of Corinth.

Pembrokeshire *see* **Dyfed.**

Penang a state of west Malaysia comprising Penang Island and the mainland province of Wellesley.

Pennines a range of hills that runs down the middle of northern England from the Scottish border to the Midlands, rising to 894 m (2087 ft) at Cross Fell.

Pennsylvania a state of the northeastern USA situated mainly in the Appalachian Mountains. The capital is Harrisburg. (117,412 sq km/45,333 sq miles; pop. 11,853,000)

Perm' an industrial port on the Kama River in the western Urals of the Russian Federation. It was known as Molotov 1940-57. (Pop. 1,049,000)

Perpignan a cathedral town in southwestern France. (Pop. 140,000)

Persia *see* **Iran.**

Persian Gulf *see* **Gulf, The**

Perth (1) the state capital of Western Australia, which includes the port of Freemantle. (Pop. 969,000). (2) a city and former capital of Scotland, 55 km (35 miles) north of Edinburgh. (Pop. 42,000)

Perthshire *see* **Central Region** and **Tayside**.

Peru (*Area* 1,285,216 sq km (496,235 sq miles); *population* 22,330,000; *capital* Lima; *other major cities* Arequipa, Callao, Cuzco, Trujillo; *form of government* Republic; *religion* RC; *currency* Sol). Peru is located just south of the Equator, on the Pacific coast of South America. The country has three distinct regions from west to east: the desert coast, the wet and cool high sierra of the Andes, and the hot and humid tropical jungle of the Amazon Basin. Most large-scale agriculture is in the oases and irrigated river valleys that cut across the coastal desert. Sugar and cotton are the main exports. The fishing industry was once the largest in the world, but recently the shoals have become depleted. The main source of wealth is oil, but new discoveries are needed as present reserves are near exhaustion.

Peshawar a historic town in northwest Pakistan at the foot of the Khyber Pass. (Pop. 555,000)

Petrograd *see* **St Petersburg.**

Philadelphia a port and city in southeast Pennsylvania, the fourth largest city in the USA. (Pop. city 1,688,700/metropolitan area 4,768,400)

Philippines (*Area* 300,000 sq km (115,830 sq miles); *population* 60,500,000; *capital* Manila; *other major cities* Cebu, Davao, Quezon City; *form of government* Republic; *religions* RC, Aglipayan, Sunni Islam; *currency* : Philippine peso). The Philippines comprise of a group of mountainous islands, in the western Pacific, which are scattered over a great area. Earthquakes are common. The climate is humid, with high temperatures and high rainfall. Typhoons are frequent. Rice and maize are the main subsistence crops and coconuts, sugar cane, pineapples and bananas are grown for export. Copper is a major export and industries include textiles, food processing, chemicals and electrical engineering.

Phnom Penh the capital of CAMBODIA, in the south of the country. (Pop. 500,000)

Phoenix the state capital of Arizona, USA. (Pop. city 853,300/metropolitan area 1,714,800)

Piedmont (Piemonte) a region of northwest Italy. The main town is Turin.

Pierre the capital of South Dakota, USA. (Pop. 121,400)

Pietermaritzburg a city in eastern South Africa and capital of Natal. (Pop. 180,000)

Pilsen *see* **Plzen.**

Piraeus the main port of Greece, close to Athens, on the Aegean Sea. (Pop. 196,400)

Pisa a city in northwestern Italy on the River Arno, famous for its leaning bell tower. (Pop. 104,300)

Pitcairn Island an island and British colony in the south Pacific, where mutineers from H.M.S. Bounty settled (after 1790).

Pittsburgh an industrial city in western Pennsylvania, USA. (Pop. city 402,600/ metropolitan area 2,172,800)

Plate, River (Rio de la Plata) the huge estuary of the Parana and Uruguay Rivers in southeast South America, with Uruguay to the north and Argentina to the south.

Plenty, Bay of the broad inlet on the north coast of the North Island of New Zealand.

Plovdiv a major market town in Bulgaria. (Pop. 373,000)

Plymouth (1) a port and naval base in southwest England and the place from which the Pilgrim Fathers set sail in the Mayflower in 1620. (Pop. 255,000). (2) the capital of the island of Montserrat. (Pop. 3200) (3) a town in Massachusetts, which has grown from the first European settlement in New England, established by the Pilgrim Fathers of the Mayflower. (Pop. 37,100)

Plzen (Pilsen) an industrial city in western Bohemia, Czech Republic. Pilsner lager beer was first produced here in 1842. (Pop. 174,100)

Po, River the longest river in Italy, flowing eastwards from the Alps across a fertile plain to the Adriatic Sea. (Length 642 km/405 miles)

Pohnpei (Ponape) the island on which Kolonia, the capital of the Federated States of Micronesia, stands.

Pointe-à-Pitre the main port of Guadeloupe. (Pop. 23,000)

Poitiers a historic university city in south central France (Pop. 80,000).

Poland (*Area* 312,677 sq km (120,725 sq miles; *population* 37,930,000; *capital* Warsaw (Warszawa); *other major cities* Gdansk, Kraków, Lódz, Wroclow; *form of government* Republic; *religion* RC; *currency* Zloty). Poland, situated on the North European Plain, consists mainly of lowlands and has long severe winters and short warm summers. Agriculture is predominantly small scale. The main crops are potatoes, wheat, barley, sugar beet and fodder crops. The industrial sector of the economy is large scale. Poland has large deposits of coal and reserves of natural gas, copper and silver. Vast forests stretching inland from the coast supply the paper and furniture industries.

Polynesia the largest of the three island divisions of the Pacific, the others being Micronesia and Melanesia. The group includes Samoa, the Cook, Society and Marquesas Islands, and Tonga.

Pomerania a region of northwest Poland, on the Baltic coast.

Pompeii an ancient city near Naples which was smothered by ash from an eruption of Vesuvius in AD79.

Ponape *see* **Pohnpei.**

Pondicherry the former capital of French India (1683–1954), in the southeast of the country. (Pop. 251,400)

Ponta Delgada a port and the capital of the AZORES, on São Miguel Island. (Pop. 21,200)

Poona (Pune) a historic and industrial city east of Bombay, in western India.

(Pop. 1,203,400)

Popocatépetl a volcano, twinned with Ixtacihuatl, 65 km (40 miles) southeast of Mexico City. (5452 m/17,887 ft)

Port-au-Prince the main port and capital of Haiti. (Pop. 888,000)

Port Elizabeth a port and industrial city in Cape Province, South Africa. (Pop. 585,400)

Port Harcourt the second port of Nigeria after Lagos. (Pop. 288,900)

Port Jackson the great natural harbour also called Sydney Harbour.

Portland (1) a port on the Atlantic coast of the USA, in Maine. (Pop. city 61,800/metropolitan area 210,000). (2) a port on the Williamette River in Oregon, USA. (Pop. city 365,900/metropolitan area 1,340,900)

Port Louis the capital and main port of MAURITIUS, on the east coast of the island. (Pop. 160,000)

Port Moresby the capital and main port of Papua New Guinea, in the southeast. (Pop. 126,000)

Porto *see* **Oporto.**

Porto Alegre a port and regional capital of southern Brazil. (Pop. city 1,126,000)

Port of Spain the capital and chief port of TRINIDAD AND TOBAGO. (Pop. city 62,700/metropolitan area 443,000)

Porto Novo the administrative capital of Benin. (Pop. 209,000)

Port Said the port at the Mediterranean end of the Suez Canal, Egypt. (Pop. 342,000)

Portsmouth a port and major naval base in southern England. (Pop. 192,000)

Port Stanley the capital of the Falkland Islands. (Pop. 1000)

Portugal (*Area* 92,389 sq km (35,671 sq miles); *population* 10,300,000; *capital* Lisbon (Lisboa); *other major cities* Braga, Coimbra, Oporto, Setúbal; *form of government* Republic; *religion* : RC; *currency* Escudo). Portugal, in the southwest corner of Europe, makes up about 15% of the Iberian peninsula. The most mountainous areas lie to the north of the Tagus river, while south of it lies the Alentajo, an area of wheat fields and cork plantations, which continues to the hinterland of the Algarve with its beautiful groves of almond, fig and olive trees. Agriculture employs one-quarter of the labour force. Manufacturing industry includes textiles and clothing for export, and footwear, food processing and cork products. Tourism, particularly in the south, is the main foreign currency earner.

Port-Vila the capital and chief port of Vanuatu. (Pop. 17,500)

Posen *see* **Poznan.**

Potsdam a city just southwest of Berlin, Germany. (Pop. 137,700)

Powys a county in mid-Wales created in 1974 out of Breconshire, Montgomeryshire, and Radnorshire. The administrative centre is Llandrindod Wells. (5077 sq km/1960 sq miles; pop. 111,000)

Poznan (Posen) a historic city in central western Poland. (Pop. 571,000)

Prague (Praha) the capital and principal city of the Czech Republic, situated on the Vltava River. (Pop. 1,235,000)

Praia the capital of Cape Verde. (Pop. 4055)

Prairies *see* **Great Plains.**

Pressburg *see* **Bratislava.**

Pretoria the administrative capital of SOUTH AFRICA, 48 km (30 miles) north of Johannesburg in the Transvaal. (Pop. 739,000)

Prince Edward Island the smallest of the provinces of Canada, an island in the Gulf of St Lawrence. The provincial capital is Charlottetown. (5660 sq km/2185 sq miles; pop. 123,000)

Principe *see* **São Tomé and Principe.**

Pristina the capital of the autonomous province of Kosovo in Serbia. (Pop. 216,000)

Provence a historical region of coastal southeast France.

Providence a port, and the state capital of Rhode Island, USA. (Pop. city 154,100/metropolitan area 1,095,000)

Prussia a historical state of Germany, centreing on its capital, Berlin.

Puebla a major city 120 km (75 miles) southeast of Mexico City, and the capital of a state of the same name. (Pop. city 835,000)

Puerto Rico (*Area* 8897 sq km (3435 sq miles); *population* 3,196,520; *capital* San Juan; *form of government* Self-governing Commonwealth (USA); *relgion* RC, Protestantism; *currency* US dollar). Puerto Rico, the most easterly of the Greater Antilles in the Caribbean, is a self-governing commonwealth in association with the USA. The climate is tropical, modified slightly by cooling sea breezes. The main mountains on Puerto Rico are the Cordillera Central. Dairy farming is the most important agricultural activity. Tax relief and cheap labour encourages American businesses to be based in Puerto Rico. Products include textiles, clothing, electrical and electronic goods, plastics and chemicals. Tourism is another developing industry.

Puglia (Apulia) a region of southeast Italy. The regional capital is Bari. (19,250 sq km/7500 sq miles; pop. 3,848,000)

Pune *see* **Poona.**

Punjab (1) a state in northwestern India. The capital is Chandigarh. (50,362 sq km/19,440 sq miles; pop. 16,789,000) (2) a fertile province in the north of Pakistan. The capital is Lahore. (205,344 sq km/79,283 sq miles; pop. 47,292,000)

Pusan a major port, and the second largest city in South Korea after Seoul. (Pop. 3,160,000)

Putumayo, River a river of northwest South America, rising in the Andes and flowing southeast to join the Amazon. (Length 1900 km/1180 miles)

Pyongyang (Pyeongyang) an industrial city and the capital of North Korea. (Pop. 1,700,000)

Pyrénées a range of mountains that runs from the Bay of Biscay to the Mediterranean, along the border between France and Spain. The highest point is Pico d'Aneto (3404 m/11,170 ft).

Qacentina *see* **Constantine.**

Qatar (*Area* 11,000 sq km (4247 sq miles); *population* 371,863; *capital* Doha (Ad Dawhah); *form of government* Monarchy; *religions* Wahhabi Sunni Islam; *currency* Qatari riyal). Qatar is a small emirate that lies halfway along the coast of The Gulf. It consists of a low barren peninsula and a few small islands. The climate is hot and uncomfortably humid in summer, and the winters are mild with rain in the north. The herding of sheep, goats and some cattle is carried out and the country is famous for its high-quality camels. The discovery and exploitation of oil has resulted in a high standard of living. In order to diversify the economy, new industries have been developed.

Qazvin (Kasvin) a historic town in northwest Iran. (Pop. 244,300)

Qingdao a city in Shangdong province in northeastern China. (Pop. 1,300,000)

Qinghai a province of northwestern China. The capital is Xining. (720,000 sq km/280,000 sq miles; pop. 3,720,000)

Qiqihar a manufacturing city in Heilongjiang province, China. (Pop. 1,000,000)

Qom (Qum) a holy city in central northern Iran. (Pop. 424,100)

Québec the largest province of Canada, in the east of the country, and also the name of the capital of the province. The majority of the population are French-speaking. (1,358,000 sq km/524,300 sq miles; pop. province 6,438,000/city 164,580)

Queen Charlotte Islands a group of some 150 islands lying 160 km (100 miles) off the west coast of Canada. (9790 sq km/3780 sq miles; pop. 5620)

Queen Charlotte Strait a waterway, some 26 km (16 miles) wide, between the northeastern coast of Vancouver Island and the mainland of Canada.

Queensland the northeastern state of Australia. The state capital is Brisbane. (1,272,200 sq km/491,200 sq miles; pop. 2,488,000)

Quercy a former province of southwestern France, around Cahors.

Quetta the capital of the province of Baluchistan, Pakistan. (Pop. 285,000)

Quezon City a major city and university town, now a part of Metro Manila, and the administrative capital of the Philippines from 1948 to 1976. (Pop. 1,165,000)

Quito the capital of Ecuador, lying just south of the Equator, 2850 m (9350 ft) high in the Andes. (Pop. 1,110,000)

Qum *see* **Qom.**

Qwaqwa a non-independent black homeland in South Africa occupied by South Sotho people, bordering Lesotho. (Pop. 305,000)

Rabat the capital of MOROCCO, in the northwest, on the Atlantic coast. (Pop. 520,000)

Radnorshire *see* **Powys.**

Ragusa *see* **Dubrovnik.**

Rainier, Mount *see* **Cascade Range.**

Rajasthan a state of northwest India. The state capital is Jiapur. (342,239 sq km/132,104 sq miles; pop. 34,261,000)

Raleigh the state capital of North Carolina, USA. (Pop. city 169,300/metropolitan area 609,300)

Ranchi an industrial town in the state of Bihar, India. (Pop. 502,800)

Rand, The *see* **Witwatersrand.**

Rangoon (Yangon) the capital of Burma, and an important port on the mouth of the Rangoon River. (Pop. 2,549,000)

Rarotonga the largest of the Cook Islands, with the capital of the islands, Avarua, on its north coast. (67 sq km/26 sq miles; pop. 9500)

Ras al Khaymah one of the United Arab Emirates, in the extreme northeast, on the Musandam peninsula. (1036 sq km/400 sq miles; pop. 83,000)

Ravenna a city in northeastern Italy, noted for its Byzantine churches. (Pop. 136,500)

Rawalpindi a military town of ancient origins in northern Pakistan. (Pop. 928,000)

Recife a regional capital of eastern Brazil. (Pop. 1,205,000)

Red River (1) a river of the southern USA, rising in Texas and flowing east to join the Mississippi. (Length 1639km/ 1018miles). (2) (Song Hong; Yuan Jiang) a river that rises in southwest China and flows southeast across the north of Vietnam to the Gulf of Tongking. (Length 800 km/500 miles)

Red Sea a long, narrow sea lying between the Arabian Peninsula and the coast of northeast Africa.

Reggio di Calabria a port on the toe of southern Italy. (Pop. 177,700)

Reggio nell'Emilia a town of Roman origins in northeastern Italy. (Pop. 130,300)

Regina the capital of the province of Saskatchewan, Canada. (Pop. 164,000)

Reims *see* **Rheims.**

Renfrewshire *see* **Strathclyde.**

Rennes a industrial city in northeastern France. (Pop. 241,300)

Reno a gambling centre in Nevada, USA. (Pop. city 105,600/metropolitan area 211,500)

Réunion an island to the east of Madagascar, an overseas department of France. The capital is Saint-Denis. (2515 sq km/970 sq miles; pop. 530,000)

Reykjavik the capital and main port of ICELAND, on the southwest coast. (Pop. 87,300)

Reynosa a town in northeastern Mexico, on the border with the USA. (Pop. 347,000)

Rheims (Reims) a historic city in France, and the centre of the production of champagne. (Pop. 204,000)

Rhine (Rhein, Rhin, Rijn), River one of the most important rivers of Europe. It rises in the Swiss Alps, flows north through Germany and then west through the Netherlands to the North Sea. (Length 1320km/ 825miles)

Rhode Island the smallest state in the USA. The state capital is Providence. (3144 sq km/1214 sq miles; pop. 968,000)

Rhodes (Rodhos) the largest of the Dodecanese group of islands belonging to Greece. (1399 sq km/540 sq miles; pop. 88,500)

Rhône, River a major river of Europe, rising in the Swiss Alps and flowing west into France, and then south to its delta on the Golfe de Lion. (Length 812 km/ 505 miles)

Richmond the state capital of Virginia. (Pop. city 219,100/metropolitan area 796,100)

Ridings, The *see* **Yorkshire.**

Riga a Baltic port, and the capital of Latvia. (Pop. 875,000)

Rijeka (Fiume) a port on the Adriatic, in Croatia. (Pop. 193,000)

Rijn, River *see* **Rhine, River.**

Rimini a popular resort on the Adriatic Sea, northeastern Italy. (Pop. 129,500)

Rio Bravo *see* **Rio Grande.**

Rio de Janeiro a major port and former capital (1763–1960) of Brazil, situated in the southeast of the country. (Pop. 5,094,000)

Rio Grande (Rio Bravo) a river of North America, rising in the state of Colorado, USA, and flowing southeast to the Gulf of Mexico. For much of its length it forms the border between the USA and Mexico. (Length 3078 km/1885 miles)

Rioja, La an autonomous area in the south of the Basque region of Spain, famous for its fine wine. (Pop. 254,000)

Riyadh the capital and commercial centre of SAUDI ARABIA. (Pop. 300,000)

Road Town the capital of the British Virgin Islands. (Pop. 3000)

Roca, Cabo da a cape sticking out into the Atlantic in central Portugal, to the west of Lisbon, the western-most point of mainland Europe.

Rockall a tiny, rocky, uninhabited island lying 400 km (250 miles) west of Ireland, and claimed by the UK.

Rocky Mountains (Rockies) a huge mountain range in western North America, extending some 4800 km (3000 miles) from British Columbia in Canada to New Mexico in the USA.

Rodhos *see* **Rhodes.**

Romania (*Area* 237,500 sq km (91,699 sq miles); *population* 23,000,000; *capital* Bucharest (Bucuresti); *other major cities* Brasov, Constanta, Timisoara; *form of government* Republic; *religions* Romanian Orthodox, RC; *currency* Leu). Apart from a small extension towards the Black Sea, Romania is almost a circular country located in southeast Europe. The Carpathian Mountains run through the north, east and centre of Romania, enclosed by a ring of rich agricultural plains and Transylvania within the Carpathian arc. Romania has cold snowy winters and hot summers. Agriculture in Romania has been neglected in favour of industry, but major crops include maize, sugar beet, wheat, potatoes and grapes for wine. There are now severe food shortages. Industry is state owned and includes mining, metallurgy, mechanical engineering and chemicals.

Rome (Roma) the historic capital of Italy, on the River Tiber, in the centre of the country near the west coast. (Pop. 2,831,300)

Rosario an industrial and commercial city on the River Parana in Argentina. (Pop. 935,500)

Roscommon a county in the northwest of the Republic of Ireland, with a county town of the same name. (2462 sq km/950 sq miles; pop. county 54,500)

Roseau the capital of Dominica. (Pop. 17,000)

Ross and Cromarty *see* **Highland region.**

Ross Sea a large branch of the Antarctic Ocean, south of New Zealand.

Rostock a major port on the Baltic coast of Germany. (Pop. 242,000)

Rostov-na-Donau (Rostov-on-Don) A major industrial city on the River Don, near the northwestern extremity of the Sea of Azov in southeastern Russian Federation. (Pop. 983,000)

Rotterdam the largest city in the Netherlands and the busiest port in the world. (Pop. city 558,800/ Greater Rotterdam 1,024,700)

Roubaix *see* **Lille-Roubaix-Turcoing.**

Rouen a port on the River Seine in northern France. (Pop. 385,800)

Rousillon *see* **Languedoc-Rousillon.**

Roxburghshire *see* **Borders.**

R.S.F.S.R. *see* **Russian Soviet Federated Socialist Republic.**

Rub al-Khali the so-called "Empty Quarter," a vast area of sandy desert straddling the borders of Saudi Arabia, Oman and Yemen. (650,000 sq km/ 251,000 sq miles)

Ruhr, River the river in northwestern Germany whose valley forms the industrial heartland of western Germany. It joins the Rhine at Duisburg. (Length 235 km/ 146 miles)

Russia the old name for the Russian Empire, latterly used loosely to refer to the former USSR. or the Russian Federation.

Russian Federation, The, (*Area* 17,075,400 sq km (6,592,800 sq miles) ; *population* 142,117,000 ; *capital* Moscow (Moskva) ; *other major cities* St Petersburg (formerly Leningrad), Nizhniy Novgorod, Novosibirsk; *form of government* Republic; *religions* Russian Orthodox, Sunni Islam, Shia Islam, RC ; *currency* Rouble). The Russian Federation, which is the largest country in the world, extends from Eastern Europe through the Ural Mountains east to the Pacific Ocean. The Caucasus form its boundary in the south. The environment ranges from vast frozen wastes in the north to subtropical deserts in the south. Agriculture is organized into either state or collective farms, which mainly produce sugar beet, cotton, potatoes and vegetables. The country has extensive reserves of coal, oil, gas, iron ore and manganese. Major industries include iron and steel, cement, transport equipment, engineering, armaments, electronic equipment and chemicals. The Russian Federation became independent in 1991.

Russian Soviet Federated Socialist Republic (R.S.F.S.R.) the former name for the Russian Federation.

Rutanzige, Lake *see* **Edward, Lake.**

Rutland once the smallest county of England, now a part of Leicestershire.

Ruwenzori a mountain range on the border between Zaïre and Uganda, also known as the Mountains of the Moon. The highest peak is Mount Ngaliema

(Mount Stanley) (5109 m/16,763 ft).

Rwanda (*Area* 26,338 sq km (10,169 sq miles); *population* 6,710,000; *capital* Kigali; *form of government* Republic; *religions* RC, Animism; *currency* Rwanda franc). Rwanda is a small republic in the heart of central Africa which lies just 2° south of the Equator. Active volcanoes are found in the north. The climate is highland tropical, with temperatures decreasing with altitude. The soils are not fertile and subsistence agriculture dominates the economy. Staple food crops are sweet potatoes, cassava, dry beans, sorghum and potatoes. The main cash crops are coffee, tea and pyrethrum.

Ryazan an industrial city 175 km (110 miles) southeast of Moscow, Russian Federation. (Pop. 488,000)

Ryukyu Islands (Nansei-shoto) a chain of islands belonging to Japan stretching 1200 km (750 miles) between Japan and Taiwan. (Pop. 1,366,600)

Saarbrücken an industrial city of western Germany, near the border with France. (Pop. 189,000)

Sabah the more easterly of the two states of Malaysia on northern coast of the island of Borneo. (73,700 sq km/28,450 sq miles; pop. 1,034,000)

Sacramento the state capital of California. (Pop. city 304,100/metropolitan area 1,219,600)

Sahara Desert the world's largest desert, spanning much of northern Africa, from the Atlantic to the Red Sea, and from the Mediterranean to Mali, Niger, Chad and Sudan.

Sahel a semi-arid belt crossing Africa from Senegal to Sudan, separating the Sahara from tropical Africa to the south.

Saigon *see* **Ho Chi Minh City.**

Saint John a port at the mouth of the Saint John River, on the Atlantic coast of New Brunswick, Canada. (Pop. 114,000)

Saipan the largest and most heavily populated of the Northern Marianas. The island group's capital, Susupe, is on the western side. (122 sq km/47 sq miles; pop. 17,000)

Sakhalin a large island to the north of Japan, but belonging to the Russian Federation. (76,400 sq km/29,500 sq miles; pop. 660,000)

Salamanca an elegant university town in western Spain, and the name of the surrounding province. (Pop. town 167,100)

Salem (1) a city in Massachusetts, USA. (Pop. city 38,600/metropolitan area 259,100). (2) the state capital of Oregon, USA. (Pop. city 90,300/metropolitan area 255,200)

Saloniki (Thessaloníki) the second largest city in Greece. (Pop. 706,200)

Salt Lake City the state capital of Utah. (Pop. city 164,800/metropolitan area 1,025,300)

Salvador a port on the central east coast of Brazil and capital of the state of Bahia. (Pop. 1,507,000)

Salvador, El *see* **El Salvador.**

Salween, River a river rising in Tibet and flowing south through Burma, forming part of the border with Thailand, to the Andaman Sea. (Length 2900 km/1800 miles)

Salzburg a city in central northern Austria, and the name of the surrounding state, of which it is the capital. (Pop. city 140,000)

Samar the third largest island of the Philippines. (13,080 sq km/5050 sq miles; pop. 1,100,000)

Samara a major industrial city and port on the River Volga in the Russian Federation. (Pop. 1,251,000)

Samarkand an ancient city in Uzbekistan. (Pop. 515,000)

Samoa, American an American territory, comprising a group of five islands, in the central South Pacific. The capital is Pago Pago. (197 sq km/76 sq miles; pop. 36,000)

Sámos a Greek island 2 km (1 mile) off the coast of Turkey. (Pop. 31,600)

Samsun a port on the Black Sea coast of Turkey, and the name of the surrounding province, of which it is the capital. (Pop. town 280,100)

San'a the capital of Yemen, situated in the middle of the country. (Pop. 210,000)

San Antonio an industrial centre in southern Texas, USA. (Pop. city 842,800/metropolitan area 1,188,500)

San Diego a major port and industrial city in southern California, USA. (Pop. city 960,500/metropolitan area 1,063,900)

San Francisco a Pacific port and commercial centre in California. (Pop. city 712,800/metropolitan area 5,684,600)

San Francisco Bay an inlet of the Pacific Ocean in western California, USA, joined to the ocean by the Golden Gate Strait.

San José the capital of Costa Rica, in its centre. (Pop. 249,000).

San Jose a city in California, USA, and the focus of "Silicon Valley." (Pop. city 686,200/metropolitan area 1,371,500)

San Juan the capital of Puerto Rico, and a major port. (Pop. 435,000)

Sankt Peterburg *see* **St Petersburg.**

San Lorenzo del Escorial *see* **Escorial, El.**

San Luis Potosi an elegant colonial city and provincial capital in north-central Mexico. (Pop. city 407,000)

San Marino (*Area* 61 sq km (24 sq miles); *population* 22,746; *capital* San Marino; *form of government* Republic; *religion* RC; *currency* : Lira). San Marino is a tiny landlocked state in central Italy, lying in the eastern foothills of the Apennines. It has wooded mountains and pasture land with a mild Mediterranean climate. The majority of the population work on the land or in forestry. Much of the country's revenue comes from tourism and duty-free sales.

San Miguel de Tucumán a regional capital in northwestern Argentina. (Pop. 497,000)

San Pedro Sula the second largest city in Guatemala. (Pop. 398,000)

San Salvador (1) the capital and major city of El Salvador. (Pop. 884,100) (2) a small island in the centre of the Bahamas, the first place in the New World reached by Columbus (1492). (Pop. 850)

San Sebastián a port and industrial city in northeastern Spain. (Pop. 175,600)

Santa Barbara a resort and industrial centre in southern California, USA. (Pop. city 76,900/metropolitan area 322,800)

Santa Fe the state capital of New Mexico, USA. (Pop. city 52,300/metropolitan area 100,500)

Santander a port and industrial city in northeastern Spain. (Pop. 180,300)

Santiago the capital and principal city of Chile. (Pop. 4,132,000)

Santiago de Cuba a port and provincial capital in southern Cuba. (Pop. 345,000)

Santo Domingo the capital and main port of the Dominican Republic. (Pop. 1,313,000)

Santorini a volcanic island in the Cyclades group of Greek islands. (84 sq km/32 sq miles; pop. 7100)

Santos the largest port in Brazil, 60 km (38 miles) southeast of São Paulo. (Pop. 417,000)

São Francisco, River a river of eastern Brazil, important for its hydroelectric dams. (Length 2900 km/1800 miles)

Saône, River a river of eastern France which merges with the River Rhône at Lyons. (Length 480 km/300 miles)

São Paulo a major industrial city in southeastern Brazil, and capital of the state called São Paulo. (Pop. city 8,500,000/metropolitan area 16,000,000)

São Tomé the capital of São Tomé and Principe. (Pop. 25,000)

São Tomé and Príncipe (*Area* 964 sq km (372 sq miles); *population* 115,600; *capital* São Tomé; *form of government* Republic; *religion* RC; *currency* Dobra). São Tomé and Príncipe are volcanic islands which lie off the west coast of Africa. The coastal areas are hot and humid, with heavy rainfall from October to May. Some 70% of the workforce work on the land, mainly in state-owned cocoa plantations.

São Vincente, Cabo de (Cape St Vincent) the southwestern corner of Portugal.

Sapporo a modern city, founded in the late 19th century as the capital of Hokkaido Island, Japan. (Pop. 1,543,000)

Saragossa *see* **Zaragoza.**

Sarajevo the capital of Bosnia Herzegovina. (Pop. 448,500)

Saransk an industrial town, capital of the republic of Mordovia in the Russian Federation. (Pop. 301,000)

Saratov an industrial city and river port on the Volga, Russian Federation. (Pop. 894,000)

Sarawak a state of Malaysia occupying much of the northwestern coast of Borneo. (125,204 sq km/48,342 sq miles; pop. 1,323,000)

Sardinia (Sardegna) the second largest island of the Mediterranean after Sicily, also belonging to Italy, lying just south of Corsica. The capital is Cagliari. (24,089 sq km/9301 sq miles; pop. 1,633,400)

Sark *see* **Channel Islands.**

Saskatchewan a province of western Canada, in the Great Plains. The capital is Regina. (651,900 sq km/251,000 sq miles; pop. 968,000)

Saskatchewan, River a river of Canada, rising in the Rocky Mountains and flowing westwards into Lake Winnipeg. (Length 1930 km/1200 miles)

Saskatoon a city on the Saskatchewan River. (Pop. 154,000)

Saudi Arabia (*Area* 2,149,690 sq km (829,995 sq miles); *population* 12,000,000;*capital* Riyadh (Ar Riyah); *other major cities* Mecca, Jeddah, Medina, Ta'if; *form of government* Monarchy; *religions* Sunni Islam, Shia Islam; *currency* Rial). Saudi Arabia occupies over 70% of the Arabian Peninsula. Over 95% of the country is desert and the largest expanse of sand in the world, "Rub'al-Khali," is found in the southeast of the country. In the west, a narrow, humid coastal plain along the Red Sea is backed by steep mountains. The climate is hot with very little rain. The main products are dates, tomatoes, water melons and wheat. The country's prosperity, however, is based almost entirely on the exploitation of its vast reserves of oil and natural gas.

Savannah the main port of Georgia, USA. (Pop. city 145,400/metropolitan area 323,900)

Savoie (Savoy) a mountainous former duchy in southeast France, which has been a part of France since 1860 and is now divided into two departments, Savoie and Haute Savoie.

Scafell Pike *see* **Lake District**.

Scandinavia the countries on, or near, the Scandinavian peninsula in northeast Europe, usually taken to include Norway, Sweden, Denmark and Finland.

Scapa Flow an anchorage surrounded by the Orkney Islands, famous as a wartime naval base.

Schelde a river rising in France and then flowing through Belgium and the Netherlands to the North Sea. (Length 435 km/270 miles)

Schlesien *see* **Silesia.**

Schleswig-Holstein the northern-most state of Germany. The capital is Kiel. (Pop. 2,614,000)

Schwarzwald *see* **Black Forest.**

Scilly, Isles of a group of islands off the southwest tip of England. The main islands are St Mary's, St Martin's and Tresco. (Pop. 2000)

Scotland a country of the UK, occupying the northern part of Great Britain. The capital is Edinburgh. (78,762 sq km/30,410 sq miles; pop. 5,035,000)

Seattle a port in Washington State, USA. (Pop. city 490,000/metropolitan area 1,677,000)

Seine, River a river of northern France, flowing through Paris to the English Channel. (Length 775 km/482 miles)

Selkirkshire *see* **Borders.**

Semarang a port and textile city on the north coast of Java, Indonesia. (Pop. 503,200)

Sendai a city in the east of Honshu Island, Japan. (Pop. 700,200)

Senegal (*Area* 196,722 sq km (75,954 sq miles); *population* 7,170,000; *capital* Dakar; *other major cities* Kaolack, Thies,St Louis; *form of government* Republic; *religions* Sunni Islam, RC; *currency* Franc CFA). Senegal is a former French colony in West Africa which extends from the most western point in Africa, Cape Verde, to the border with Mali. Senegal is mostly low-lying and covered by savanna apart from the Fouta Djalon mountains in the south. The climate is tropical. Almost 80% of the labour force work in agriculture, growing groundnuts and cotton for export and millet, maize, rice and sorghum as subsistence crops.

Senegal River a West African river that flows through Guinea, Mali, Mauritania, and Senegal to the Atlantic. (Length 1790 km/1110 miles)

Seoul (Soul) the capital of South Korea, in its northwest. (Pop. 8,364,000)

Sepik a major river of Papua New Guinea. (Length 1200 km/750 miles)

Seram (Ceram) an island in the Maluku group, Indonesia. (17,148 sq km/6621 sq miles)

Serbia (Srbija) the largest republic of former Yugoslavia. The capital is Belgrade. (88,361 sq km/34,107 sq miles; pop. 9,314,000)

Sevastopol' a Black Sea port of the Ukraine. (Pop. 335,000)

Severn, River the longest river in the UK, flowing through Wales and the west of England. (Length 350 km/220 miles)

Seville (Sevilla) a historic, now industrial city in southern Spain, and also the name of the surrounding province. (Pop. city 653,800)

Seychelles (*Area* 280 sq km (108 sq miles); *population* 67,378*capital* Victoria; *form of government* Republic; *religion* RC; *currency* Seychelles rupee). Seychelles a group of volcanic islands which lie in the western Indian Ocean about 1200 km (746 miles) from the coast of East Africa. The climate is tropical maritime, with heavy rain. The staple food is coconut, imported rice and fish. Tourism accounts for about 90% of the country's foreign exchange earnings and employs one-third of the labour force.

's-Gravenhage *see* **Hague, The.**

Shaanxi a province of northwestern China. The capital is Xi'an. (190,000 sq km/ 73,000 sq miles; pop. 28,070,000)

Shandong a province of northern China, with its capital at Jinan. (150,000 sq km/ 58,000 sq miles; pop. 72,310,000)

Shanghai the largest city in China. An important port, it is situated on the delta of the Chang Jiang (Yangtze) River. (Pop. 11,860,000)

Shannon, River a river of the Republic of Ireland, and the longest river in the British Isles. It flows southwest into the Atlantic Ocean near Limerick. (Length 386 km/240 miles)

Shanxi a province of northern China, with its capital at Taiyuan. (150,000 sq km/ 58,000 sq miles; pop. 24,472,000)

Sharjah the fourth largest of the United Arab Emirates. Its capital is also Sharjah. (159,000 sq km/61,000 sq miles; pop. emirate 184,000/ city 126,000)

Shatt al Arab a waterway flowing into The Gulf along the disputed border between Iran and Iraq, formed where the Rivers Euphrates and Tigris converge some 170 km (105 miles) from the coast.

Sheffield a major industrial city in South Yorkshire, England. (Pop. 545,000)

Shenyang the capital of Liaoning province, China. (Pop. 4,000,000)

Shetland Islands a group of some 100 islands lying 160 km (100 miles) northeast of mainland Scotland. The capital is Lerwick. (1426 sq km/550 sq miles; pop. 28,000)

Shijiazhuang the capital of Hebei province, China. (Pop. 973,000)

Shikoku the smallest of the four main islands of Japan. (Pop. 4,227,200)

Shiraz a provincial capital of Iran, southeast of Tehran. (Pop. 801,000)

Shropshire a county of west central England; the county town is Shrewsbury. (3490 sq km/1347 sq miles; pop. 390,000)

Siberia a huge tract of land, mostly in northern Russian Federation, that extends from the Ural Mountains to the Pacific coast. It is renowned for its inhospitable climate, but parts of it are fertile, and it is rich in minerals.

Sichuan (Szechwan) the most heavily populated of the provinces of China, in the southwest of the country. The capital is Chengdu. (570,000 sq km/220,000 sq miles; pop. 97,740,000)

Sicily (Sicilia) an island hanging from the toe of Italy, and the largest island in the Mediterranean. The capital is Palermo. (25,708 sq km/9926 sq miles; pop. 5,065,000)

Siena (Sienna) a historic town of Tuscany, in central Italy. (Pop. 60,500)

Sierra Leone (*Area* 71,740 sq km (27,699 sq miles); *population* 4,140,000*capital* : Freetown; *form of government* Republic; *religion* Animism, Sunni Islam, Christianity; *currency* : Leone). Sierra Leone, on the Atlantic coast of West Africa, consists of wide swampy forested plains and these rise to a mountainous plateau in the east. The climate is tropical. The main food of Sierra Leoneans is rice, and this is grown in the swamplands at the coast. On the plateau much forest has been cleared for growing of groundnuts. Most of the country's revenue comes from mining. Diamonds are panned from the rivers, and there are deposits of iron ore, bauxite, rutile and some gold.

Sierra Madre Occidental the mountain range of western Mexico.

Sierra Madre Oriental the mountain range of eastern Mexico.

Sierra Nevada (1) a mountain range in southern Spain. (2) a mountain range in eastern California, USA.

Si Kiang *see* **Xi Jiang.**

Sikkim a state in northeastern India. The capital is Gangtok. (7096 sq km/2739 sq miles; pop. 316,400)

Silesia (Schlesien) a region straddling the borders of the Czech Republic, Germany and Poland.

Simpson Desert an arid, uninhabited region in the centre of Australia.

Sinai a mountainous peninsula in northeastern Egypt, bordering Israel, between the Gulf of Aqaba and the Gulf of Suez.

Sind a province of southeastern Pakistan. The capital is Karachi. (140,914 sq km/ 54,407 sq miles; pop. 19,029,000)

Singapore (*Area* 618 sq km (239 sq miles); *population* 2,690,000; *capital* Singapore; *form of government* Republic; *religions* 0Buddhism, Sunni Islam, Christianity; *currency* Singapore dollar). Singapore, one of the world's smallest yet most successful countries, comprises 60 islands which are located at the foot of the Malay peninsula in southeast Asia. The main island, Singapore Island, is very low-lying, and the climate is hot and wet throughout the year. Only 3% of the land area is used for agriculture, and most food is imported. It is self-sufficient in fish. Singapore has the largest oil refining centre in Asia. The country has a flourishing manufacturing industry for which it relies heavily on imports. Tourism is an important source of foreign revenue.

Sinkiang Uygur Autonomous Region *see* **Xinjiang Uygur Autonomous Region.**

Sint Maarten *see* **St Martin.**

Siracusa *see* **Syracuse.**

Síros *see* **Cyclades.**

Sirte, Gulf of a huge indent of the Mediterranean Sea in the coastline of Libya.

Sivas an industrial town in central Turkey. (Pop. 197,300)

Sjaelland *see* **Zealand.**

Skagerrak the channel, some 130 km (80 miles) wide, separating Denmark and Norway. It links the North Sea to the Kattegat and Baltic Sea.

Skiathos the westernmost of the Greek Sporades (Dodecanese) Islands. (Pop. 4200)

Skopje the capital of Macedonia, a republic in the south of former Yugoslavia. (Pop. 506,500)

Skye an island off the northwest coast of Scotland; the largest of the Inner Hebrides. The main town is Portree. (1417 sq km/547 sq miles; pop. 8000)

Slavonia (Slavonija) a part of Croatia, southeast of Zagreb, mainly between the Drava and Slava Rivers.

Sligo a county on the northwest coast of the Republic of Ireland, with a county town of the same name. (1796 sq km/693 sq miles; pop. county 55,400)

Slovakia (*Area* 49,032 sq km (18,931 sq miles); *population* 5,013,000; *capital* Bratislava; *other major city* Kovice; *form of government* Republic; *religion* RC; *currency* Koruna). Slovakia was constituted on 1 January 1993. Landlocked in central Europe, the northern half of the republic is occupied by the Tatra Mountains, which have vast forests and pastures used for intensive sheep grazing, and is rich in high-grade minerals. The southern part of Slovakia is a plain drained by the Danube and its tributaries, with farms, vineyards, orchards and pastures for stock.

Slovenia (*Area* 20,251 sq km (7817 sq miles); *population* 1,998,912; *capital* Ljubljana; *other major cities* Maribor, Celje; *form of government* Republic; *religion* RC; *currency* Slovene Tolar). Slovenia made a unilateral declaration of independence from former Yugoslavia on June 25 1991. Most of Slovenia is situated in the Karst Plateau and in the Julian Alps. Although farming and livestock raising are the chief occupations, Slovenia is very industrialized and urbanized. Iron, steel and aluminium are produced, and mineral resources include oil, coal and mercury. Tourism is an important industry. The northeast is famous for its wine production.

Smolensk an industrial city in the Russian Federation, on the River Dnieper. (Pop. 326,000)

Smyrna *see* **Izmir.**

Snake, River a river of the northwest USA, which flows into the Columbia River in Washington State. (Length 1670 km/1038 miles)

Snowdonia a mountainous region in the north of Wales. The highest peak is Mount Snowdon (1085 m/3560 ft).

Snowy Mountains a range of in southeastern Australia, where the River Snowy has been dammed to form the complex Snowy Mountains Hydroelectric Scheme. The highest peak is Mount Kosciusko (2230 m/7316 ft).

Society Islands a group at the centre of French Polynesia. They are divided into the Windward Islands, which include Tahiti and Moorea; and the Leeward Islands, which include Raiatea and Bora-Bora. (Pop. 142,000)

Socotra an island in the northwestern Indian Ocean, belonging to Yemen.

Sofia (Sofiya) the capital of Bulgaria, in the west of the country. (Pop. 1,093,800)

Solent, The a strait in the English Channel that separates the Isle of Wight from mainland England.

Solomon Islands (*Area* 28,896 sq km (11,157 sq miles); *population* 308,796; *capital* Honiara; *form of government* Constitutional Monarchy; *religions* Anglicanism, RC, other Christianity; *currency* Solomon Island dollar). The Solomon Islands lie in an area between 5° and 12° south of the Equator to the east of Papua New Guinea, in the Pacific Ocean. The nation consists of six large islands and innumerable smaller ones. The climate is hot and wet, and typhoons are frequent. The main food crops grown are coconut, cassava, sweet potatoes, yams, taros and bananas. The forests are worked commercially, and the fishing industry is developing.

Somalia (*Area* 637,657 sq km (246,199 sq miles); *population* 6,260,000; *capital* Mogadishu; *other major cities* Hargeisa, Baidoa, Burao, Kismaayo; *form of government* Republic; *religion* Sunni Islam; *currency* Somali shilling). Somalia is shaped like a large number seven and lies on the horn of Africa's east coast. The country is arid, and most of it is low plateaux with scrub vegetation. Most of the population live in the mountains and river valleys, and there are a few towns on the coast. Main exports are live animals, meat, hides and skins. A few large-scale banana plantations are found by the rivers. Years of drought have left Somalia heavily dependent on foreign aid.

Somerset a county in the southwest of England; the county town is Taunton. (3458 sq km/1335 sq miles; pop. 440,000)

Somme, River a river of northern France, the scene of a devastating battle during World War I. (Length 245 km/152 miles)

Song Hong *see* **Red River.**

Soul *see* **Seoul.**

South Africa (*Area* 1,221,037 sq km (471,442 sq miles); *population* 30,190,000; *capital* Pretoria (Administrative), Cape Town (Legislative); *other major cities.* Johannesburg, Durban, Port Elizabeth, Bloemfontein; *form of government* Republic; *religions* Dutch reformed, Independent African, other Christianity, Hinduism; *currency* Rand). South Africa is a republic that lies at the southern tip of the African continent and has a huge coastline on both the Atlantic and Indian Oceans. The country occupies a huge saucer-shaped plateau, surrounding a belt of land which drops in steps to the sea. In general the climate is healthy, with plenty of sunshine and relatively low rainfall. This varies with latitude, distance from the sea, and altitude. Of the total land area, 58% is used as natural pasture. The main crops grown are maize, sorghum, wheat, groundnuts and sugar cane. It is South Africa's extraordinary mineral wealth which overshadows all its other natural resources. These include gold, coal, copper, iron ore, manganese and chrome ore.

Southampton a major port in southern England. (Pop. 206,000)

South Australia a state in central southern Australia, on the Great Australian Bight. Adelaide is the state capital. (984,380 sq km/380,069 sq miles; pop. 1,347,000)

South Carolina a state in the southeast of the USA, with a coast on the Atlantic Ocean. The state capital is Columbia. (80,432 sq km/31,055 sq miles; pop. 3,347,000)

South China Sea an arm of the Pacific Ocean between southeast China, Malaysia and the Philippines.

South Dakota a state in the western USA. The state capital is Pierre. (199,552 sq km/77,047 sq miles; pop. 708,000)

Southern Alps a range of mountains on the South Island of New Zealand.

Southern Ocean *see* **Antarctic Ocean.**

South Georgia an island in the South Atlantic, and a dependency of the Falkland Islands. (3755 sq km/1450 sq km)

South Glamorgan a county in south Wales. The administrative centre is Cardiff. (416 sq km/161 sq miles; pop. 384,700)

South Island *see* **New Zealand.**

South Korea *see* **Korea.**

South Pole the most southerly point of the Earth's axis, in Antarctica.

South Sandwich Islands a group of islands in the South Atlantic which are dependencies of the Falkland Islands. (340 sq km/130 sq miles)

Soweto a group of black townships to the south of Johannesburg, South Africa. (Pop. 829,400)

Spain (*Area* 504,782 sq km (194,896 sq miles); *population* 39,540,000; *capital*

Madrid; *other major cities* Barcelona, Seville, Zaragosa, Malaga, Bilbao; *form of government* Constitutional Monarchy; *religion* RC; *currency* Peseta). Spain occupies the greater part of the Iberian peninsula, sealed off from the rest of Europe by the Pyrénées Much of the country is a vast plateau, the Meseta Central, cut across by valleys and gorges. Its longest shoreline is the one that borders the Mediterranean Sea. It has a climate with mild moist winters and hot dry summers. Spain's principal agricultural products are cereals, vegetables and potatoes, and large areas are under vines for the wine industry. Industry represents 72% of the country's export value, and production includes textiles, paper, cement, steel and chemicals. Tourism is a major revenue earner.

Spitsbergen A large island group in the Svalbard archipelago, 580 km (360 miles) to the north of Norway. (39,000 sq km/15,060 sq miles; pop. 2000)

Split the largest city on the coast of Dalmatia, Croatia. (Pop. 236,000)

Sporades (Sporadhes) *see* **Dodecanese.**

Spratly Islands a group of islands in the South China Sea between Vietnam and Borneo. Occupied by Japan during World War II, they are now claimed by almost all the surrounding countries.

Springfield (1) the state capital of Illinois, USA. (Pop. city 101,600/metropolitan area 190,100). (2) a manufacturing city in Massachusetts, USA. (Pop. city 150,300/metropolitan area 515,900)

Srbija *see* **Serbia.**

Sri Lanka (*Area* 65,610 sq km (25,332 sq miles); *population* 16,810,000; *capital* Colombo; *other major cities* Dehiwela-Mt. Lavinia, Moratuwa, Jaffna; *form of government* Republic; *religions* Buddhism, Hinduism, Christianity, Sunni Islam; *currency* Sri Lankan rupee). Sri Lanka is a teardrop-shaped island in the Indian Ocean, lying south of the Indian peninsula. The climate is equatorial, but it is affected by both the northeast and southwest monsoons. Agriculture engages 47% of the work force, and the main crops are rice, tea, rubber and coconuts. Amongst the chief minerals mined and exported are precious and semiprecious stones. The main industries are food, beverages and tobacco, textiles, clothing and leather goods, chemicals and plastics.

Srinagar the capital of the state of Jammu and Kashmir, northern India. (Pop. 606,000)

Staffordshire a Midlands county of England. The county town is Stafford. (2716 sq km/1049 sq miles; pop. 1,018,000)

Stanley *see* **Port Stanley.**

Stanley Falls *see* **Boyoma Falls.**

Stanley, Mount *see* **Ngaliema, Mount.**

Stanleyville *see* **Kisangani.**

St Barthélémy a small island dependency of Guadeloupe. (Pop. 3000)

St Christopher (St Kitts) and Nevis (*Area* 261 sq km (101 sq miles); *population* 43,410; *capital* Basseterre; *form of government* Constitutional Monarchy; *religions* Anglicanism, Methodism; *currency* : East Caribbean dollar). The islands of St Christopher (popularly known as St Kitts) and Nevis lie in the Leeward group in the eastern Caribbean. St Kitts consists of three extinct volcanoes linked by a sandy isthmus to other volcanic remains in the south. Sugar is the chief export crop, but market gardening and livestock are being expanded on the steeper slopes above the cane fields. Nevis, 3 km (2 miles) south, is an extinct volcano. Farming is declining and tourism is now the main source of income.

St Croix the largest of the US Virgin Islands. The main town is Christiansted. (218 sq km/84 sq miles; pop. 50,000)

Saint-Denis the capital of Réunion island. (Pop. 110,000)

St-Etienne an industrial city southwest of Lyons, France. (Pop. 319,500)

Stettin *see* **Szczecin.**

St George's the capital of Grenada, and the island's main port. (Pop. 30,800)

St Helena a remote island and British colony in the South Atlantic. (122 sq km/ 47 sq miles; pop. 5500)

St Helena Dependencies the islands of Ascension and Tristan da Cunha are so-called dependencies of St Helena, a British colony.

St Helens, Mount an active volcano in the Cascade Range of western Washington State, USA. It last erupted in 1980. (2549 m/8364 ft)

St John's (1) the capital and main port of Antigua. (Pop. 30,000). (2) a port and the capital of Newfoundland, Canada. (Pop. 155,000)

St Kitts and Nevis *see* **St Christopher and Nevis.**

St Lawrence, River a commercially important river of southeast Canada, which flows northeast from Lake Ontario to the Gulf of St Lawrence, forming part of the border with the USA. (Length 1197 km/744 miles)

St Lawrence, Gulf of an arm of the Atlantic Ocean in northeastern Canada, into which the St Lawrence River flows.

St Lawrence Seaway a navigable waterway that links the Great Lakes, via the St Lawrence River, to the Atlantic Ocean.

St Louis a city in eastern Missouri, USA, on the River Mississippi. (Pop. city 429,300/metropolitan area 2,398,400)

St Lucia (*Area* 622 sq km (240 sq miles); *population* 146,600; *capital* Castries; *form of Government* Constitutional Monarchy; *religion* RC; *currency* East Caribbean dollar). St Lucia is one of the Windward Islands in the eastern Caribbean, formed of extinct volcanoes. The climate is wet tropical, with a dry season from January to April. The economy depends on the production of bananas and, to a lesser extent, coconuts. Production, however, is often affected by hurricanes, drought and disease. Tourism is becoming an important industry and Castries, the capital, is a popular calling point for cruise liners.

St Martin one of the Leeward Islands in the southeastern Caribbean. It is divided politically into two, one a part of Guadeloupe (France); the other (Sint Maarten) a part of the Netherlands Antilles. The capital of the French side is Marigot; of the Dutch side Philipsburg. (54 sq km/21 sq miles; pop. 24,000)

Stockholm the capital of Sweden, and an important port on the Baltic Sea. (Pop. 1,435,500)

Stockton-on-Tees a town in Cleveland, England. (Pop. 173,000)

Stoke-on-Trent a major city in the "Potteries" of the Midlands of England. (Pop. 250,000)

St Paul the state capital of Minnesota, twinned with the adjoining city of Minneapolis. (Pop. city 265,900/ metropolitan area 2,230,900)

St Petersburg (Sankt Peterburg) a former capital of Russia and the current Russian Federation second-largest city. It is an industrial city, important cultural centre and major port on the Baltic Sea. From 1914-24 it was known as Petrograd; then, until 1991, Leningrad.

St Pierre and Miquelon two islands to the south of Newfoundland, Canada, which are administered by France. (240 sq km/93 sq miles; pop. 6100)

Strasbourg an industrial city and river port in eastern France, the capital of the Alsace region, and the seat of the European Parliament. (Pop. 378,500)

Stratford-upon-Avon a town in Warwickshire, England, the home of William Shakespeare (1564–1616). (Pop. 22,000)

Strathclyde an administrative region in western Scotland, with its administrative centre in Glasgow. It was created in 1975 out of the former counties of Ayrshire, Lanarkshire, Renfrewshire, Bute, Dunbartonshire and parts of Stirlingshire and Argyll. (13,856 sq km/5350 sq miles; pop. 2,373,000)

Stromboli an island with an active volcano in the Eolian Islands, to the north of Sicily. (Pop. 400)

St Thomas the principal tourist island of the US Virgin Islands. The capital is Charlotte Amalie. (83 sq km/32 sq miles; pop. 44,000)

Stuttgart a major industrial centre and river port of the Neckar river in southwestern Germany. (Pop. 600,000)

St Vincent, Cape *see* **São Vincente, Cabo de.**

St Vincent and the Grenadines (*Area* 388 sq km (150 sq miles); *population* 113,950; *capital* Kingstown; *form of government* Constitutional Monarchy; *religions* : Anglicanism, Methodism, RC; *currency* : East Caribbean dollar). St Vincent is an island of the Lesser Antilles, situated in the eastern Caribbean, separated from Grenada by a chain of some 600 small islands known as the Grenadines, the northern islands of which form the other part of the country. The climate is tropical, with very heavy rain in the mountains.The volcano, Soufrière (1234 m/4049 ft), is active and its last eruption was in 1979. Farming is the main occupation on the island. Bananas for the UK are the main export, and it is the world's leading producer of arrowroot starch.

Sucre the legal capital of Bolivia. (Pop. 70,000)

Sudan (*Area* 2,505,813 sq km (967,494 sq miles); *population* 25,560,000; *capital* Khartoum (El Khartum); other major cities : Omdurman, Khartoum North, Port Sudan; *form of government* Republic; *religions* Sunni Islam, Animism, Christianity; *Currency* Sudanese pound). Sudan, the largest country in Africa, covers much of the upper Nile basin. The climate is tropical and temperatures are high throughout the year. Rainfall increases in amount from north to south, the northern areas being virtually desert. Sudan is an agricultural country, subsistence farming accounting for 80% of production. Cotton is farmed commercially and accounts for about two-thirds of Sudan's exports. Sudan is the world's greatest source of gum arabic used in medicines and inks.

Sudd a vast swampland on the White Nile in Sudan.

Sudety (Sudetenland) a mountainous region straddling the border between the Czech Republic and Poland.

Suez Canal a canal in northeast Egypt, linking the Mediterranean to the Red Sea. It was completed in 1869.

Suez (El Suweis) a town at the south end of the Suez Canal. (Pop. 195,000)

Suez, Gulf of a northern arm of the Red Sea that leads to the Suez Canal.

Suffolk a county in East Anglia, England. The county town is Ipswich. (3800 sq km/1467 sq miles; pop. 619,000)

Sulawesi (Celebes) a large, hook-shaped island in the centre of Indonesia. (179,370 sq km/69,255 sq miles; pop. 10,409,600)

Sulu Archipelago a chain of over 400 islands off the southwest Philippines, stretching between the Philippines and Borneo.

Sulu Sea a part of the Pacific Ocean which lies between the Philippines and Borneo.

Sumatra the main island of western Indonesia. (473,607 sq km/182,860 sq miles; pop. 28,016,200)

Sumba one of the Lesser Sunda Islands, Indonesia, to the south of Sumbawa and Flores. (11,153 sq km/4306 sq miles; pop. 251,100)

Sumbawa one of the Lesser Sunda Islands, Indonesia, between Lombok and Flores. (15,448 sq km/5965 sq miles; pop. 195,000)

Sunda Islands *see* **Lesser Sunda Islands.**

Sunda Strait the strait, 26 km(16 miles) across at its narrowest, which separates Java and Sumatra.

Sunderland an industrial town in Tyne and Wear, England. (Pop. 200,000)

Superior, Lake the largest and most westerly of the Great Lakes. (82,400 sq km/ 31,800 sq miles)

Surabaya the second largest city of Indonesia after Jakarta, on the northeast coast of Java. (Pop. 2,470,000)

Surat a port on the west coast of India, in western Gujarat. (Pop. 913,800)

Suriname (*Area* 163,265 sq km (63,037 sq miles); *population* 416,839; capital Paramaribo; *form of government* Republic; *religions* Hinduism, RC, Sunni Islam; *currency* Suriname guilder). Suriname in northeast South America, comprises a swampy coastal plain, a forested central plateau, and southern mountains. The climate is tropical, with heavy rainfall. Rice and sugar are farmed on the coastal plains, but the mining of bauxite is what the economy depends on. This makes up 80% of exports. Suriname has resources of oil and timber but these are so far underexploited.

Surrey a county of central southern England. The county town is Guildford. (1655 sq km/639 sq miles; pop. 1,012,000)

Sussex, East a county in southeast England; the county town is Lewes. (1795 sq km/693 sq miles; pop. 655,000)

Sussex, West a county in southeast England; the county town is Chichester. (1989 sq km/768 sq miles; pop. 660,000)

Susupe the capital of the Northern Marianas, on Saipan. (Pop. 8000)

Suva the capital of Fiji. (Pop. city 74,000/metropolitan area 133,000)

Suzhou a city in Jiangshu province, China. (Pop. 900,000)

Svalbard an archipelago in the Arctic Ocean to the north of Norway, which has sovereignty. (62,049 sq km/23,958 sq miles; pop. 3500)

Swansea a port in south Wales. (Pop. 168,000)

Swaziland (*Area* 1736 sq km (670 sq miles); *population* 681,059; capital Mbabane; *other major cities* Big Bend, Manzini, Mhlume; *form of government* Monarchy; *religion* Christianity, Animism; *currency* emalangeni). Swaziland is a landlocked hilly enclave almost entirely within the borders of the Republic of South Africa. The mountains in the west of the country rise to almost 2000 m (6562 ft), then descend in steps of savanna toward hilly country in the east. The climate is subtropical, moderated by altitude. Oranges, pineapple and sugar cane are the masin crops, and asbestos is mined. Swaziland attracts a lot of tourists from South Africa.

Sweden (*Area* 449,964 sq km (173,731 sq miles); *population* 8,500,000; *capital* Stockholm; *other major cities* Göteborg, Malmö, Uppsala, Orebro; *form of government* Constitutional Monarchy; *religion* Lutheranism; *currency* krona). Sweden is a large country in northern Europe, which makes up half of the Scandinavian peninsula. The south is generally flat, the north mountainous. Summers are warm but short, and winters are long and cold. Dairy farming is the predominant agricultural activity. Only 7% of Sweden is cultivated. About 57% of the country is covered in forest, and the sawmill, wood pulp and paper industries are important. Sweden is one of the world's leading producers of iron ore. Other main industries are engineering and electrical goods, vehicles and furniture making.

Switzerland (*Area* 41,293 sq km (15,943 sq miles); *population* 6,700,000; *capital* Berne (Bern); *other major cities* : Zürich, Basle, Geneva, Lausanne; *form of government* Federal republic; *religions* RC, Protestantism; *currency* : Swiss franc). Switzerland is a landlocked country in central Europe. The Alps occupy the southern half of the country, forming two main eastwest chains divided by the rivers Rhine and Rhône. Summers are generally warm and winters cold, and both are affected by altitude. Northern Switzerland is the industrial part of the country and where its most important cities are located. It is also in this region that the famous cheeses, clocks, watches and chocolates are produced. Switzerland has huge earnings from international finance and tourism.

Sydney the largest city and port in Australia, and the capital of New South Wales. (Pop. 3,332,600)

Syracuse (1) a city in the centre of New York State. (Pop. city 164,200/ metropolitan area 650,000). (2) (Siracusa) an ancient seaport on the east coast of Sicily, Italy. (Pop. 119,200)

Syrdar'ya, River a river of central Asia, flowing through Kazakhstan to the Aral Sea. (Length 2860 km/1780 miles)

Syria (*Area* 185,180 sq km (71,498 sq miles); *population* 11,300,000; *capital* Damascus (Dimashq); *other major cities* Aleppo, Homs,Lattakia, Hama; *form of government* Republic; *religion* Sunni Islam; *currency* Syrian pound). Syria is a country in southwest Asia that borders on the Mediterranean Sea in the west. Much of the country is mountainous desert behind the narrow fertile coastal plain that has hot dry summers and mild wet winters. About 50% of the workforce get their living from agriculture. Sheep, goats and cattle are raised, and cotton, barley, wheat, tobacco, fruit and vegetables are grown. Reserves of oil are small compared to neighbouring Iraq but it has enough to make the country self-sufficient and provide three quarters of the nation's export earnings. Textile, leather, chemical and cement industries have developed rapidly in the last 20 years.

Szczecin (Stettin) a port in northwest Poland. (Pop. 390,200)

Szechwan *see* **Sichuan.**

Table Mountain a flat-topped mountain overlooking Cape Town in southwest South Africa. (1087 m/3567 ft)

Tabriz a city in northwest Iran. (Pop. 599,000)

Tadmor *see* **Palmyra.**

Tadzhikistan *see* **Tajikistan.**

Taegu the third largest city of South Korea. (Pop. 1,608,000)

Tagus (Tajo; Tejo), River a major river of southwest Europe, which rises in eastern Spain and flows west and southwest through Portugal to the Atlantic Ocean west of Lisbon. (Length 1007 km/626 miles)

Tahiti the largest of the islands of French Polynesia in the South Pacific. The capital is Papeete. (1005 sq km/388 sq miles; pop. 96,000)

T'aichung a major commercial and agricultural centre in western Taiwan. (Pop. 1,608,000)

T'ainan a city in southwest Taiwan. (Pop. 595,000)

T'aipei the capital and largest city of Taiwan, in the north. (Pop. 2,272,000)

Taiwan (*Area* 36,179 sq km (13,969 sq miles); *population* 20,300,000; *capital* Taipei; *other major cities* Kaohsiung, Taichung, Tainan; *form of government* Republic; *religions* Taoism, Buddhism, Christianity; *currency* New Taiwan dollar). Taiwan is a large mountainous island that about 160 km (99 miles) off the southeast coast of mainland China. The climate is warm and humid for most of the year. Winters are mild and summers rainy. The soils are fertile, and a wide range of crops, including tea, rice, sugar cane and bananas, is grown. Taiwan is a major international trading nation. Exports include machinery, electronics, textiles, footwear, toys and sporting goods.

Taiwan Strait the stretch of water between Taiwan and China.

Taiyuan the capital of Shanxi province, China. (Pop. 1,838,000)

Tajikistan (*Area* 143,100 sq km (55,250 sq miles); *population* 5,100,000; *capital* Dushanbe; *form of Government* Republic; *religion* Shia Islam; *currency* Rouble). Tajikistan, a republic of southern central former USSR, declared itself independent in 1991. More than half the country lies over 3000 m (9843 ft). Most of the country is desert or semi-desert, and pastoral farming of cattle, sheep, horses and goats is important. The lowland areas are irrigated so that cotton, mulberry trees, fruit, wheat and vegetables can be grown. The republic is rich in deposits of coal, lead, zinc, oil and uranium, which are now being exploited.

Tajo *see* **Tagus.**

Taklimakan Desert the largest desert in China, consisting mainly of sand, in the west of the country.

Takoradi a main port of Ghana, in its southwest. (Pop. 165,000)

Tallahassee the state capital of Florida, USA. (Pop. city 112,000/metropolitan area 207,600)

Tallinn a port on the Baltic Sea, and the capital of ESTONIA. (Pop. 458,000)

Tamil Nadu a state in southeast India. The state capital is Madras. (130,357 sq km/50,839 sq miles; pop. 48,298,000)

Tammerfors *see* **Tampere.**

Tampa a port and resort on the west coast of Florida, USA. (Pop. city 275,000/ metropolitan area 1,811,000)

Tampere (Tammerfors) the second largest city in Finland after Helsinki, in the southwest of the country. (Pop. 167,000)

Tana (Tsana), Lake a lake in the mountains of northwest Ethiopia, and the source of the Blue Nile. (3673 sq km/1418 sq miles)

Tanganyika *see* **Tanzania.**

Tanganyika, Lake the second largest lake in Africa after Lake Victoria, in the Great Rift Valley, between Tanzania and Zaïre, although Burundi and Zambia also share the shoreline. (32,893 sq km/12,700 sq miles)

Tangier (Tanger) a port on the north coast of Morocco, on the Strait of Gibraltar. (Pop. 188,000)

Tangshan an industrial city in Hebei province, China. (Pop. 1,087,000)

Tanzania (*Area* 945,087 sq km (364,898 sq miles); *population* 24,800,000; *capital* Dodoma; *other major cities* Dar es Salaam, Zanzibar, Mwanza, Tanga; *form of government* Republic; *religions* Sunni Islam, RC, Anglicanism, Hinduism; *currency* Tanzanian shilling). Tanzania lies on the east coast of central Africa and comprises a large mainland area as well as the islands of Pemba and Zanzibar. The mainland consists mostly of plateaux, broken by mountainous areas, and the Great Rift Valley. The coast is hot and humid, the central plateau drier, and the mountains semi-temperate. Some 80% of Tanzanians make a living from the land. Cash crops include cotton and coffee. The islands are more successful agriculturally and have important coconut and clove plantations.

Tarabulus *see* **Tripoli.**

Taranto a port and naval base on the south coast of Italy. (Pop. 245,000)

Taranto, Gulf of an inlet of the Mediterranean Sea between the "toe" and the "heel" of Italy.

Tarawa the main atoll and capital of Kiribati. (Pop. 23,000)

Tarragona a port of ancient origins on the Mediterranean coast of northeastern Spain, and the name of the surrounding province. (Pop. city 111,700)

Tarsus an agricultural centre in southeast Turkey, the birthplace of St Paul. (Pop. 160,000)

Tashkent the capital of UZBEKISTAN, in the northeast. (Pop. 1,987,000)

Tasmania an island state to the south of Australia, separated from the mainland by the Bass Strait. The capital is Hobart. (68,332 sq km/26,383 sq miles; pop. 435,000)

Tasman Sea a branch of the Pacific Ocean that separates Australia and New Zealand.

Tatar Republic (Tatarstan) an autonomous republic of the Russian Federation, southwest of Moscow, around the River Volga. The capital is Kazan'. (68,000 sq km/26,250 sq miles; pop. 394,000)

Tatra Mountains a range of mountains that lines the border between Poland and Slovakia The highest peak is Gerlachovka (2663 m/8737 ft).

Tatung *see* **Datung.**

Tayside an administrative region of Scotland formed in 1975 out of the former counties of Angus, Kinrossshire and part of Perthshire. The administrative centre is Dundee. (7511 sq km/2900 sq miles; pop. 392,000)

Tbilisi the capital of GEORGIA, in the centre of the republic. (Pop. 1,140,000)

Tegucigalpa the capital of HONDURAS, in its south. (Pop. 473,700)

Tehran the capital of IRAN, in the central north of the country. (Pop. 6,000,000)

Tejo *see* **Tagus.**

Tel Aviv-Jaffa the largest city of Israel, former capital and the main financial centre. It was combined with the old port of Jaffa in 1950. (Pop. 324,000)

Tenerife the largest of the Canary Islands. The capital is Santa Cruz. (2058 sq km/ 795 sq miles; pop. 558,000)

Tennessee a state in southern central USA. The state capital is Nashville. (109,412 sq km/42,244 sq miles; pop. 4,762,000)

Tennessee, River a river which flows southwest from the Appalachian Mountains of North Carolina and then through Alabama, Tennessee and Kentucky to join the Ohio River. (Length 1049km/ 652miles)

Tevere, River *see* **Tiber.**

Texas a state in the southwest of the USA, bordering Mexico. It is the nation's second largest state. The capital is Austin. (678,927 sq km/262,134 sq miles; pop. 16,370,000)

Thailand (*Area* 513,115 sq km (198,114 sq miles); *population* 55,900,00; *capital* Bangkok (Krung Thep); *other major cities* Chiengmai, Hat Yai, Songkhla; *form of government* Constitutional Monarchy; *religions* Buddhism, Sunni Islam; *currency* Baht). Thailand, a kingdom located in southeast Asia, is a tropical country of mountains and jungles, rain forests and green plains. It has a subtropical climate with heavy monsoon rains. The central plain of Thailand contains vast expanses of paddy fields which produce enough rice to rank Thailand as the world's leading exporter. The narrow southern peninsula is very wet, and it is here that rubber is produced. Thailand is the world's third largest exporter of rubber.

Thailand, Gulf of a branch of the South China Sea lying between the Malay peninsula and the coasts of Thailand, Cambodia and Vietnam.

Thames, River a major river of southern England flowing eastwards from its source in the Cotswold Hills, past London to its estuary on the North Sea. (Length 338 km/210 miles)

Thar Desert a desert in northwest India, covering the border between Rajasthan and Pakistan.

Thebes the ruins of an ancient city on the River Nile in central Egypt. It was the capital of Ancient Egypt for about 1000 years from 1600bc.

Thessaloníki *see* **Saloniki.**

Thimphu (Thimbu) the capital of BHUTAN, in its west. (Pop. 8922)

Thon Buri a city on the west side of the River Chao Phraya, oppposite Bangkok, in Thailand. (Pop. 919,000)

Thousand Islands a group of over 1000 islands scattered in the upper St Lawrence River, between the USA and Canada.

Tianjin (Tientsin) a major industrial city in Hebei province, the third largest city in China after Shanghai and Beijing. (Pop. 7,390,000)

Tiber (Tevere) a river of central Italy, rising to the east of Florence and flowing south to Rome and into the Mediterranean. (Length 405 km/252 miles)

Tibet (Xizang Autonomous Region) a region of southwest China, consisting of a huge high plateau high beyond the Himalayas. Formerly a Buddhist kingdom led by its spiritual leader, the Dalai Lama, it was invaded by China in 1950 and has been gradually desecrated. (1,221,600 sq km/471,660 sq miles; pop. 1,893,000)

Tientsin *see* **Tianjin.**

Tierra del Fuego the archipelago at the southern tip of South America, belonging to Argentina and Chile and separated from the mainland by the Strait of Magellan.

Tigray a province of northern Ethiopia, bordering Eritrea, whose people have been fighting a separatist war against the central government. The capital is Mekele. (Pop. 2,045,000)

Tigris a major river of the Middle East, rising in eastern Turkey, flowing through Syria and Iraq and joining the Euphrates to form a delta at the Shatt al Arab waterway as it enters The Gulf. (Length 1900 km/1180 miles)

Tijuana a border city and resort in northwest Mexico, at the northern end of the Baja California. (Pop. 567,000)

Timbuktu a town in central Mali at the edge of the Sahara. (Pop. 20,000)

Timisoara an industrial city in southwest Romania. (Pop. 288,000)

Timor an island at the eastern end of the Lesser Sunda Islands, Indonesia. The eastern half of the island was a possession of Portugal, but was annexed in 1975 by Indonesia. (30,775 sq km/11,883 sq miles; pop. 3,085,000)

Timor Sea the arm of the Indian Ocean between the northwest coast of Australia and the island of Timor.

Tipperary a county in the south of the Republic of Ireland. It includes the town of Tipperary, but Clonmel is the county town. (4255 sq km/1643 sq miles; pop. 135,000)

Tiranë (Tirana) the largest city and the capital of ALBANIA, in the centre of the country. (Pop. 220,000)

Tiruchiràppalli (Trichinopoly) an industrial city in central Tamil Nadu in southern India. (Pop. 609,500)

Titicaca, Lake the largest lake in South America, in the Andes, on the border between Bolivia and Peru. (8135 sq km/3141 sq miles)

Tobago an island to the northeast of Trinidad, forming part of the republic of Trinidad and Tobago. (Pop. 40,000)

Togo (*Area* 56,785 sq km (21,925 sq miles); *population* 3,400,000; *capital* Lomé; *form of government* Republic; *religions* Animism, RC, Sunni Islam; *currency* Franc CFA). Togo is a tiny West African country with a narrow coastal plain on the Gulf of Guinea and the heavily forested .Togo Highlands inland. Over 80% of the population are involved in agriculture, with yams and millet as the principal crops. Coffee, cocoa and cotton are grown for cash. Minerals, especially phosphates, are the main export.

Tokyo the capital of Japan, a port on the east coast of Honshu Island. Its original name was Edo (until 1868). (Pop. city 8,353,700/Greater Tokyo 11,680,000)

Toledo (1) a historic city of central Spain, on the River Tagus. (Pop. 60,100). (2) a city and Great Lake port in Ohio, USA. (Pop. city 343,900/metropolitan area 610,800)

Tonga (*Area* 750 sq km (290 sq miles); *population* 95,200; *capital* Nuku'alofa; *form of government* Constitutional Monarchy; *religions* Methodism, RC; *currency* Pa'anga). Tonga is situated about 20° south of the Equator and just west of the International Date Line in the Pacific Ocean. It comprises over 170 islands and only about one-fifth of which are inhabited. The climate is warm, with heavy rainfall. Yams, cassava and taro are grown as subsistence crops, and fish from the sea supplements the diet. Bananas and coconuts are grown for export. The main industry is coconut processing.

Tongking (Tonkin) *see* **Mien Bac**.

Tonle Sap a lake in central Cambodia which swells and quadruples in size when the River Mekong floods. (In flood 10,400 sq km/4000 sq miles)

Topeka the state capital of Kansas, USA. (Pop. city 119,000/metropolitan area 159,000)

Torino *see* **Turin.**

Toronto the largest city of Canada, and the capital of Ontario, situated on Lake Ontario. (Pop. 2,999,000)

Torres Strait between the northeastern tip of Australia and New Guinea.

Toscana *see* **Tuscany.**

Toulon a major naval base and port in southeast France. (Pop. 418,000)

Toulouse a city of southwest France, on the Garonne River. (Pop. 551,000)

Touraine a former province of northwest France, around Tours.

Tours a town in western France, on the River Loire. (Pop. 268,000)

Trabzon (Trebizond) a port on the Black Sea in northeastern Turkey. (Pop. 156,000)

Trafalgar, Cape the southwestern tip of Spain.

Transkei a Bantu homeland in eastern Cape Province, South Africa, declared independent by South Africa in 1976. The capital is Umtata. (41,000 sq km/ 15,831 sq miles; pop. 3,300,000)

Transvaal a province of northern South Africa. The capital is Pretoria. (Pop. 8,950,500)

Transylvania a region of central and northwestern Romania.

Trebizond *see* **Trabzon.**

Trent, River is the main river of the Midlands of England, flowing northeast from Staffordshire to the Humber. (Length 270 km/170 miles)

Trenton a city in eastern USA on the Delaware River in western New Jersey, of which it is the capital. (Pop. 92,124)

Trieste a port on the Adriatic Sea in northeast Italy. (Pop. 251,000)

Trichinopoly *see* **Tiruchiràppalli.**

Trinidad and Tobago (*Area* 5130 sq km (1981 sq miles); *population* 1,240,000; *capital* Port-of-Spain; *form of government* Republic; *religions* RC, Hinduism, Anglicanism, Sunni Islam; *currency* Trinidad and Tobago dollar). Trinidad and Tobago, situated off northeastern Venezuela, are the most southerly of the Lesser Antilles. Trinidad consists of a mountainous region in the north and undulating plains in the south. Tobago is more mountainous. The climate is tropical. Trinidad is one of the oldest oil-producing countries in the world. Output is small but provides 90% of Trinidad's exports. Sugar, coffee and cocoa are grown for export, but imports of food now account for 10% of total imports. Tobago depends mainly on tourism to make a living.

Tripoli (Tarabulus) (1) the capital and main port of Libya, in the northwest. (Pop. 620,000). (2) a port in northern Lebanon. (Pop. 175,000)

Tristan da Cunha a group of four remote, volcanic islands in the middle of the South Atlantic Ocean, which form part of the St Helena Dependencies. (100 sq km/40 sq miles; pop. 325)

Trivandrum a port on the southern tip of India, and the state capital of Kerala. (Pop. 520,000)

Trujillo a city and provincial capital in northwest Peru. (Pop.750,000)

Tsana, Lake *see* **Tana, Lake.**

Tsushima Strait *see* **Korea Strait.**

Tucson a city in southern Arizona, USA. (Pop. city 365,400/metropolitan area 594,800)

Tulsa a city in northeastern Oklahoma, on the Arkansas River. (Pop. 375,000/ metropolitan area 725,000)

Tunis the capital and main port of TUNISIA. (Pop. 550,000)

Tunisia (*Area* 163,610 sq km (63,170 sq miles); *population* 7,750,000; *capital* Tunis; *other major cities* Sfax, Bizerta, Djerba; *form of government* Republic; *religion* Sunni Islam; *currency* Tunisian dinar). Tunisia is a North African country consisting of hills, plains and valleys in the northern central mountains and the Sahara Desert in the south. Climate ranges from warm temperate in the north, to desert in the south. Some 40% of the population are engaged in agriculture. The mainstay of Tunisia's modern economy, however, is oil, phosphates and tourism.

Turin (Torino) a major industrial town on the River Po, and the capital of the Piedmont region, in northwest Italy. (Pop. 1,103,500)

Turkey (*Area* 779,452 sq km (300,946 sq miles); *population* 50,670,000; *capital* Ankara; *other major cities* Istanbul, Izmir, Adana, Bursa; *form of government* Republic; *religion* Sunni Islam; *currency* Turkish lira). With land on the continents of Europe and Asia, Turkey forms a bridge between the two. It guards the sea passage between the Mediterranean and the Black Sea. Its landscapes vary from fertile lowlands in European Turkey to high coastal mountains and central plains in Asian Anatolia. The climate ranges from Mediterranean on the coasts to hot summers and bitterly cold winters in the central plains. Agriculture employs over half the workforce. Major crops are wheat, rice, tobacco and cotton. Manufacturing industry includes iron and steel, textiles, motor vehicles and the production of carpetsfor which the country is famous. Tourism is a fast-developing industry.

Turkmenistan (*Area* 488,100 sq km (186,400 sq miles); *population* 3,600,000; *capital* Ashkhabad; *form of government* Republic; *religion* Sunni Islam; *currency* Rouble). Turkmenistan, a central Asian republic of the former USSR, declared itself a republic in 1991. Much of the west and central areas are covered by the sandy Kara Kum Desert, while the east is a plateau. The climate is extremely dry, and most of the population live in oasis settlements near the rivers, where agriculture is intensive. There are rich mineral deposits, especially natural gas. Silk is also produced.

Turks and Caicos Islands a British colony in the northeastern West Indies consisting of some 14 main islands. The capital is Cockburn Town on Grand Turk. (430 sq km/166 sq miles; pop. 7400)

Turku (Åbo) a port in southwest Finland, on the Gulf of Bothnia. (Pop. 161,400)

Tuscany (Toscana) a region of central western Italy. The capital is Florence. (Pop. 3,600,000)

Tuvalu (*Area* 26 sq km (10 sq miles); *population* 8229; *capital* Funafuti; *form of government* Constitutional Monarchy; *religion* Protestantism; *currency* Australian dollar). Tuvalu is located just north of Fiji, in the South Pacific, and consists of nine coral atolls. The climate is tropical. Coconut palms are the main crop, and fruit and vegetables are grown for local consumption. Sea fishing is extremely good although largely unexploited. Most export revenue comes from the sale of elaborate postage stamps.

Tver an industrial city on the navigable part of the River Volga, Russian Federation, 160 km (100 miles) northwest of Moscow. (Pop. 437,000)

Tyne and Wear a metropolitan county in northeast England, created in 1974 out of parts of Durham and Northumberland. The administrative centre is Sunderland. (540 sq km/208 sq miles; pop. 1,145,000)

Tyrol a province of western Austria, in the Alps. The capital is Innsbruck. (Pop. 586,200)

Tyrone a county in the west of Northern Ireland. The county town is Omagh. (3266 sq km/1260 sq miles; pop. 160,000)

Tyrrhenian Sea a part of the Mediterranean Sea between Sicily, Sardinia, and mainland Italy.

UAE *see* **United Arab Emirates.**

Udaipur a historic city in southern Rajasthan, India. (Pop. 233,000)

Ufa an industrial city and capital of Bashkiria, in the Russian Federation. (Pop. 1,048,000)

Uganda (*Area* 235,880 sq km (91,073 sq miles); *population* 17,000,000; *capital* Kampala; *other major cities* Jinja, Masaka, Mbale; *form of government* Republic; *religions* RC, Protestantism, Animism, Sunni Islam; *currency* Uganda shilling). Uganda is a landlocked country in east central Africa, and for the most part it is a richly fertile land, well watered, with a kindly climate. The lowlands around Lake Victoria, once forested, have now mostly been cleared for cultivation. Agriculture employs over three-quarters of the labour force, and the main crops grown for subsistence are plantains, cassava and sweet potatoes. Coffee is the main cash crop and accounts for 90% of the county's exports.

Ujung Padang a major port in the southwest of Sulawesi, Indonesia. It was formerly known as Makassar. (Pop. 709,000)

Ujvidek *see* **Novi Sad.**

UK *see* **United Kingdom.**

Ukraine (*Area* 603,700 sq km (233,100 sq miles); *population* 51,700,000; *capital* Kiev; *other major cities* Dnepropetrovsk, Donetsk, Kharkov, Odessa; *form of government* Republic; *religions* Russian Orthodox, RC; *currency* Rouble). Ukraine, formerly a Soviet socialist republic, declared itself independent of the former USSR in 1991. It consists largely of fertile steppes. The climate is continental, although this is greatly modified by the proximity of the Black Sea. It is one of the chief wheat-producing regions of Europe. Other major crops include corn, sugar beet, flax, tobacco, soya, hops and potatoes. There are rich reserves of coal and raw materials for industry. The central and eastern regions form one of the world's densest industrial concentrations. Manufacturing industries include ferrous metallurgy, machine building, chemicals, food processing, gas and oil refining.

Ulan Bator (Ulaanbaatar) the capital of MONGOLIA, in the central north of the country. (Pop. 440,000)

Ulan-Ude the capital of the Buryat Republic, in the Russian Federation. (Pop. 330,000).

Ulster one of the four ancient provinces into which Ireland was divided, covering the north. It is often used to refer to Northern Ireland, but three counties of Ulster are in the Republic of Ireland (Donegal, Monaghan and Cavan).

Ul'yanovsk a city of the eastern Urals, in the Russian Federation, on the River Volga. (Pop. 525,000)

Umbria a land-locked region of central, eastern Italy. (Pop. 816,000).

Umm al Qaywayn one of the seven United Arab Emirates, on The Gulf. (518 sq km/200 sq miles; pop. emirate 14,000/town 3000)

United Arab Emirates (UAE) (*Area* 83,600 sq km (32,278 sq miles); *population* 1,600,000; *capital* Abu Dhabi; *other major cities* Dubai, Sharjh, Ras al Khaymah; *form of government*: Monarchy (emirates); *religion* Sunni Islam; *currency* Dirham). The United Arab Emirates is a federation of seven oil-rich sheikdoms located in The Gulf. The land is mainly flat sandy desert. The summers are hot and humid, with temperatures reaching 49°C, but from October to May the weather is warm and sunny with pleasant, cool evenings. Abu Dhabi and Dubai are the main industrial centres, and, using their wealth from the oil industry, they are now diversifying industry by building aluminium smelters, cement factories and steel-rolling mills.

United Kingdom (UK) (*Area* 244,100 sq km (94,247 sq miles); *population* 57,240,000; *capital* London; other major cities Birmingham, Manchester, Glasgow, Liverpool; *form of government* Constitutional Monarchy; *religion* Anglicanism, RC, Presbyterianism, Methodism; *currency* Pound sterling). Situated in northwest Europe, the United Kingdom comprises the island of Great Britain and the northeast of Ireland, plus many smaller islands, especially off the west coast of Scotland. The south and east is low-lying and fertile, while the rest is hilly, with large areas of rugged mountains in northern Scotland. The climate is cool temperate with mild conditions and an even annual rainfall. Mixed farming is highly mechanized. Fishing is important off the east coast. It is primarily an industrial country, although the recent recession has led to the decline of some of the older industries, such as coal, textiles and heavy engineering.

United States of America (USA) (*Area* 9,372,614 sq km (3,618,766 sq miles); *population* 249,630,000; *capital* Washington D.C.; *other major cities* New York, Chicago, Detroit, Houston, Los Angeles, Philadelphia, San Diego, San Francisco; *form of government* Federal Republic; *religion* Protestantism, RC, Judaism, Eastern Orthodox; *currency* US dollar). The United States of America stretches across central North America, from the Atlantic Ocean to the Pacific Ocean. It consists of fifty states, including outlying Alaska and Hawaii. The climate varies from polar conditions to the subtropical. Although agricultural production is high, it employs only 1.5% of the population because of advanced technology. The United States is a world leader in oil production. The main industries are iron and steel, chemicals, motor vehicles, aircraft, telecommunications equipment, computers, electronics and textiles. It is the richest and most powerful nation in the world.

Upper Volta *see* **Burkina.**

Uppsala an old university town in eastern central Sweden. (Pop. 154,000)

Ural Mountains (Urals, Uralskiy Khrebet) a mountain range in western Russian Federation. Running north to south from the Arctic to the Aral Sea, the Urals form the traditional dividing line between Europe and Asia. The highest point is Mount Narodnaya (1894 m/6214 ft).

Uruguay (*Area* 177,414 sq km (68,500 sq miles); *population* 3,100,000; *capital* Montevideo; *form of government* Republic; *religions* RC, Protestantism; *currency* Uruguayan nuevo peso). Uruguay, a small country lying on the east coast of South America, consists of low plains and plateaux. About 90% of the land is suitable for agriculture but only 10% is cultivated, the remainder being used to graze vast herds of cattle and sheep. Uruguay has only one major city in which half the population live. The country has no mineral resources, oil or gas, but has built hydroelectric power stations.

Ürümqi (Urumchi) the capital of the Xinjiang Autonomous Region of northwest China. (Pop. 1,200,000)

USA *see* **United States of America.**

US Virgin Islands *see* **Virgin Islands, US**

Utah a state in the west of the USA. The state capital is Salt Lake City. (212,628 sq km/82,096 sq miles; pop. 1,645,000)

Utrecht a historic city in the central Netherlands. (Pop. city 231,000/Greater Utrecht 498,900)

Uttar Pradesh the most populous state of India, in the north of the country. The capital is Lucknow. (294,364 sq km/113,654 sq miles; pop. 110,865,000)

Uzbekistan (*Area* 449,500 sq km (173,546 sq miles); *population* 20,300,000; *capital* Tashkent; *other major city* Samarkand; *form of government* Republic; *religion* Sunni Islam; *currency* Rouble). Uzbekistan, a central Asian republic of the former USSR, declared itself independent in 1991. It has varied landcsapes: mountainous Tian Shan, the oil-rich Kyzlkum Desert, the stony Usturt Plateau, and the irrigated and fertile Fergana and lower Amudar'ya river regions. Uzbekistan is a major cotton producer, and Karakul lambs are reared for wool and meat.

Vadodara (Baroda) an industrial city in southeast Gujarat, India. (Pop. 745,000)

Valencia (1) a port on the Mediterranean coast of Spain, and the capital of the province of the same name. (Pop. city 752,000). (2) An industrial city in northern Venezuela. (Pop. 540,000)

Valladolid an industrial city in northwest Spain. (Pop. city 330,200)

Valle d'Aosta a French-speaking region of northwest Italy. The capital is Aosta. (Pop. 114,000)

Valletta the capital of MALTA. (Pop. 14,000)

Valparaíso the main port of Chile, in the centre of the country. (Pop. 267,000)

Van, Lake a salt lake in eastern Turkey. (3675 sq km/1419 sq miles)

Vancouver a major port and industrial centre in southeast British Columbia, Canada, on the mainland opposite Vancouver Island with access to the Pacific Ocean. (Pop. 1,268,000)

Vancouver Island the largest island off the Pacific coast of North America, in southwest Canada. The capital is Victoria. (32,137 sq km/12,408 sq miles; pop. 390,000)

Vanuatu (*Area* 12,189 sq km (4706 sq miles); *population* 142,630; *capital* Vila; *form of government* Republic; *religion* Protestantism, Animism; *currency* Vatu). Vanuatu, located in the western Pacific, comprises about eighty islands, some of which are mountainous and include active volcanoes. Vanuatu has a tropical climate that is moderated by the southeast trade winds from May to October. The majority of the labour force are engaged in subsistence farming, and the main exports include copra, fish and cocoa.

Varanasi (Benares) a holy Hindu city on the banks of the River Ganges in Uttar Pradesh, northeastern India. (Pop. 798,000)

Vatican City State (*Area* 44 hectares (108.7 acres); *population* 1000; *capital* Vatican City (Citta del Vaticano); *form of government* Papal Commission; *religion* RC; *currency* Vatican City lira). Vatican City State, in the heart of Rome, is the world's smallest independent state and headquarters of the Roman Catholic Church. It has its own police, newspaper, coinage, stamps and radio station. Its main tourist attractions are the frescoes of the Sistine Chapel, painted by Michelangelo. The Pope exercises sovereignty and has absolute legislative, executive and judicial powers.

Veglia *see* **Krk.**

Veneto a region of northeastern Italy, centreing upon Venice. (Pop. 4,367,000)

Venezia *see* **Venice.**

Venezuela (*Area* 912,050 sq km (352,143 sq miles); *population* 9,250,000; *capital* Caracas; *other major cities* Maracaibo, Valencia, Barquisimeto; *form of government* Federal Republic; *religion* RC; *currency* Bolívar). Venezuela forms the northernmost crest of South America. In the northwest a spur of the Andes runs southwest to northeast. The River Orinoco cuts the country in two, and north of the river run the undulating plains known as the Llanos. South of the river are the Guiana Highlands. The climate ranges from warm temperate to tropical. In the Llanos area, cattle are herded across the plains. Sugar cane and coffee are grown for export, but petroleum and gas account for 95% of export earnings. The oil fields lie in the northwest, near Lake Maracaibo.

Venice (Venezia) a historic port built on islands at the head of the Adriatic Sea in northeastern Italy. The principal thoroughfares are canals. (Pop. 346,000)

Vermont a state in the northeast of the USA, bordering Canada. The state capital is Montpelier. (24,887 sq km/9609 sq miles; pop. 535,000)

Verona a historic and industrial city in Veneto, northern Italy. (Pop. 260,000)

Versailles a town just to the west of Paris, France, which grew up around the palace built there by Louis XIV in the 1660s. (Pop. 96,000)

Vesuvius an active volcano to the southeast of Naples, in southwest Italy, notorious for having buried Pompeii. (1281 m/4203 ft)

Viangchan *see* **Vientiane.**

Victoria (1) a state in southeastern Australia. The state capital is Melbourne. (227,620 sq km/87,884 sq miles; pop. 4,054,000). (2) a port on the southeastern coast of Vancouver Island, southwest Canada, and the capital of British Columbia. (Pop. 233,000). (3) former port and capital of Hong Kong, in the northwest of Hong Kong Island. (Pop. 1,026,900) (4) the capital of the Seychelles, on the island of Mahé. (Pop. 25,000)

Victoria Falls one of the world's greatest waterfalls, where the River Zambezi tumbles some 108 m (355 ft), on the border Zambia-Zimbabwe.

Victoria, Lake the largest lake in Africa, and the second largest freshwater lake in the world after Lake Superior. Its shoreline is shared by Uganda, Kenya and Tanzania. (69,485 sq km/26,828 sq miles)

Vienna (Wien) the capital of Austria, on the River Danube, in the northeast of the country. (Pop. 1,531,000)

Ventiane (Viangchan) the capital of Laos, on the River Mekong in the northeast of the country, near the border with Thailand. (Pop. 177,000)

Vietnam (*Area* 331,689 sq km (128,065 sq miles); *population* 65,000,000; *capital* Hanoi; *other major cities* Ho Chi Minh City, Haiphong; *form of government* Socialist Republic; *religion* Buddhism, Taoism, RC; *currency* Dong). Vietnam is a long narrow country in southeast Asia, which runs down the coast of the South China Sea. It has a central hilly area that links broader plains centred on the Red and Mekong rivers. The climate is humid with tropical conditions in the south and subtropical in the north. The far north can be very cold when polar air blows over Asia. Agriculture employs over three-quarters of the labour force. The main crop is rice. Rubber, tea and coffee are grown for export. Vietnam, however, remains underdeveloped and is still recovering from the ravages of many wars this century.

Vilnius the capital of Lithuania. (Pop. 536,000)

Virginia a state in the east of the USA, with a coast on the Atlantic Ocean. The capital is Richmond (103,030 sq km/39,780 sq miles; pop. 5,706,000).

Virgin Islands, British a British Crown colony in the eastern Caribbean, to the east of Puerto Rico. The British islands are in the east of the Virgin Island group. Sixteen of the islands are inhabited, including Virgin Gorda and Tortola, the site of the capital, Road Town. (103 sq km/50 sq miles; pop. 12,000)

Virgin Islands, US a territory of the USA in the eastern Caribbean, to the east of Puerto Rico. (344 sq km/133 sq miles; pop. 100,000)

Visayan Islands a group of islands in the centre of the Philippines, which includes Negros, Cebu, Leyte, Masbate, Bohol, Panay and Samar.

Vistula a river of central and northern Poland, flowing northwards through Cracow and Warsaw to the Baltic Sea. (Length 1090 km/677 miles)

Vlaanderen *see* **Flanders.**

Vladivostok a major port on the Pacific coast in the far east of the Russian Federation, 50 km (30 miles) from the border with China. (Pop. 590,000)

Vlissingen *see* **Flushing.**

Vojvodina an autonomous province in the north of Serbia. The capital is Novi Sad. (21,506 sq km/8301 sq miles; pop. 2,035,000)

Volga, River a largely navigable river of western Russian Federation, flowing south from its source, to the northeast of Moscow, to the Caspian Sea. It is the longest river in Europe. (Length 3690 km/2293 miles)

Volgograd a port and major industrial city on the Volga. (Pop. 990,000)

Volta, Lake a major artificial lake that occupies much of eastern Ghana, formed by the damming of the Volta River. (8480 sq km/3251 sq miles)

Volta a river in Ghana, fed by the Black Volta and the White Volta, which flows south to the Bight of Benin. (Length 480 km/298 miles)

Voronezh an industrial city 450 km (280 miles) south of Moscow, Russian Federation. (Pop. 842,000)

Voroshilovgrad *see* **Lugansk.**

Wahran *see* **Oran.**

Wales a principality in the southwest of Great Britain, forming a part of the UK. Cardiff is the capital. (20,768 sq km/8017 sq miles; pop. 2,749,600)

Wallis and Fortuna Islands three small islands forming an overseas territory of France in the southwest Pacific, to the northeast of Fiji. The capital is Mata-Utu. (367 sq km/143 sq miles; pop. 13,500)

Warsaw (Warszawa) the capital of Poland, on the River Vistula, in the eastern central part of the country. (Pop. 1,641,000)

Warwickshire a county of central England. The county town is Warwick. (1981 sq km/765 sq miles; pop. 475,000)

Wash, The a shallow inlet formed by the North Sea in the coast of East Anglia, between the counties of Lincolnshire and Norfolk.

Washington a state in the northwest USA, with a coast on the Pacific. The capital is Olympia. (172,416 sq km/66,570 sq miles; pop. 4,409,000)

Washington D.C. the capital of the USA, on the Potomac River. It stands in its own territory, called the District of Columbia (D.C.), between the states of Virginia and Maryland, close to the Atlantic coast. (179 sq km/69 sq miles; pop. city 622,800/metropolitan area 3,429,400)

Waterford a county in the south of the Republic of Ireland. The county town is also called Waterford. (1838 sq km/710 sq miles; pop. county 89,000)

Weimar a historic city in southern central Germany. (Pop. 65,000)

Wellington the capital of New Zealand and a port in the southwest of North Island. (Pop. 342,000)

Weser a river in the northwest of Germany, flowing through Bremen and Bremerhaven to the North Sea. (477 sq km/196 sq miles)

West Bank a piece of disputed territory to the west of the River Jordan, including a part of Jerusalem, which was taken by Israel from Jordan in the Arab-Israeli war of 1967. (5858 sq km/2262 sq miles)

West Bengal a state in eastern India, bordering Bangladesh. Calcutta is the capital. (88,752 sq km/34,258 sq miles; pop. 54,581,000)

Western Australia a state occupying much of the western half of Australia. The capital is Perth. (2,527,636 sq km/975,920 sq miles; pop. 1,300,000)

Western Isles the regional island authority covering the Outer Hebrides of western Scotland. The administrative centre is Stornaway, on the Isle of Lewis. (2900 sq km/1120 sq miles; pop. 32,000)

Western Sahara a disputed territory of western Africa, with a coastline on the Atlantic Ocean. Consisting mainly of desert, it is rich in phosphates. The main town is Laâyoune (El Aaiún). (266,770 sq km/103,000 sq miles; pop. 200,000)

Western Samoa (*Area* 2831 sq km (1093 sq miles); *population* 163,000; *capital* Apia; *form of government* Constitutional Monarchy; *religion* Protestantism; *currency* Tala). Western Samoa, lying in the Polynesian sector of the Pacific Ocean, consists of seven small islands and two larger volcanic islands. The climate is tropical, with high temperatures and very heavy rainfall. Subsistence agriculture is the main activity, and copra, cocoa and bananas are the main exports. Many tourists visit the grave of the Scottish writer Robert Louis Stevenson, who died here and whose home is now the official home of the king.

West Glamorgan a county in South Wales, created in 1974 from part of Glamorgan and the borough of Swansea, with Swansea as the administrative centre. (817 sq km/315 sq miles; pop. 368,000)

West Indies a general term for the islands of the Caribbean Sea.

Westmeath a county in the central north of the Republic of Ireland. The county town is Mullingar. (1764 sq km/681 sq miles; pop. 61,500)

West Midlands a metropolitan county of central England, created in 1974, with its administrative centre in Birmingham. (889 sq km/347 sq miles; pop. 2,658,000)

West Virginia a state of eastern USA. The capital is Charleston. (62,341 sq km/24,070 sq miles; pop. 1,936,000)

Wexford a county in the southeast of the Republic of Ireland. The county town is also called Wexford. (2352 sq km/908 sq miles; pop. county 13,293)

White Sea an arm of the Barents Sea off the northwest of the Russian Federation, which is almost enclosed by the bulge of the Kola peninsula.

Whitney, Mount a mountain in the Sequoia National Park in eastern California, with the highest peak in the USA outside Alaska. (4418 m/14,495 ft)

Wichita a city in southern Kansas, USA, on the Arkansas River. (Pop. city 283,500/metropolitan area 428,600)

Wicklow a county in southwest Republic of Ireland. The county town is also called Wicklow. (2025 sq km/782 sq miles; pop. county 87,000)

Wien *see* **Vienna.**

Wiesbaden an old spa town in western Germany, and capital of the state of Hessen. (Pop. 272,000)

Wight, Isle of an island and county off the south coast of England, separated from the mainland by the Solent. The county town is Newport. (380 sq km/147 sq miles; pop. 120,000)

Wiltshire a county in central southern England. The county town is Trowbridge. (3481 sq km/1344 sq miles; pop. 510,000)

Winchester a historic city in southern England, and the county town of Hampshire. (Pop. 31,000)

Windward Islands *see* **Leeward and Windward Islands.**

Winnipeg the capital of Manitoba, Canada, in the south of the state. (Pop. 585,000)

Winnipeg, Lake a lake in the south of Manitoba, Canada, which drains into Hudson Bay via the Nelson River. (23,553 sq km/9094 sq miles)

Wisconsin a state in the north central USA, bordering Lake Superior and Lake Michigan. The state capital is Madison. (141,061 sq km/54,464 sq miles; pop. 4,775,000)

Witwatersrand (The Rand) a major gold-mining and industrial area of south Transvaal, South Africa.

Wollongong a major port and industrial centre in New South Wales, Australia, 80 km (50 miles) south of Sydney. (Pop. 235,000)

Wolverhampton an old industrial town in the West Midlands of England. (Pop. 255,000)

Worcestershire *see* **Hereford and Worcester.**

Wroclaw (Breslau) an industrial city on the River Oder in southwest Poland. (Pop. 631,000)

Wuhan (Hankow) the capital of Hubei province, southeast China. (Pop. 3,885,000)

Wyoming a state in the west of the USA. The state capital is Cheyenne. (253,597 sq km/97,914 sq miles; pop. 509,000)

Xiamen a port on the east coast of China, in Fujian province. (Pop. 1,006,000)

Xi'an the capital of Shaanxi province, China, and an industrial centre and former capital of China. (Pop. 2,330,000)

Xi Jiang (Si Kiang) the third longest river in China, flowing across the southwest of the country from Yunnan to its delta on the South China Sea near Guangzhou (Canton). (Length 2300 km/1437 miles)

Xining an industrial city and the capital of Qinghai province, in western China. (Pop. 860,000)

Xinjiang (Sinkiang) Uygur Autonomous Region a region of northwest China, bordering Mongolia, the Russian Federation, Afghanistan, Pakistan and India. It is also known as Dzungaria. The capital is Ürümqi. (1,646,799 sq km/635,829 sq miles; pop. 12,830,000)

Xizang Autonomous Region *see* **Tibet.**

Yamoussoukro the new capital of Côte d'Ivoire, in its centre. (Pop. 45,000)

Yamuna (Jumna), River a major river of north India, a tributary of the Ganges. (Length 1376 km/855 miles)

Yangon *see* **Rangoon.**

Yangtze Kiang *see* **Chang Jiang.**

Yaoundé the capital of Cameroon, in its southwest. (Pop. 500,000)

Yaren the capital of Nauru. (Pop. 400)

Yekaterinburg an industrial city to the east of the Ural Mountains, Russian Federation. (Pop. 1,288,000)

Yellowknife a city on the Great Slave Lake, Canada, and capital of the Northwest Territories. (Pop. 11,077)

Yellow River *see* **Huang He.**

Yellow Sea a branch of the Pacific Ocean between the northeast coast of China and the peninsula of Korea.

Yemen (*Area* 195,000 sq km (75,290 sq miles); *population* 12,000,000; *capital* Sana'a, Commercial *capital* Aden; *form of government* Republic; *religion* Zaidism, Shia Islam, Sunni Islam; *currency* Riyal and dinar). Yemen is bounded by Saudi Arabia in the north, Oman in the east, the Gulf of Aden in the south, and the Red Sea in the west. Most of the country comprises rugged mountains and trackless desert lands. It is almost entirely dependent on agriculture even though a very small percentage is fertile. The main crops are coffee, cotton, millet, sorghum and fruit. Fishing is an important industry. Other industry is on a very small scale.

Yerevan an industrial city and the capital of Armenia. (Pop. 1,114,000)

Yinchuan the capital of Ningxiahui Autonomous Region, in north central China. (Pop. 635,000)

Yogyakarta (Jogjakarta) a city of south central Java, and a cultural centre. (Pop. 40,000)

Yokohama the main port of Japan, and it's second largest city after neighbouring Tokyo, on the southeast coast of Honshu. (Pop. 3,012,900)

Yorkshire an old county of northeast England which used to be divided into the East, West and North Ridings. In 1974, however, the county was redivided into North Yorkshire (administrative centre Northallerton; 8309 sq km/3207 sq miles; pop. 666,000); West Yorkshire (administrative centre Wakefield; 2039 sq km/787 sq miles; pop. 2,038,000); and South Yorkshire (administrative centre Barnsley; 1560 sq km/602 sq miles; pop. 1,302,000).

Yucatán a state on a broad peninsula of southeast Mexico. (Pop. 1,100,000)

Yugoslavia (*Area* 127,886 sq km (49,377 sq miles); *population* 11,807,098;

capital Belgrade (Beograd); *other major cities* Nis, Skopje, Titograd; *form of government* Federal Republic; *religions* Eastern Orthodox; *currency* Dinar). Yugoslavia today refers only to the republics of Serbia, Montenegro and Macedonia, the other republics having gained independence in 1991–1992. Macedonia may follow suit. The economy is largely agricultural, but exports include chemicals, machinery, textiles and clothing.

Yukon Territory a mountainous territory in northwest Canada centreing upon the River Yukon and including the River Klondike. (536,372 sq km/207,076 sq miles; pop. 23,500)

Yünnan a province in southwestern China. The capital is Kunming. (436,200 sq km/168,400 sq miles; pop. 34,000,000)

Zagreb the capital of Croatia. (Pop. 1,180,000)

Zagros Mountains a mountain range in southwest Iran, running parallel to the border with Iraq. The highest point is Zard Kuh (4548 m/14,918 ft).

Zaïre (*Area* 2,345,409 sq km (905,562 sq miles); *population* 34,140,000; *capital* Kinshasa; *other major cities* Lubumbashi, Mbuji-Mayi, Kananga,; *form of government* Republic; *religion* RC, Protestantism, Animism; *currency* Zaïre). Situated in west central Africa, Zaïre is a vast country with a short coastline on the Atlantic Ocean. Mountain ranges and plateaux surround the Zaïre Basin, drained by the river Zaïre and its main tributaries. The climate is equatorial, and rainforests, containing valuable hardwoods, cover about half the country. Agriculture employs 75% of the population yet less than 3% of the country can be cultivated. Grazing land is limited by the infestation of the tsetse fly. Cassava is the main subsistence crop, and coffee, tea, cocoa, rubber and palms are grown for export. Minerals, mainly copper, cobalt, zinc and diamonds, account for 60% of exports.

Zaïre (Congo), River a major river of central Africa (the second longest river in Africa after the Nile) and, with its tributaries, forming a massive basin. It rises as the Lualaba in the south of Zaïre, then flows north and northwest, and finally southwest, forming the border between Zaïre and the Congo before entering the Atlantic Ocean. (Length 4800 km/3000 miles)

Zambezi, River a river of southern Africa. It rises in Zambia, then flows south to form the border with Zimbabwe, and then southeast across Mozambique to the Indian Ocean. (Length 2740 km/1700 miles)

Zambia (*Area* 752,614 sq km (290,584 sq miles); *population* 8,500,000; *capital* Lusaka; *other major cities* Kitwe, Ndola, Mufulira; *form of government* Republic; *religion* Christianity, Animism; *currency* Kwacha). Zambia, situated in central Africa, is made up of high plateaux. The climate is tropical, modified somewhat by altitude. The country has a wide range of wildlife, and there are large game parks on the Luangwa and Kafue rivers. Agriculture is underdeveloped, and most foodstuffs are imported. The economy relies heavily on the mining of copper, lead, zinc and cobalt.

Zanzibar an island lying just off the east coast of Tanzania, in the Indian Ocean. The main town is the port also called Zanzibar. (2461 sq km/950 sq miles; pop. 556,000)

Zaporozh'ye a major industrial city on the River Dnieper in the Ukraine. (Pop. 844,000)

Zaragoza (Saragossa) a historic and industrial city and surrounding province in northeastern Spain, on the River Ebro. (Pop. city 590,000)

Zealand (Sjaelland) the largest island of Denmark, on which the capital, Copenhagen, is sited. (7014 sq km/2708 sq miles; pop. 1,855,500)

Zhangjiakou a city in Hebei province, in northeast China. (Pop. 630,000)

Zhejiang a province of eastern China, with a coast on the East China Sea. The capital is Hangzhou. (102,000 sq km/39,780 sq miles; pop. 37,920,000)

Zhengzhou the capital of Henan province, in east central China. (Pop. 1,271,000)

Zibo an industrial city in Shangdong province, northeastern China. (Pop. 2,000,000)

Zimbabwe (*Area* 390,580 sq km (150,803 sq miles); *population* 9,370,000; *capital* Harare; *other major cities* Bulawayo, Mutare, Gweru; *form of government* Republic; *religion* Animism, Anglicanism, RC; *currency* Zimbabwe dollar). Zimbabwe, landlocked, in southern Africa, is a country with spectacular physical features and is teeming with wildlife. It is bordered in the north by the Zambezi river, which flows over the mile-wide Victoria Falls before entering Lake Kariba. In the south, the River Limpopo marks its border with South Africa. A great plateau between 1200 m (3937 ft) and 1500 m (4922 ft) occupies the central area. Massive granite outcrops, called *kopjes*, also dot the landscape. The climate is tropical in the lowlands and subtropical in the higher land. About 75% of the labour force are employed in agriculture. Tobacco, sugar cane, cotton, wheat and maize are exported and form the basis of processing industries. Tourism is a major growth industry.

Zululand *see* **KwaZulu.**

Zürich the largest city in Switzerland, in the northeast of the country, and a major industrial and financial centre. (Pop. 422,000)

INDEX TO THE MAP SECTION

A

C

D

E

F

I

J

K

N

Q

R

S

T

U

V

W

X

Y

Z

TIME ZONES

At Greenwich Mean Time, the time is:

Place	Local Time	Place	Local Time
Addis Ababa (Ethiopia)	3pm	Copenhagen (Denmark)	1pm
Alexandria (Egypt)	2pm	Dehli (India)	5.30pm
Amsterdam (Netherlands)	1pm	Dublin (R. of Ireland)	12 noon
Athens (Greece)	2pm	Edinburgh (Scotland)	12 noon
Baghdad (Iraq)	3pm	Florence(Italy)	1pm
Bangkok (Thailand)	7pm	Frankfurt (Germany)	1pm
Barcelona (Spain)	1pm	Geneva (Switzerland)	1pm
Belfast (N. Ireland)	12 noon	Glasgow (Scotland)	12 noon
Belgrade (Serbia)	1pm	Halifax (Canada)	12 noon
Berlin (Germany)	1pm	Hanoi (Vietnam)	7pm
Bogotá (Colombia)	7am	Havana (Cuba)	7am
Bombay (India)	5.30pm	Helsinki (Finland)	2pm
Brasília (Brazil)	9am	Ho Chi Minh City (Vietnam)	7pm
Brussels (Belgium)	1pm	Hong Kong (Hong Kong)	8pm
Bucharest (Romania)	2pm	Istanbul (Turkey)	3pm
Budapest (Hungary)	1pm	Jakarta (Indonesia)	7pm
Buenos Aires (Argentina)	9am	Jerusalem (Israel)	2pm
Cairo (Egypt)	2pm	Johannesburg (South Africa)	2pm
Calcutta (India)	5.30pm	Karachi (Pakistan)	5pm
Cape Town (South Africa)	2pm	Kuala Lumpur (Malaysia)	8pm
Caracas (Venezuala)	8am	Leningrad (Russia)	3pm
Casablanca (Morocco)	12am	Lima (Sweden)	1pm